Through the Dragon's Gate

Memories of a Hong Kong childhood

JEAN O'HARA

MEREO
Cirencester

Mereo Books

1A The Wool Market Dyer Street Cirencester Gloucestershire GL7 2PR
An imprint of Memoirs Publishing www.mereobooks.com

Through the Dragon's Gate: 978-1-86151-736-4

First published in Great Britain in 2016
by Mereo Books, an imprint of Memoirs Publishing

Copyright ©2017

Jean O'Hara has asserted her right under the Copyright Designs and Patents Act 1988 to be identified as the author of this work.

A CIP catalogue record for this book is available from the British Library.

The address for Memoirs Publishing Group Limited can be found at www.memoirspublishing.com

The Memoirs Publishing Group Ltd Reg. No. 7834348

The Memoirs Publishing Group supports both The Forest Stewardship Council® (FSC®) and the PEFC® leading international forest-certification organisations. Our books carrying both the FSC label and the PEFC® and are printed on FSC®-certified paper. FSC® is the only forest-certification scheme supported by the leading environmental organisations including Greenpeace. Our paper procurement policy can be found at www.memoirspublishing.com/environment

Typeset in 10/15pt Century Schoolbook
by Wiltshire Associates Publisher Services Ltd. Printed and bound in Great Britain by Printondemand-Worldwide, Peterborough PE2 6XD

CONTENTS

Dedication

Acknowledgements

To my family, who have given so much to make this journey possible; to my husband, who has walked beside me; to the many patients I have met along the way; and to those who have inspired me. To Jamie and Heather, with all my love. This memoir is written for you and dedicated to my grandmother; and for Sara – because I promised.

Acknowledgements

In researching for this memoir I have drawn on: *The Fall of Hong Kong* by Philip Snow; *The Heritage Hiker's Guide to Hong Kong*, by Pete Spurrier; *A Visitor's Guide to Historic Hong Kong*, by Sally Rodwell; and *Fragments of the Past*, by Randolph O'Hara.

All descriptions of clinical encounters have been anonymised. Where more detail is given, it is already in the public domain.

1

Early days in Sheung Wan

The bamboo cane hung behind a thin partition door which did not reach the ceiling. Thin and flexible, it could slash through the air with such devastation that not even a child's cry could muffle the sound. That child seems many worlds away from the adult I have become. For several years into my adult life, the flesh on the backs of my thighs and buttocks vasodilated in an autonomic physiological response whenever I felt I had said something which might have provoked unintended anger or tension. The wheals it left in its wake healed quickly; the emotional self continues on a journey.

To be fair, caning was a reprimand used in many households and schools when I was growing up. But often I felt the punishment meted out to me was for a minor infringement; I would never have dared anything worse. I don't recall transgressions, apart from not turning down the volume on a television set one evening. We were sitting together, watching a television programme as a family. No one had asked me to turn the volume down, no one had said or even hinted that it was too loud; somehow I was just expected to know. The other reason would have been any hint of criticism in the end-of-term or yearly school report. This would be construed as unsatisfactory performance and in need of reprimand, but it did not happen often.

Sudden, inexplicable, incomprehensible bouts of danger or violence peppered my childhood. I remember being given a toy rifle for my birthday. I was a tomboy and enjoyed playing with such things. This rifle was very special. To my young mind it looked like the real thing, similar to those expertly handled by cowboys in the Wild West films of the 1950s, or by the US Marshall in the American television series 'Gunsmoke'. I was thrilled. I had visions of lying in wait behind some boulder, for what was probably only minutes but felt like hours, as someone came into my field of vision... and I would secretly, quietly, take them out with a gentle squeeze of the trigger. Then the shootout would begin. When I came to London to start medical school, one of the first extra-curricular clubs I joined was the rifle club. I didn't pursue it for long, finding the reality of lying in the rifle range not as satisfying as I had imagined, but I was a pretty good shot.

I also had recurrent dreams of flying, or running away. One day, probably in my pre-teens, I decided that if I was ever beaten again, or locked out of home, I would run away. Nothing was planned. It was just a promise I made to myself. Luckily I never needed to put my resolve to the test.

Perhaps it was because I was physically bigger and stronger and more independent, but I think it was actually because life at home got easier. We were no longer living hand to mouth, there was the promise of promotions with increased salaries and my father on the threshold of being eligible for a government-sponsored flat. I was 15.

Home before then was in the oldest part of Hong Kong island, the most traditional Chinese part where foreigners did not enter. Sheung Wan District was directly west of Central District, and during my early childhood my home street was very near the waterfront. It was named after Sir Samuel Bonham, governor of Hong Kong in the early 1850s. He brought trade into Queen Victoria's new colony with American whaling ships calling in for supplies; it soon became the embarkation port for mainland China. Sheung Wan was a warren of streets and the 'hongs' of Chinese trading, from rice, bird's nest, dried seafood, tea and traditional medicines. We lived above a watch shop. Early in the morning I would hear the foghorns sound, and the rattle of carts going down the gentle sloping road outside. By day the streets would be thronged with the local Chinese going to nearby wet markets, street stalls, teahouses and small businesses. In the early evening there would likely be the sound of merriment as local youngsters played Chinese shuttlecock. By night, I would hear, and often smell, the weekly stench as 'night soil' ladies came up the stairs to our landing to collect buckets of human excrement. We had very basic sanitation. Although we had running water, I also remember months of rationing during the Cultural Revolution, when older cousins who lived with us would join long queues to bring water home every few days.

Nothing remains of the street where I lived. At least, not the street of my childhood. It has been engulfed in a wave of expansion as small residential streets in the heart of an old Chinese neighbourhood give way to the sprawling concrete jungle of new office blocks, banks and even gleaming posh hotels and landscaped gardens, complete with statues and water fountains. When I was a child, one would not see a *'gweilo'* (foreign devil) walking the streets of my home. The Colonial elite merely passed by in their private cars, or rickshaws, on their way to pick up an artefact in the famous curio market of Cat Street, or on their way home in the affluent surroundings of the mid-levels or Victoria Peak. No *gweilos* would stop in the lanes and alleyways I called home. It was the haunt of the Chinese working class - a village atmosphere - where everyone knew their neighbours, and the streets were full of clatter as wooden carts tumbled down the road alongside the occasional motorized vehicle. The banter of warm greetings and the slamming of steel gates marked the beginning of another trading day, as shops opened for business.

In the afternoon, a lone 'flying olive pedlar' often sauntered down the street in his *kung fu* slippers, carrying a satchel of preserved olives, and playing on the strings of his *erhu* (Chinese fiddle). When lucky enough to gain a ten cent coin from my grandmother, I would rush out onto our balcony, shout out what I wanted to buy and throw the money onto the pavement below. On pocketing payment, he would kick a small bag of olives, sending it flying up in the air to land on our balcony. He never missed.

Home was a two-hundred-square foot second-floor flat. The tenement building was typical of the many low-rise residential properties in the area; a rather curious mix of Chinese-Western styles, with its small balconies and wrought iron railings; windows and doors with round arches, tiled roofs, wooden floors and staircases. Access was up a steep flight of steps in a dark, narrow hallway at the side of the watch shop. Tin letterboxes of various sizes, painted in a lucky red, adorned the side of a dilapidated wall. Our letterbox was different; it was larger and made of wood, with our address painted in English and Chinese on the front. I remember my father painting the words on it. Our front door was different too; whilst others had batten doors which could be pushed open from the middle, ours was a sturdy wooden door secured in position by a thick wooden bar.

Until the age of ten, I shared a bed with my grandmother and younger sister. It was a raised platform. Instead of a mattress we had a straw mat. We shared this small space, enclosed on two sides by thin partition walls, and the third by a length of purpose-built shelves for our toys and a single built-in wardrobe. The fourth side of this room was open, and allowed an old wooden chest to be wedged at one end, under the bed and my grandmother's dressing table to stand at the other. There was less than one square metre of standing space. A curtain hung from a beam above our heads; when drawn it was the only means of privacy. I grew up unaware I had no privacy, or that seven of us were living in overcrowded conditions.

Next door was my parents' bedroom, the only room to have its own door, and a small window, although the partitions which enclosed the room did not reach the high ceiling. A short communal passageway led from our living room to the kitchen, and this was lined with a small cupboard for crockery, glassware and 'fine china', a simple wooden crate converted into a wardrobe for my cousins to hang their clothes, spare folding chairs and a removable round table top used for special occasions. At night, to create more sleeping space, my grandmother wedged a wooden plank by the side of her bed, propped up at one end on an open drawer of her dressing table and the other on top of her Chinese chest. This allowed the three of us to sleep in relative comfort, although I remember waking many times, with my leg strewn across my grandmother's diminutive figure, pinning her down. She never once complained.

During the summer months it would be unbearably hot in her box room, and we would then join my cousins, who slept on straw mats on the living room floor. My grandmother would sit up, fanning us with her black feather fan as we lay in the humidity and heat of the stifling tropical weather, calamine lotion painted over our bodies to calm the prickly heat which attacked with a vengeance. The highly-polished wooden floorboards were clean, and swept daily. Sleeping on them allowed me to peep, cautiously, through the wide cracks into the flat below.

One of my earliest memories in this flat was being bathed in the kitchen sink. It was deep, white and made of stone, and when I sat in it I could see into the small square concrete courtyard below. Through the window I was aware of neighbours going up and down the stairwell, and the odd item of clothing caught in the wiry metal contraption surrounding the external walls. Occasionally there would be blasts of 'God Save the Queen' as a local youngster practised on his trumpet, rather badly. We rarely ventured into the courtyard unless it was to retrieve an item that had fallen. Entry was via the front of the watch shop; walking through their dinghy kitchen and cramped living quarters, past their black and white television set (which was a treat before we had one of our own) and into the daylight afforded by the courtyard.

At Christmas we shared a paper plate of goodies with each of our neighbours: slices of Christmas cake bought from the church fair, homemade mince pies, colourful foil wrapped chocolates, jelly sweets covered in desiccated coconut, dried fruits and other seasonal treats. I loved this part of Christmas best of all. I loved putting the plates together, wrapping them in cellophane, knocking on the door and saying 'Merry Christmas' in Cantonese, and seeing their faces light up at the gift. Even though we were relatively poor we celebrated Christmas, the only family who did in our neighbourhood, so it felt important to bring some festive cheer to others. But it was not as easy as it sounds. Below us lived the bogey man, and above us the mad woman.

I had been up Bonham Strand East to collect our copy of the English-language *South China Morning Post* from the newspaper stall at the top of our street. '*Jo-sun*,' the elderly lady called as she saw me coming towards her. 'Where's your grandmother today? Ask her to come for *yum char*. They make good *dim sum* here, especially their roast pork buns,' she enthused, throwing her head to one side in the direction of the teahouse just behind her.

'My thanks to you. When she has the time,' I replied in Cantonese, imitating my grandmother's social chatter. 'And you, have you had *dim sum* today?'

'When do I have the time?' the woman answered in her squatting position. 'I have to look after this stall. No one else will do it for me. But my husband's in there,' she continued, tilting her head once more towards the teahouse. 'He'll treat you'.

'Thank you kindly in advance then,' I said. 'Perhaps another day'.

'And your mother?' the woman enquired again, handing a Chinese daily newspaper to a customer as he threw the coinage onto her pile of magazines spread neatly on the pavement.

'She's at work, of course, like every other day,' I answered. My attention was drawn to the Indian security guard standing a little further up the road. I waved and he nodded in acknowledgement. He was a rather large man, tucked neatly into a beige safari-like uniform, with a turban on his head and a healthy growth of beard covering his well-endowed chin. A loaded rifle stood innocuously on his shiny black leather boots, his left hand over the barrel. It was his daily duty to guard the bank, and he stood outside on the pavement when the day was fine and in the lobby when it was not. My sister and I passed him almost every afternoon on our way back from school, and he welcomed us into the air-conditioned banking hall to cool off before continuing the last short distance home. Often he had boiled sweets tucked away in his uniform, and we gladly shared them with him. His co-worker, a much slimmer guard, was on duty at other times - and then we would give the bank a miss.

The jewellers next door must also have benefited from their presence, for they often had an obscenely expensive display of 24-carat gold ornaments and jade in their window.

The jade was of the most exquisite emerald green - Imperial Jade - but none of the items were as attractive or perfect as the bangle my grandmother wore on her wrist. It had the feel of life, unlike the coldness of an unowned precious stone. Most people in Hong Kong wore a jade talisman as they are meant to protect against disasters, disease and evil spirits, but to the Chinese, jade is more than a talisman. It is a precious link between Heaven and Earth, between Life and Immortality. Its hard stone is believed to take on the spiritual personality of its wearer, and this most traditional gift could then be passed down through the generations.

My grandmother had worn her bangle for many years, and the longer she had it on, the more beautiful it became. She never parted with it when I was a child, although I know she had pawned it several times before when poverty was extreme and she had little choice. When I visited her from England in 1988, she gave me a small piece of jade. To Chinese people, the giving of jade can have a very poignant, symbolic and special meaning. I was so excited and honoured, as throughout my childhood she had rarely given me anything material, but I was also filled with silent dread. I feared she was actually preparing to say goodbye and that it would be the last time I would see her alive. That foreboding was real, as she died suddenly a few months later.

There was a knock on our door. I peeped on tiptoe and caught a glimpse of our upstairs neighbour, the eldest boy, who must have been no more than twenty. I lifted the heavy beam and unbarred the door, inviting him in, but he refused. He looked subdued and was wringing his hands together incessantly. My grandmother came to the door as

I called for her, wiping her hands on an old flowery apron that was fastened to her waist. She was already seventy, but walked with the vigour and posture of a woman twenty years her junior. Her long black hair was pinned back in a bun, and her small frame belied the fact that she had borne seventeen children.

After some gentle persuasion in hushed tones, the young man came into our flat and stood silently by the door, his wane features almost as neglected as the clothes he had on.

'I'm going upstairs for a while,' my grandmother announced as she made safe what she was doing in the kitchen and untied her apron. 'I won't be long. You open the door for me when I get back.'

Fifteen minutes later, she returned alone. 'The old man is very sick. In fact, he is dying. If he lives through this week, long enough to open the New Year, he'll be all right.'

He did not. I went upstairs to pay my condolences. That day the family had already consulted several specialists, to ensure that the old man's soul had an easy journey to the Western Heaven. I approached their door, more fearful of the widow than I was of the deceased, for she was a very volatile woman with episodes of inexplicable, frightening behaviour. I never knew what was troubling her, but looking back on it now I can only assume she had either a schizophrenic or manic-depressive disorder, for at times she would be withdrawn and almost catatonic, and at other times we would hear screams and shouts as she argued with family members, and on one occasion she bit her elderly husband, causing injury. I remember one terrifying evening when she started throwing meat cleavers down into the back courtyard below. I caught the deadly glint of their sharp edges as they hurtled down past our kitchen window. At other times, often breaking the peacefulness of the night, police would arrive to escort her away, when she spent time in the asylum of Castle Peak Mental Hospital.

This time her youngest son opened the door, but I wasn't really aware of him or his mother's presence. She was mostly silent throughout, apart from when she spoke to my grandmother. I noticed instead how dark and simple everything was. The balcony shutters were almost completely closed. The only light came from a small flickering candle burning in a bowl of sesame oil. It stood on a nearby makeshift altar, a black and white photograph of the old man on one side, a vase of paper flowers on the other, in blue and white, the colours of death and mourning. My attention was drawn to the curved contours of his coffin, laid out on two high black stools, its foot pointing towards the door. He was dressed in his best Chinese gown reminiscent of old Chinese films. A snuffbox lay beside him and in his mouth he held a gold leaf and a twist of red paper, containing ashes of incense. Covering him was a length of silk, probably the most expensive gift he had ever been presented with in his lifetime.

I looked down on him, not quite knowing what to expect. His skin was so pale, his wrinkles almost smoothed out over his slightly puffy face. I noticed fine wisps of white hair, the almost disappearing eyebrows and the long hairy mole on his cheek. His eyes were closed, and a strange sense of tranquillity exuded from his lifeless body. I spoke to him in my head, in English and in Cantonese, but there was no answer. Perhaps his spirit had already left his body as the astrologer had predicted. If so, he had begun his inevitable journey into the Ten Halls of Hell. How could such a frail old man survive seven weeks of this? Would he be made to languish and suffer in excruciating agony or would the judgement in each Hall allow him to move on? I thought about the awful depictions of torture and hell on brash sculptures and grottoes I had seen when we had visited Tiger Balm Gardens. He did not look as though he was going through hell; he seemed serene, lying there in state, oblivious to the numbness and despair he had left behind.

His widow seemed so small now, not the frightening, towering madwoman I had feared. Had grief immobilised her, keeping check on that unpredictable and dangerous part of her being? Her glazed expression betrayed a world of isolation and pain. Perhaps it was she who was going through hell, braving that lonely path, for her husband's soul to follow.

On the eve of the old man's funeral I asked my grandmother why he had died. He had been ill with cancer. Cancer was often terminal in those days, and nobody really spoke of it. 'If only he had hung on a few more days to see in the New Year,' she said. 'Anyway, he lived to a good age. One cannot expect to have life for much longer than that.'

Out on the balcony I could see a group of people gathered below, burning paper offerings in a small bonfire outside the entrance to our building. An attendant, dressed in a simple robe, was beating the offerings with a long pole to prevent any 'wandering spirits' who might snatch the objects for their own use in the next world. Ornate paper servant dolls, hell money, a model of a furnished and inhabited house and an expensive-looking car were burnt. Specks of ash and amber-edged paper flew into the air as a gentle gust of wind swept down our street. I continued to watch as he scooped some cooked rice and shoved it into the heart of the fire. The flames rose slightly. From a small tin container, the attendant poured a little water into the bonfire. The flames began to hiss and sizzle, but the noise soon died down as the food and drink were lapped up in burning tongues of fire. The 'Hungry Ghosts' who lived all around our world would be distracted by this, allowing the old man to continue his journey with his possessions intact.

The next morning my grandmother was dressed suitably for the funeral procession. Since dawn priests had begun their incessant chant. It soon became noticeable only by its absence, for when they stopped a strange uneasy silence fell. At about two o'clock I listened out for the breaking of an earthenware saucer, a signal that the coffin had reached the door to begin its journey to the crematorium. I had seen such saucers before, in stalls by the Market Square. They were meant as drinking utensils for the deceased, but had a hole in the middle through which water could leak away. Ingenious really, as it was believed that all water wasted in life had to be drunk by the deceased after death. The hole ensured that such a penalty was lessened.

Shortly afterwards the procession came into view and the chanting and music started again. I watched as two men assisted the old man's eldest son down the street. It was their duty to sustain him in his grief. A three-pronged banner, inscribed with a few Chinese characters in bold, was clasped tightly in his hand, proclaiming his father's name. A little way behind were the female mourners, his widow and my grandmother amongst them. Immediately after and in front of the long coffin, came the old man's sedan chair. In it rode his soul, represented by a photograph. Minutes later, the funeral procession snaked round the corner of Bonham Strand and disappeared from view, leaving a trail of hell money in its path, to once again distract the attention of malignant wandering spirits.

'Did grandpa have all this when he died?' I remember asking.

'Of course. Your grandfather was the head of a very large family you know, what with so many sons. He had to have a proper service, even though we couldn't really afford it. I had to borrow money from everywhere. And not only that, we had a Requiem Mass too. The monks and nuns chanted the whole day long, just for him. It's very important, you know, to do things right - to comfort his soul on his journey.'

I couldn't begin to imagine a whole day of sitting still through some long and drawn-out service. Just listening to the fifteen-minute sermon in the cathedral church every Sunday was boring enough, especially when a particular preacher insisted on delivering his sermon by mumbling all the way through.

'Oh, it's not like in your church,' my grandmother continued, as if reading my mind. 'It's a whole day ceremony, but you don't have to worry. The monks and nuns do all the chanting. You just have to be there, to pay respects and to honour the departed and his family. You can talk to people if you want to, or you can just sit there, or you can help fold gold and silver paper squares into ingots for the treasure chests. It's not really something children go to anyway. But you know, traditions have changed. These ceremonies aren't performed much these days. Just a simple service now. And most people are cremated instead of buried. But I have seen bodies being burnt, on pyres back home in the village. Can you believe it, they actually sit up in the flames? I saw it with my own eyes.'

2

The dissection room

The body in front of me was partially covered, but it was obvious that it had been mutilated. Some bits actually looked like textbook dissections, showing in detail the routes of main nerves and arteries, muscle insertions and how various organs lay in relation to one another. Our cadaver had been with us for two and a half terms now, and was regarded as a familiar companion. She had given us many hours of study as my group of eight students took it in turns to dissect, whilst others read out instructions from a well-thumbed softback copy of Zuckermann, our anatomy bible. We knew her intimately by now and respected her greatly.

I don't know how many people are inspired to donate their bodies to medical science after death. It must take a great deal of forethought and may possibly be a reflection of gratitude. I remember one afternoon trying to locate our subject's uterus and delving into her pelvic cavity, only to discover it was a futile exercise, as she had had it removed in her lifetime. I never thought of that before. For some reason, I expected a perfect body, with everything intact, as it should be. After all, we were working to a textbook and we had no knowledge of her medical history.

On another occasion, we cut right down onto the femoral head, intent on examining the hip joint, only to hit metal. The woman had had a hip replacement, and I remember one of the boys in my group removing it from the bone and taking it home as a memento. It was smooth, shiny and cool to the touch - unlike the other hip, which showed the wear and tear of years of weight bearing and movement. I am sure it was against any of the rules, but nobody said anything. In fact, a rumour going round at the time, whether fact or fiction, concerned a male student in the year above who had reportedly removed a leg from the dissection room, dressed it and taken it home on the tube train. Everyone said it was true, and that he was suspended, but I remain sceptical.

'For those of you who want to help, you can stay behind. The others can leave after you've cleared your tables,' the anatomy instructor concluded as we approached the end of another Zuckermann chapter.

After the weekend, we were to begin studying the head - and that meant disposing of the rest of the body. But in order to do so, it meant not only decapitation but sawing right down the middle of the head. For me it was a line too far; it was not something I wished to be involved in or to witness. Very few of us stayed.

When we returned the following Monday, our dissection table looked unusually empty. At the end of each was a large jar, and in it we found our woman's head, split down the middle vertically – a sagittal split - so that we could see her brain tissue and airways and gullet. It looked like a specimen rather than a person, and I was glad of it. We spent the following weeks prodding and poking, examining and reading and ultimately memorizing all we could about the anatomy of the head.

The systematic dissection of human cadavers for medical study dates back to 200 BC, but medical students do not spend much time around a dissection table in the anatomy theatre any longer. These days it is more usual for them to have expertly produced 'landscaped specimens' already prepared, supplemented by computer models, digital images and videotapes of almost anything. I remember how impressed I was by one of our anatomy tutors who was able to draw out for us the human chest cavity, building it layer upon layer, so we were able to appreciate a three-dimensional perspective of how organs, blood vessels and muscles related to one another. I have since seen a similar approach in textbooks, with layered acetate sheets as pages.

For us, the dissection room was a large part of our first year at medical school; an initiation and a rite of passage. We spent much of our time in sterile environments overwhelmed by the smell of formalin. It got into everything; our belongings, our clothing, under our fingernails and into our hair. We were still smelling of it when we went to the canteen for lunch, already having removed our white lab coats and washing our hands.

That memorable first scalpel incision into the back we all had to make on the first day as medical students is still etched in my mind. I remember vividly the feel of the blade in my hand and the different resistance as the scalpel went through the skin (rather rubbery), into the subcutaneous tissue and hitting muscle.

"We were introduced to our own cadaver today," I said to a friend that night from a public telephone box at the end of my road when I returned to my bedsit a few stops along the District Line.

"I suppose that was your first dead body," she replied, rather sympathetically, as if knowing it must have been a tough day for all sorts of reasons. It wasn't - but I didn't tell her that.

3

Hong Kong, mid-1960s

In the 1960s, Hong Kong was filled with crooked lanes, hawkers, street markets, sampans, junks and the clatter of rickshaws and double-decker trams, affectionately called 'ding dings'. The harbour was wider than it is now and the waterfront gave one a feeling of space. There were few gleaming skyscrapers, and the skyline on Kowloon-side was low because of the airport a few miles away.

One of my favourite buildings was a grand striped red-bricked Edwardian construction on the junction of Des Voeux Road Central and Pedder Street, which served as the General Post Office. It had been built on newly-reclaimed land in 1911, apparently by mistake, using plans which were intended for the General Post Office in Nairobi. Whether this was true or not, it felt a rather curious building, different and quite magical. It was demolished in 1976 to make way for the construction of the Mass Transit Railway. I also remember how special we felt about the two buildings of City Hall, opened when I was a toddler. It was our first multi-purpose cultural complex on Edinburgh Place, and had safe walkways dotted with plants and unobstructed views of the famous harbour. City Hall low block had an outstanding concert hall where we sang in school choir competitions and watched Christmas pantomimes; high block housed our first public library where my father worked, and with its twelve floors, was one of the tallest buildings in Central District when I was growing up.

Nearby Statue Square was built entirely on reclaimed land, to commemorate Queen Victoria's Golden Jubilee. Many of the original statues were taken abroad to be melted down by the occupying Japanese forces during the Second World War. However, the statue of Queen Victoria survived and was moved to its current location in Victoria Park, close to the hospital where I was born. Thankfully, the two bronze lions, so beloved of young children, were also returned to their place outside the Hong Kong and Shanghai Banking Corporation Headquarters, at the prestigious No 1 Queen's Road. The shrapnel damage is still clearly visible. I so enjoyed touching the lions' paws, climbing onto their backs and entering the banking hall, its mix of classical and art deco design adding to a sense of awe and adulthood. Being the first building to be air conditioned in Hong Kong, it was also such a welcome treat from the intense heat of the Hong Kong summer. Demolished after I left Hong Kong, it was replaced in 1985 with an expensive steel and aluminum construction. This 'bank of mirrors', with its unobstructed views of the harbour, a spacious ground floor atrium seemingly without walls and the absence of an internal supporting structure to the building, was certainly expertly designed with good *feng shui* in mind. The cenotaph, a memorial to those who had died during WWII, stood at the northern end of the square, and in the mid-1960s, with the addition of plants and fountains, the square became a beautiful little oasis of calm and tranquillity amongst the increasingly hectic bustle of modern Hong Kong life.

I loved visiting Statue Square and the surrounding areas around City Hall and the Star Ferry pier. There were memorial gardens in classical Bauhaus style with clean lines. There was safe space to run around, water to play with, low ledges to climb, columns to hide behind, cool benches to sit on and shade from the midday sun. When it got too hot, we would pop into the adjacent Prince's Building to cool off in its luxurious air-conditioned arcade of shops. My parents or grandmother would allow extra time when we were travelling in the area for us kids to play, more often than not on our way across the harbour.

One time, I must have been about five or six, and was playing tag and chase with my younger sister, who was four at the time. It was a blissful afternoon, and we had so much fun. And then she fell. She tripped, scraped her knees and started crying. Boy, did I get a telling off that day. It was all my fault because I was running too fast. I should have known better, being the older sister. I should have slowed down to let her catch me.

Later that year, 1966, large scale riots erupted. Originally a minor labour dispute, it soon escalated to massive, violent confrontations between pro-Communist demonstrators and British colonial rule. My beloved Central District was transformed into an ugly 'no go' area for us children. The Bank of China, so close to Statue Square, bristled with loudspeakers inciting revolution as they broadcasted pro-Communist rhetoric and propaganda. It stood out as a Maoist citadel in the heart of a capitalist Central District, and yet we knew from newspaper and television coverage that in the cricket ground across the road, cricketers continued to play on regardless. It was as if such chaos and tensions were a normal part of everyday life, or perhaps it was to give this impression to the outside world. It felt chaotic though, and at times frightening. Crowds of protesters shouted 'blood for blood!' as they thrust copies of Mao's Little Red Book into the air.

I think it was around this time that I was taken to the cinema to see 'The Red Detachment of Women', the most famous Chinese ballet, produced at the height of Chairman Mao's 'Great Proletarian Cultural Revolution'. It tells the story of a woman's journey into the People's Liberation Army. Instead of fragile women dressed in tutus, women were depicted in military uniforms with rifles. Instead of soft, elegant movements, they had strong arms and clenched fists and danced with vigour and strength. It shook the entire foundation of bourgeois art. I remember the posters and billboards vividly.

Rumours began to circulate that China was preparing to take back control of Hong Kong. Emergency restrictions and a curfew was imposed. The Leftists retaliated, resorting to terrorist tactics and planting fake and real bombs in the city. Members of the press who had voiced opposition to violence were threatened and murdered. As children we were warned not to step on loose sheets of newspapers lying on the road, nor to pick up toys in our path. Explosives were often found in innocuous-looking objects, and they caused considerable injury. A seven-year-old girl and her two-year-old brother had been killed by a bomb wrapped like a gift and placed outside their residence. To this day, I do not relish walking through a pile of autumn leaves; nor do I step onto anything I cannot see. It might explain why I would rather contemplate sky diving than jumping into ocean waters when on holiday.

The police raided a bomb-making factory in my local Western District, and had tracked down a number of Communist schools in which the students and their teachers were also making bombs. Returning home one late afternoon with my grandmother and sister, I could see as we approached our home street that it had been cordoned off by police, and no one was allowed to enter. As usual, a crowd soon gathered – and then a bomb disposal van arrived, and we were all told to remain calm, and that everything would soon be over. It did not take long. I remember the sound of the muted explosion, and the young bomb disposal man, who lost his right arm as he attempted to make it safe. The media reported his return to duty, prosthesis in place. Living, modern heroism - not just in the annuals of history but in the street where I lived.

The waves of bombing subsided in October 1967. In all, the dispute lasted 18 months and became known as the Cultural Revolution. It ceased only when Zhou En Lai gave orders for it to stop. I've since read that during that time the police and British military defused over 8,000 home-made bombs. Statistics show that one in every eight was genuine. As a result, laws were passed prohibiting fireworks without the permission of the government. The Queen granted the Hong Kong Police Force the privilege of the Royal title, still in use after the 1997 handover of the colony back to China. Apart from the human toll, it caused millions of dollars' worth of damage and confidence in Hong Kong's future declined. As many sold their property and moved overseas, HK tycoon Li Ka-Shing amassed his fortune by buying property at rock-bottom prices at the height of the riots.

4

First steps in medicine

"When your patient dies, it doesn't end there," our pathology lecturer informed us in a matter-of-fact manner. There was such a detached air of authority about him; he was so knowledgeable about such grave matters, so fascinated by the science he was imparting, and yet seemingly so impervious to the humanity of it all.

He had been showing us slides of diseased organs: blood vessel walls furred with thick flaking gunge, lungs destroyed by smoking and chronic bronchitic changes, brains and heart muscle starved of oxygen, stomach walls eaten away with cancerous ulceration, fungating tumours of every description and visceral organs in different stages of discolouration and disease.

"You follow your patient through their hospital stay, into

the mortuary, and through the post mortem. You find out all you can about how and why they died. You look at everything the body can tell you. How many of you have been to the post-mortems held every lunchtime?" Not many of us put our hands up, but we could guess who would.

"Every lunch time there is a notice pinned up on the board, with the names and times of all the post-mortem demonstrations," the lecturer continued, probably appalled by the low uptake. "I want to see you all here."

The first patient I ever clerked as a clinical year student (the third year of medical school training in those days) was a middle-aged man with spiky silvery hair. I cannot remember his name, just his diagnostic label and the outcome – is that sad? - but I can still see him sitting up in his hospital bed as I approached. A gentle man, softly spoken and with a warm and engaging manner. Whatever he was going through, he had a reassuring smile. I spent over an hour with him that first day, talking to him as he told me his personal and medical history, the symptoms he had and how he first noticed them, how they had developed and how he felt.

I examined him - awkwardly; a small hand on a large firm, slightly jaundiced body, palpating and percussing his abdomen to examine the organs that we had been taught were in there - flicking for the liver edge, pushing deep for the spleen and kidneys, checking for fluid and listening for the tinkling noises of intestinal gurgles. He did not flinch when I asked him to turn onto his side so that I could probe into his rectum ("examine your back passage", we had been taught to say, and "breathe through your mouth as I put my finger in"). No need for a chaperone either. Patients were like that - they seemed to let us medical students poke around in all sorts of awkward ways as we attempted to master the clinical skills that would become the bread and butter of our work. I checked his X-rays, his temperature and blood pressure charts hanging at the foot of his bed, and most mornings I would come to talk to him to find out how he was doing and just to have a social chat. That was the real bonus - for both patient and student - to have the time to talk to each other. It was often at these more informal and personal times when patients asked about what they feared most. Sadly, we were never taught how to handle it apart from being told to direct such questions to the doctors. I am told things are different now; difficult situations and the breaking of bad news are role played by medical students under supervision.

But back to my first patient. The day of his surgery arrived, and I followed him into the operating theatre, talking to him and being with him as he entered the anaesthetic room. I attempted, unsuccessfully, to put a venflon and intravenous drip into the back of his hand, and when he was under the anaesthetic I was shown his windpipe, and how to intubate him. He had a laparotomy to open up his abdomen - just to see if there was anything surgically that could be done to alleviate some of his symptoms. There was not, so he was stitched up again and wheeled out of theatre and back to the ward.

As the days passed, he became more and more jaundiced, but his hands held mine with the same warmth and reassurance as they had before. One autumnal morning ... I remember his name now, but I shall call him Ernest...

he died. I never had a chance to say goodbye, or to see his relatives. My next encounter with Ernest was at his post-mortem, with his naked body cut open and his cancerous pancreas on display for all to see. Somehow, I had to detach myself, to forget that he had been that warm, welcoming human being, and just concentrate on his diseased organs and the medical jargon that went with it. I think that was the way most of us dealt with it. A lot of black humour and laughter. Making macabre jokes of quite awful human tragedies - either in the context of the annual medical college Christmas show, or when relaxing within our own social group of friends.

Some years ago I read a most extraordinary and disturbing novel called 'Being Dead'. It spoke about the physical nature of death in great detail, the decay and decomposition, yet at the same time it tried to convey a sense of life through the relationship of an ordinary middle-aged couple. I still do not know whether or not I like the book, though it was undoubtedly extremely well written. But I found it too raw, too detached. I think we lived life as medical students, in a rather theme park or fairground manner – getting into rides one after the other, not knowing where they might take us and without the time to think about of the consequences. We were pushed along the queue by peers and supervisors herding us into the jaws of exhilarating uncertainty and adrenaline-driven encounters. We went through rollercoasters of emotions and experiences no one in their teens should have to go through; the hurdles and horrors, the dizzy highs and the gut-wrenching lows. There was little in the way of pastoral care. We did have a professor assigned to a small group of us, but I think we only met up once or twice a year at most. I recall going to his home and being served curried eggs. A fellow student found them so awful he hid his in a flower pot in the professor's garden.

As the months went by, every long day was immersed in disease, illness, surgery and death. But what I remember most was our unquenchable thirst for life - to experience life, to marvel at the natural beauty that was all around us. On our regular Wednesday afternoons off, my boyfriend and I would take the underground train to Lancaster Gate, running through the greenery and fresh air of Hyde Park, along the Serpentine and onto the familiar statue of Peter Pan. Sometimes we played like school children, he kicking up the fallen autumn leaves whilst I tried to catch one as they fell. We looked for squirrels as they scurried about, burying nuts for the coming winter, or fed the ducks and swans in the nearby lake outside Kensington Palace. In the evening, we would queue outside a West End theatre box office, waiting for student standby tickets, or secret ourselves in the darkness of a cinema, where the huge screen and loud soundtrack overwhelmed the senses - and made us forget.

That summer London was filled with life, and a real sense of a new beginning. Prince Charles was to marry Lady Diana Spencer, a young, shy woman who stood with her head down, but had a rather awkward, secretive smile that made one warm to her. She was demure and looked regal, despite her schoolgirlish charm. There was much talk about how she had to submit to 'an internal examination' to make sure she was untouched by another man, so as to avoid any possible scandal. Lady Diana was even younger than myself, and I was astounded that a contemporary of mine, who lived in Kensington (a place I frequented every Saturday when I visited a school friend who was studying at one of the colleges nearby) was taking on such an enormous role.

When I was about nine, my parents came home with our first rented television, a small black and white Rediffusion set with little knobs down the side. It was always breaking down, and the technician would take ages to repair it as he waited for parts. Except on special occasions, we were allowed one hour viewing a day. We seldom used the allocation. One of the first broadcasts I ever saw was the investiture of the Prince of Wales at Caernarfon Castle. I remember watching his solemn oath to the Queen. Later, the oath was published in full in the *South China Morning Post*, the main English newspapers in Hong Kong. We soon had a popular version of our own in the school playground, where I was a member of a group akin to that in Enid Blyton's Secret Seven stories, with our own little adventure house hidden at the end of a pebbly path.

My boyfriend and I spent the eve of the Royal Wedding up in Hyde Park, watching, along with thousands of others, the spectacular fireworks display that was held in the couple's honour. It was an historic and unforgettable evening, made more so by the fact that all tube stations closed before the crowds had a chance to get to them. They even closed the gates to the park, with thousands still in the grounds, and we had to climb over. The few night buses that were around were packed with people, so in the end we had no option but to walk home - from Hyde Park to Bromley by Bow, past some of the most iconic London landmarks and through some of the most famous streets of London. Luckily, the weather was perfect for walking. Surprisingly, it did not feel in any way unsafe either, walking through the streets of London in the early hours of the morning. Everyone we passed along the way was merry and happy, as a wave of euphoria swept the nation. It made the whole royal fireworks event all the more memorable, and 'something to tell the grandchildren' in the years to come.

When we arrived back at our small hard-to-let council flat on the seventh floor of a run-down East End council estate, there was no time to sleep. Instead, my flatmate, my boyfriend and I sat glued in front of our small television, feet soaking in basins of warm water, drinking a bottle of champagne to toast the royal couple. It was like a fairytale made real, from the majestic music to the rousing cathedral bells, from the crowds lining the route waving their flags to the pomp and ceremony of the wedding itself and from the appearance of the newlyweds on the balcony of Buckingham Palace to that first kiss. Yet there was more. There was the shyness of the bride in her dazzling wedding dress, and the nervousness in her voice when making her wedding vows. The groom, on the other hand, seemed rather used to it all as he nonchalantly placed his gloves back on his hands without looking at his bride as they came out of St Paul's Cathedral. One could sense that he was ready for the show.

5

Chinese marriage

'Me? Sixteen I was married. No, fifteen,' my grandmother told me one hot summer's day when I was recovering from mumps. My cheeks were painted with a topical herbal remedy, and I was lying on my grandmother's wooden bed, watching as she combed her long hair. It reached down to her waist.

'But you were allowed to marry at thirteen,' my grandmother continued. 'The age when girls become fertile. Everyone starts looking for men then, as suitable husbands, for their daughters and girls. I must have been about fourteen when I first saw your mother's father. He was older than me by twenty-one years. But it was an arranged marriage - all arranged. He had agreed to marry me. My foster father's eldest son, Ah So, was sent along with two large baskets full of food as a dowry. It so happened that your grandfather was living only two hamlets away from me at the time. In fact, he even knew who I was, although I didn't know him. My foster family were from the same village as his, and they knew one another through business.'

'How come?' I asked.

'You know he was in the clock and watch business, right? I had been to Hong Kong before, and had helped his friend look after the shop. Buying and selling things, you know. Your mother's father said to the others, "this girl is very good". But they told him I was a wild one, full of life. "Just don't know if you can ride her, that's all. She's very strong willed, and bad tempered," that's what they said of me. But your grandfather said to them, "that's no matter. If she's bad tempered, all I have to do is to teach her slowly." They challenged him. "Go on then," they said. "See if you can tame the wild horse."'

I couldn't imagine my grandmother being such a maverick, but looking back on her life now, she was a very determined woman, hard-working, strong, industrious and wise. And quite surprisingly, for someone who was traditional and old-fashioned at heart, she embraced not only her own culture and tradition but those of other cultures with a tolerant and compassionate interest. After all, my father was not Chinese, and she had been under a great deal of pressure from well-meaning family and friends not to go ahead with it when she gave her blessing for my parents' marriage.

'Was it a big celebration when you were married?' I asked. Some quick mental arithmetic put the wedding at about 1912 or 1913.

My grandmother reminisced, with that dancing twinkle in her eye I often saw. 'Weddings back in the village were such happy events, and many guests were invited. Marrying a *tin fong* (a bride who filled the place of a first wife after her death) was like marrying a first wife. So I had all the trimmings; there was a *tai hung fa kui* (a sedan chair), *tai long san* (large patterned umbrella) and *hei cheung* (cloth embroidered with symbols of happiness). I married your grandfather as a *tin fong*, and my foster brother bought two large baskets full of coconuts, betel nuts, sweet rice cakes and buns. It lasted three days, the wedding ceremony, with big banquets on each day for relatives and friends. It's very different now, of course. We had at least twenty tables at the banquet. When your second and third uncles were married, back in the village, they had over forty tables. Their celebrations each lasted for three days too.'

China was such a foreign country to me. Her borders were closed, and at the time there was little chance of my ever visiting the village my grandmother spoke so often about. It was the ancestral village of the Mok clan, in the southern province of Guangdong.

'Why three days? I'll tell you why. Each day had a special meaning. On the first day, the day of the wedding itself, the banquet is to welcome in the dowry; then the second day's banquet is to celebrate the wedding and the third day's is for *ching chi* (the ritual tea ceremony to one's elders). On the day of the wedding, the bride has to offer tea to all the family elders in the Ancestral Hall. A middleman called out each of the groom's relatives by name, sat them down in the centre of the Hall, in order of seniority, and I then offered them their tea. They each gave me a *laisee* (red lucky packet), with money, jewellery or gold. They all wore those long black, silk damask gowns with auspicious emblems woven into the fabric. And those funny hats, you know, the ones with the red knob on top.'

I smiled at the traditional image I recognised from the old black and white Chinese operas, iconic stage productions reprised for television. Although I couldn't understand them, I was able to follow the gist of the story line mainly by the mood expressed in the music, and I often found my grandmother enjoying their screeching high-pitched singing and their stilted mime. The Cantonese opera star Yum Kim Fai was her favourite by far. Renowned for her ability to sing in the lower register, she was able to play both male and female roles, although she often performed the male lead opposite famous actresses of the day.

'You know, it was customary for the guests to make fun of the bride during the banquet, as a way of testing her temperament,' my grandmother went on. 'Sometimes they would tease the bride, other times they might goad her to drink a sip of alcohol, or sing a song or recite some poetry. Guests asked me to make up a poem.' She chuckled. 'But I just made up a funny joke and sipped a little bit of wine. Then of course, on the third day, I went back home and we had a roast pig,' she boasted.

'What! You roasted a whole pig?'

'Of course. Your grandfather's family sent a whole roast pig back to my home. If there was no pig, it would have brought dishonour to the family name.'

I didn't understand any of this, so my grandmother explained. 'If there was no pig, it means the bride had lost her virginity before the wedding night. Chastity was the most important thing, not like nowadays. You know, a man could have his new bride thrown out if he discovered she was not a virgin.'

'What, you mean even after they are married?'

'Yes. The marriage ceremony goes on for three days, right? Well, after the first day, the man takes his new bride by his bedside. If he discovers then that she has already given herself to another man, he can have her thrown out and the wedding is called off. It would have been the ultimate disgrace. That is why girls were not allowed out unchaperoned after they were thirteen. You know, in case they became acquainted with men. We all had our own little back streets in which we maidens could wander freely.'

My grandmother looked at herself in the mirror as she put the finishing touches to her hair. 'But some men, they really went too far. After taking their bride, they wiped her down below with a handkerchief, and then took it out for their elders to inspect. Just to prove whether or not she was a virgin. They had no sense of decency. No shame.'

'Where exactly were you married?' I asked.

'Guangzhou. Well - the village. Very close really. Once I got into the bridal sedan chair, I was there! Crying all the way, of course. The go-between said to me, 'you can throw down your handkerchief now, we're here.' Hmm, how come so quick, my heart was thinking within. You know, back in those days, the bride was locked in a small cockloft for a month before the wedding, and not allowed to come out. Her maiden friends had to bring in food and comb her hair and keep her company. We all cried together, singing bridal laments.'

My grandmother gave me a short rendition, her waxing modulating tones gracefully rippled the surface of the still air. I couldn't understand the words, but judging from her coy expression it must have been a little mischievous. I enjoyed its lyrical melody, and the way in which my grandmother swayed her head and relived a very different world.

'OK, that's all. You don't really want to hear any more. It goes on and on, there are so many things to sing about, you know. All about the family, and what we are doing, and how we are feeling, and what we wish for.' There was that smile again. 'Then afterwards, they went out to gather *chee tau mong* (plants which stick to clothes and hair) to throw at the wedding procession.'

'Oh, a little like the Western custom of throwing rice and confetti and things like that?' I offered, trying to compare and contrast what I knew about English traditions and customs.

'They do that in Western weddings too?' my grandmother was rather surprised. 'I didn't know they threw rice. In Chinese weddings, when they scatter rice we had to open an umbrella to shelter ourselves. It was to prevent bad luck falling upon the new bride. But you know, years ago, we never had to do that. Do you know the story of how it came about that we use rice in the village? I will tell you why.

'Many years ago it was said that two Immortals, Chow Kung and Tao Fa Kuo, had been battling for some time to determine who was the more powerful of the two. You see, they both had the power to help people by predicting their futures. But although they both had this power, Chow Kung was also a judge.

'One day, an old woman went to him to ask about her

son's future. She was horrified to learn that her son would die at a certain time, on a certain date. Naturally, the woman was very distressed, and she cried and cried, and begged him to save her son. But Chow Kung told her there was no way he could help her. So the woman's friends and relatives implored her to plead with Tao Fa Kuo instead. She went to see her, and recounted her story. Tao Fa Kuo told her to go home, and at the time and date predicted for her son's demise, she was to hold up his clothing and shout his name very loudly. The time arrived, and the woman did everything she was told. Her son heard his mother calling him, woke up from his sleep and rushed outside to her – just as his house collapsed.

Now the old woman was overjoyed that she had been able to save her son, but she soon became very angry with Chow Kung for refusing to help her. She went to him and announced, in no uncertain terms, how his long-time rival, Tao Fa Kuo had come to her rescue. This annoyed Chow Kung, so he thought up a plan to get the better of her. Using his position as a judge, he ordered Tao Fa Kuo to marry his son. His scheme was this. He planned to use his gold cockerel to peck the new bride to death as she rode in her sedan chair on her way to the wedding. Should that fail, he planned to kill her on the wedding night, when the newlyweds dine together in their bridal room on a special dish that was meant to symbolise good luck and long life. They would take this meal together at midnight, and his plan was to hide a white tiger in their bed, so that the bride would be eaten when she got in.'

'Wouldn't the tiger eat his own son too?' I asked, a little puzzled.

My grandmother had anticipated the query and had the answer waiting. 'It's customary for the bride to sit on the bed and wait for her meal to be uncovered, and then be invited to take it by her new husband. But luckily Tao Fa Kuo saw through his evil plan. She realised when she was ordered to marry his son that Chow Kung was out for revenge. Cleverly, she arranged for her relatives and friends to prepare bags of rice, and told them to throw the rice over her sedan chair as she was getting in. That way, the gold cockerel would be too busy pecking at the grains of rice to pay any attention to her. Then she asked the cook to prepare another pork dish, and just before their midnight meal on her wedding night, she threw the dish onto the bed to attract the white tiger. She pushed the groom in as well, and he soon got eaten. That is how it came to be that people in the village throw rice on the sedan chair, and why Leun Cheong Fan (the special dish of pork and rice) is customary on the wedding night in order to protect the bride.'

I remember being more than a little confused by the story, for I had a bad recall of traditional Chinese names. To make matters worse, it was difficult to tell male characters from female characters, as there are no gender pronouns in Cantonese, like 'he' or 'she'. Maybe I was thinking in English and I should have been thinking in Cantonese. But it was always fun to listen to my grandmother talking. She had a lyrical quality about her voice, and intensity in her speech and manner which was hard to resist.

I watched her as she put away her brushes and combs. Her dressing table had served her well over the past sixty years. She had the top drawer, and my sister and I had one each of the lower drawers for almost all the clothes we owned. It is a little strange to know that this dressing table, which featured so prominently in our little flat, is now a permanent exhibit in the Museum of Hong Kong. I wonder if one can still smell the grain of wood, so richly perfumed by a collection of medicinal oils my grandmother kept in her little side drawer next to the mirror; oils of lavender, eucalyptus, cinnamon, lemon grass, peppermint and white flower. Sometimes when I walk into a Chinese medicinal store, I get a subtle reminder, and it takes me back to a time and a place that seems so far away.

6

A family divided

Every morning my grandmother woke before the sun rose. As everyone else in the flat stirred to the distant hoot of vessels in the harbour, Grandmother would be found in the kitchen, brewing a fresh thermos flask of green leaf tea, or perhaps returning from the local market with freshly-fried dough sticks to accompany the tasty congee (rice gruel) she sometimes cooked for our breakfast.

I stood on the pavement in the Sheung Wan (Western) District, much of it reclaimed land. It is the oldest settled part of Hong Kong. The British moved out when the island was seized in January 1841, leaving the then malaria-infested area to the Chinese. I loved our trips to the nearby market and lanes. It was a web of balconied tenements, busy street markets, hawker stalls, traditional open-fronted shops and fascinating traders, from the craftsmen at work on soapstone or tusks of ivory and the flourishing snake shop just a stone's throw away. Even though I knew the snakes were kept coiled in caged baskets outside the shop, the thought of walking too close to them frightened me. But as a young child, I watched, from a safe distance, a young man in a sleeveless vest pick up a long thin snake, and skin it, live, before my eyes. Bottles of wine made from snake gall bladders and bile were on sale, giving his customers the extra strength they needed to see them through the winter months.

The restaurants nearby were renowned for their snake delicacies and soups, whilst a little further down the road, glass cabinets fronting my home street displayed an array of Chinese medicinal ingredients, dried sea horses, birds' nests, antlers and horns, and the highly prized ginseng roots. Tea shops with large gold urns served tortoise jelly; made from powdered tortoise shell, this bitter black jelly-like medicine is also served as a dessert when sweetened with honey or cane sugar. The tortoise is an auspicious creature, not only representing the beginning of creation but symbolising strength, longevity and endurance. My grandmother knew the owners, but I don't remember ever stopping by to taste even a spoonful. I suspect it was outside our price bracket.

Along the tram, we would often go to my grandmother's favourite stores, selling various grades of dried Chinese mushrooms, salted and preserved fish, flat duck, dried scallops, prawns, seaweed and aromatic strings of sun and wind-dried sausages. All around me were hawkers, squatting on the roadside with their wares spread out on sheets of yesterday's newspaper, or standing by their wooden carts brimming with fruits or vegetables, clothing, plastic sandals and reams of fabric. A few trotted past me, their flip-flops slapping against their heels, a bamboo pole across their shoulders as they balanced baskets full of goods at either end. Along Queens Road, red London double-decker buses spewed their exhaust into the humid atmosphere as private cars and taxis swerved in and out to avoid being caught in the inevitable traffic. On the tramlines of Des Voeux Road, rickety double-decked trams carrying advertisements for cigarettes and brandy dinged and clicked in constant succession, their regular stops allowing one to glimpse the working harbour just a few feet away. Riding a tram gave one the feeling of safety whilst travelling down the heart of a busy road, though I'm not sure about the trailers which were introduced for a short period during my childhood. They were somewhat of a novelty but didn't last long.

Fruit stalls, with crates and baskets piled high, created the most tantalising aromas of delicious, juicy goodness. Large watermelons hung in carriers from the bamboo poles overhead. My eyes feasted on the guavas, papayas, mangoes, lychees, dragon eyes, pineapples, oranges, apples and bananas spread out before me. For fifty cents, one could choose whatever fruit juice one wanted, and have it freshly squeezed; heavenly, on a hot summer's day.

My grandmother fingered the imported oranges in front of her. 'Are these sweet? How are they selling' she shouted to the fat hawker woman trying to tie up a paper bag with twine, one end gripped firmly between her decaying teeth. My grandmother never bothered with the prices displayed on small placards wedged between the fruits. They were there for the benefit of others who would inevitably end up paying more for their goods. After sampling a few soft fruits we ended up with a catty of lychees instead.

'Now, I must stop by the letter writer, before he closes up for the morning', she said, 'and then, if we have time, I will buy you and your sister some roast pork, as a treat. Now come, let's cross the road.'

A passer-by spat. He missed the manhole cover by a fraction of an inch. I could hear the cursing of hawkers as they cajoled one another; *cho hou* or *lann hou*, literally meaning coarse or rotten mouth. Their curses and swearing were never translated for me, though there were times when I heard my grandmother shout similar expletives on the rare occasions when she lost her temper. From a short distance away, the dulcet chirping and twittering of birds, perched in their individual cages, ascended the mundane noise of the main road traffic. Only a few blocks away, hidden from view, was the site of my grandmother's watch shop, long since demolished to make way for a modern financial building. Bamboo poles stuck out overhead, outer garments threaded along their length to dry in the sun. At street level, stalls piled with dried salty fish added their own distinct smell to the busy market district. *Dai pai* dongs (open air food stalls) were already doing a roaring business as manual workers and office staff stood side by side, slurping their soups and congee and shovelling fresh rice or noodles down their gullets. The stall holder, clad in a sleeveless vest and trousers, a half-apron round his flabby belly, tossed noodles over an open fire, whilst a cauldron of broth bubbled fiercely nearby. In his glass cabinet were freshly fried dough sticks, fishcakes, minced fish balls and stacks of clean bowls and plates. Clouds of steam wafted through the air, carrying with it the tantalising smell of spring onions and freshly cooked foods.

'Ah, Mrs Mok. *Jo-sun*. You going out?' called one of the newspaper sellers squatting outside a medicinal shop.

'Ah, good morning. Have you eaten rice yet?' my grandmother enquired politely, so as not to betray the fact that time was of the essence and that we were in a bit of a hurry.

'Yes, thank you. And you?'

'Thank you, yes,' my grandmother replied, though we had not yet had our midday meal. 'No problems with the big wind?' she continued, referring to the typhoon we had had a few days before.

'No, no. You are very kind to enquire,' the man said with a toothless grin. I noticed then how long his left little fingernail was. At least an inch and a half.

'I'm just on my way to the letter writer. See you again another day. Good business to you,' and with that my grandmother forged her way back into the crowds, with me tagging along for good measure.

The letter writer was an elderly man, dressed in black trousers and a mandarin-collared shirt. Bronzed and wrinkled, he had the appearance of a learned old scholar. In fact, to my mind he was exactly how I had imagined a Confucian scholar to be: a studious, learned man who had successfully taken his examinations and earned his place as an official despite his humble beginnings. If it had been one of the traditional Cantonese films my grandmother was so fond of watching on television in the early afternoons, he would not have stopped there, but instead would have risen to the rank of a local district judge.

'Lao Pak!' my grandmother called, though she was not much younger. I knew that was not his real name; in fact, it was not a name at all, merely a polite form of address. Lao Pak literally means 'old man of a hundred surnames', and is used as a respectful address to an older man whose name is not known to you.

'Mrs Mok, please, you are invited to sit down,' he greeted her, reaching for his thick rimmed spectacles. 'Haven't seen you here for a while. Are you well?'

'Much the same really, you know how it is at our age. And yourself? Good business?'

My grandmother rested on a low stool, her fingers brushing against the rough edges of an overturned wooden crate serving as a small writing desk. A pad of thin tissue-like rice paper lay in the middle beside two Chinese ink brushes and a small ink block. A short distance away, women were having their eyebrows plucked and threaded, their hairlines pulled back with tight bands to expose the forehead. I watched as the threader worked, expertly rolling a taut length of cotton thread over her customer's eyebrows and forehead, pulling out unwanted hair from their roots in what seemed to be a most painful manner. My grandmother had had it done too, but ceremonially, on the eve of her wedding, almost sixty years before. She had told me how the elderly 'good luck lady' pulled two red threads across her forehead, in order to '*hoi min*' (open up her face) as a way of blessing the new bride-to-be with many sons. This practice of threading had waned in popularity by the late 1960s, but could still be found flourishing in the back streets of Hong

Kong Island. It has made something of a resurgence in recent times, or perhaps it has just been embraced by Western cultures, as threading services are now commonly found in shopping malls in the UK and offered in salons as fairly pricey beauty treatments.

My home streets offered much more of which casual visitors were unaware, from the skinning of live snakes for winter soup to the circular tables with a hole in the middle. Monkeys would be chained to these tables, their heads secured into the hole so that there was no way of escape. I was told at night customers gladly paid for the privilege of scooping out monkey brains whilst the animal was still alive, and eating it as a rare delicacy. This was not a blood sport; it was supposed to release a massive flow of adrenaline in the poor animal, resulting in more tender and delicious organs. Some people now say that tales of this practice were just mythology, but I remember my parents pointing out where this took place, and it was not far from our flat.

The professional letter writer proceeded to set down, in formal Chinese script, what my grandmother wanted to say to her family back in Guangzhou. She spoke to him in common everyday language, explaining her thoughts and messages. He listened attentively, sometimes with his eyes closed, seemingly nodding in approval and understanding as he assimilated her sentiments. He then rephrased them for the written word. Half an hour later he was reading the letter back aloud, checking its accuracy and suggesting a suitable closing phrase. Now that it was written, my grandmother would be able to send off the sacks she had been preparing all week, having filled them with our unwanted or outgrown clothes.

The authorities in mainland China only allowed second-hand clothes into the country, so nothing was thrown out. Whatever we could send would be recycled. On this occasion, my grandmother was sending sacks to her third, seventh, eighth and ninth sons, to be shared amongst their families. Just prior to the Japanese invasion of Hong Kong in 1941 my uncles had taken refuge in China. According to my mother this was a shameful and unforgiveable act as they left my grandmother and my mother, their only sister, to fend for themselves. It was an action difficult to justify in the cold light of day, particularly during peace time, and I'm not sure if it was ever spoken of. Perhaps it was out of a feeling of retribution and anger, for my grandmother had decided to run the watch shop herself instead of giving it to her sons after her husband died a few months before. Or perhaps it was them taking advantage of the Japanese enforced repatriation because of the scarcity of food in Hong Kong soon after the occupation. My family never spoke about it, but whatever the reality, it was an act which divided the family for many years.

During the three years of Japanese occupation, and the following years of civil unrest as the Communists fought to gain control of China, my grandmother lost contact with many of her sons. Some were undoubtedly killed during the years of fighting, many having joined Chiang Kai Shek's Nationalist army. We were told years later that two of my uncles were executed as spies.

My grandmother never laughed. Well, I don't remember a time when she laughed out loud, with her face, yet her eyes danced. A lateral palsy on one eye, and early cataracts, served to restrict this for a while, but she still danced her laughter with her good eye. She never complained about her ailments but she did once say to me, 'you will understand when you get older'. She looked forward to the peace death would bring, and was philosophical about it, but she also loved life and loved learning from and talking with others. One day, many years after I had left home and she was living with my parents, both busy with full time working hours, she described herself by saying: 'I sit there like a grain of rice, with my mouth shut. I have nothing to say. I haven't done anything all day. It was so much more fun when young people were around.'

She was never one to dwell in the past; she lived for the present and for the future. Gradually, over time, she began receiving more and more letters from her long-lost sons, pleading for help and financial assistance. To my mother's chagrin and through much personal sacrifice and hardship, my grandmother scraped together money and clothes to send back to them from time to time. They, in turn, sent to her one grandchild after another, smuggled through the guarded borders of China, expecting her to raise them in the freedom and prosperity of Hong Kong. I suspect her sons must have thought she was well off, and perhaps in comparison she was, but in reality she often took in sewing from the local shops in order to supplement my parents' income. Our flat became home to a number of cousins, sometimes for several weeks,sometimes for years.

I recall two hundred Hong Kong dollars being mentioned, equivalent at the time to about twelve pounds sterling (British pounds). That sum was the budget my grandmother had to feed the whole household - me and my sister, four cousins, my parents, herself and the family cat - for an entire month, as well as to put my cousins through school.

One afternoon, after a trip to Causeway Bay, perhaps to Victoria Park, as we were jostling with the crowd as we tried to board a tram back to our home district, my father was pickpocketed. That was a whole month's salary gone, in one careless moment. I was not aware how we managed then, but as children I suppose many hardships were kept from us and we did not know any different.

The family must have sacrificed much to put me and my sister through what they considered the best education available in Hong Kong. After early years at the nursery school attached to the Cathedral Church of St John, we enrolled into Glenealy Junior School, which opened in 1959. It was designed to provide a modern liberal education for expatriate children, providing a curriculum based on the British curriculum for when they returned. It was also the first step in my parents' plans to get us into a British university. But in order to be eligible, one's mother tongue had to be English. My father told me he was therefore very worried when the first word I uttered was in Cantonese, in fact calling my grandmother. Accordingly my parents made a deliberate effort to keep us two children from learning Chinese, a decision I regret to this day. I was able to speak enough Cantonese to communicate with my beloved grandmother, but it became a language I reserved for her, and for our relationship, and I hardly speak it otherwise. It is as if it has been frozen in time, though over the years I have made many half-hearted attempts to be more fluent in the spoken language.

Initially we had a little carton of milk during morning break and the usual school dinners, where I remember the fuss so many children made about eating all their greens. After the first few years we took packed lunches into school. These were in Thermos flasks with boiled rice at the bottom, and a portion of steamed meats and vegetables at the top. My grandmother often made them from food she had prepared for dinner the evening before. I felt very special carrying my little flask into school. My sister was not so appreciative; she chose instead to feed much of her lunch to a small dog we saw almost every day at the bus stop before we began our steep walk up to the school gates. As we got older, we travelled to primary school together but I was allowed to walk the few miles home alone on the return journey. After school, waiting at the gates, would be an ice-cream man on his bicycle, with an icebox at either end filled with ice cream cones such as nutty nibbles, tubs of Dairy Farm ice creams, ice Popsicles and little packets of frozen oriental fruits; papaya being my favourite. 'Icey-cream! Icey-cream!' he would call out. I watched with envy as my classmates crowded around him, buying their afternoon treat in the hot sunshine and dearly wished I had money to do the same. It was around this time that my friends asked me to fold origami creations for them. My entrepreneurial self surfaced, and I charged 10 cents for labour! If I was lucky enough, I was able to afford an ice lolly once a week.

The walk home took us close to the Botanic Gardens, one of the oldest zoological and botanical gardens in the world.

Sometimes I would walk through it to catch sight of the small mischievous golden lion tamarins at play in their rather outdated enclosures, or the large but handsome Burmese python, coiled and looking deceptively innocent. The space wasn't big enough to house larger mammals, and I didn't much care for the birds, but the gardens were full of indigenous tropical and sub-tropical plants, like camellias, magnolias and bauhinias as well as the Hong Kong orchid tree. There were Victorian gas lamp posts too and a fine bronze statue of King George VI, erected in 1941 to commemorate one hundred years of colonial rule.

As children we were actively discouraged from inviting anyone over to play after school, let alone stay the night, and as a consequence we were hardly invited over to theirs either. I do remember one occasion when a primary school teacher 'happened to be in the neighbourhood' with her children and called in on us unexpectedly over the school holidays. I think it was a visit she was quite unprepared for. They didn't stay long. After all, it was basically a small one-bedroomed flat; we had no bathroom, went to the toilet in a chamber pot kept under my grandmother's bedside table, and slept on straw mats on the floor in the living room. I was pretty apt at carrying the chamber pot, filled to the brim with stagnant urine, to our kitchen sluice and cleaning it out. Although I felt different at school, I didn't make a big deal of it, and it certainly did not dominate my world. I felt fully accepted by my peers, and was never bullied or made to feel in any way inferior. But then again, I never talked about home, and particularly our limited sanitation, and I don't remember friends and school mates ever asking either.

I guess they all assumed that the world they knew and inhabited was the world everyone knew and inhabited. We all unintentionally make assumptions about others, their life experiences or their political persuasion just because they happen to be our peers. Both my primary and secondary schools were multi-cultural, with students of every race, colour and creed treated as equals, but I don't recall ever discussing or considering difference. It was only when I came to the United Kingdom in 1978 that I became aware of difference and indeed experienced the undertones and unspoken effects of racism.

'Okay, let's go home now,' my grandmother called, 'or I shan't be able to cook lunch in time for your mother and father's return.'

Across the street, an elderly man was checking through a pile of invoices, the sharp clacking of his abacus resonating on the glass counter. A cigarette hung innocuously from one corner of his mouth.

Our return route took us along the tramway, with a brief detour down onto the waterfront. I watched out for young boys fishing with their tackle, squatting precariously on the edge of a short wooden jetty. Further up the street, a mass of colourful placards and signboards hung from our local restaurants, many four or five storeys up and famed for their hospitality. One displayed a huge flower-board, announcing the wedding party it was hosting that day. Next door, workmen had begun setting up scaffolding outside the building, long bamboo poles tethered together with lashings of reed.

Approaching the corner of our little street from the west

gave me the first reminder that we were so close to the financial centre of Hong Kong Island. In the midst of little shops and hawker stalls stood the imposing Bank of China, its gold-coloured gates swung wide open. It was like entering the portals of a different world. The building was air-conditioned, yet there was a sparsity about it, and I never ceased to be struck by the simplicity of each teller's window, such was the contrast to the other banking halls of the Hong Kong and Shanghai Bank, or the Chartered Bank in Central District. And inside, hanging on the main wall was a large framed portrait of the great chairman, Mao Tse-tung. Dominating the adjacent wall was an enormous mural, which literally spanned the whole width of the banking hall. Its two-dimensional perspective was quite striking. It featured a crowd of young people, grouped together in one corner and spreading out all along the lower border, giving the impression of hundreds of thousands more just like them. Their faces were a glowing bronze, their black hair blown back over their ears and their eyes fuelled with a sense of determination and purpose. Their fists were clenched and held above their shoulders. Rising out like a phoenix from the ashes were red flags waving in defiance against the ceaseless wind that blew against them. Poetically, as if ordained from above, the image of the Chinese leader became the focus of the picture, a halo of radiating glory and promise emanating from his presence.

I had been taken to see films at our local cinema, able to afford to sit only in the front stalls. They were filled with loud, stirring and emotionally-charged music, with choruses of peasants singing about their patriotic duty and the glory of the motherland. Powerful dancers leapt effortlessly in brightly-coloured costumes, offering leadership and hope. I could not follow the story line in any detail, mainly because it was all sung in a Chinese dialect, but it was always the same. The hero and heroine of the film end up having to make a choice between personal, and often marital happiness or fighting for the good of the country. China always won.

Such films were not the only cinematic experience to make an impact on my childhood. One very different experience happened when I was about five years old. In fact, it was my first experience of being taken to the cinema, with its enormous auditorium and massive screen, unlike the multiplexes of today. As the auditorium darkened, tantalisingly gentle music filled the crowded space, and immediately I was transported into a world of majestic natural beauty. I had never seen such a world before. The film was 'The Sound of Music', and the opening sequence with Julie Andrews coming up over the hilltop has become one of the most powerful images in my life. I fell in love with the film immediately: the scenery, the music, the story and most of all, its gentle and breathtaking beauty. It seemed to transcend my humdrum everyday life, the protagonist and heroine bringing to seven emotionally-deprived children the love they had longed for and the joy of music and childhood. Of course, we were only able to see it once - videotapes were unheard of at the time - and it was a one-off treat my parents could ill afford. But it filled my young heart with promise and hope, love and inspiration. I remain a passionate fan of the film, and of Julie Andrews, its star.

7

In at the deep end

It came as a rude awakening when I arrived at Heathrow Airport in September 1978, ready to take up my post as a medical student at the London Hospital. The immigration officer scrutinised my travel documents, demanding to see my letter confirming the offer of a place at medical school. He brusquely quizzed me over how much money I had with me and whether or not there would be sufficient funds for me to pay my university fees as well as my daily living expenses. He eyed me up and down with derogatory suspicion and promptly carted me off to the medical centre as though I were some infected foreign subspecies. I was examined by a male doctor who was the rudest medical practitioner I have ever had the unfortunate pleasure of meeting, although at the time I was too young and intimidated to make an issue of it. I was required to have a chest X-ray, and was led, topless, through a fairly public corridor to the radiography room, while a number of strangers, mainly male, walked past us.

It was also mandatory that I should be inoculated against smallpox, cholera and tetanus. Luckily, I had already had all the necessary vaccinations - but Hong Kong was not some third world country living in poverty. By the time I came to Britain it was one of the world's strongest financial centres, and my family were pretty well off - the emerging Eurasian middle class. We had already moved out of the traditional Sheung Wan District, and had secured a spacious 3-bedroomed flat in the mid-levels, courtesy of my father's position in the civil service. My sister and I shared our own room, we had two bathrooms complete with bathtubs and flushing toilets, a living room, a dining room, servants' quarters and a veranda which overlooked a private courtyard. Sure, there were times when hawkers would come up the hill to sell their wares, but they were not there permanently - and there were no restaurants nearby, or newsagents, or shops, only a park and private gardens filled with flowers and tended by a paid gardener. There was even a sheltered sports area, with ping pong tables, and access to the green mountain behind us by way of a private path.

I know from hearing second-hand accounts of other people's experiences, especially those of women from the Indian sub-continent, that my own story bears little resemblance to the humiliation they must have been put through when they arrived in Britain to join their husbands already living here. Imagine being subjected to an internal examination to prove that one is no longer a virgin, with the conclusion that they must therefore be married.

When I was informed that I had secured a place at the London Hospital Medical College, I was in fact in London on a visitor's visa, having had to sign something to the effect that I would leave the country immediately after my six-week holiday. So, despite coming to the end of my long summer trip in Britain, I had to return to Hong Kong, apply for a student visa, repack my bags and once more make the 19-hour flight. In those intervening two weeks, apart from celebrating Moon Festival and my father's birthday, I was so busy getting all the necessary formalities sorted that I don't think I realised the enormity of the undertaking and what lay ahead. On the same day that I collected my new visa, passport and air ticket, I kissed my family goodbye once more at Hong Kong's Kai Tak airport. I was committing myself to five years away from home and had no idea when I would see them again.

On a grey, drizzly, late September morning, I arrived in Britain with no one to meet me at the airport and nowhere to stay.

'Oh no, you have left it too late,' said the woman who was in charge of university halls of residence when I enquired on accepting the university offer. 'There are no spaces for you in any of the halls. No, I cannot help you find anywhere to stay. Sorry dear, I know you are coming from Hong Kong. You will need to see the accommodation officer when you arrive.'

Very helpful, that was. Luckily, a friend had managed, at the last minute, to book me a room in the Catholic Chaplaincy near the University of London. Travelling by underground train from the airport, it was another hour before I arrived at Goodge Street underground station. Eventually, lugging a heavy suitcase, and with a British Airways cabin bag stacked full of cassette tapes to bring some familiarity and sanity to my rather fragile world, I arrived at the Catholic hostel and checked in.

My first port of call was the Post Office tower (now known as the BT tower), which I could see up in the skyline. I went there in order to make my long-distance phone call home; just a short call, to let everyone know that I had arrived safe and well. Then it was time to visit the University's accommodation officer, where after a little to-ing and fro-ing, I was given a short list of possible bedsits. They were all in the East End of London, or a little further out on the Central or District lines if one looked at the underground tube map. However, time was not on my side, and I didn't dally around trying to find a place to stay. Anywhere that was half-decent would do, until I could sort myself out with more suitable accommodation.

I went to the pay phone and tried one telephone number, but did not get an answer. The next number led me to visit a Pakistani family, living in a small terraced three-bedroomed house in East Ham. The landlady, a rather large woman who was always smiling and chewing on betel nut, opened the door and showed me their spare back room overlooking an overgrown and rather neglected garden. The room looked very dark and unused, but it had a bed, a small bedside table, a wardrobe, a desk and an armchair. The floor was carpeted and I had shared use of the bathroom next door as well as the kitchen downstairs. The woman was at home all day, her husband worked at the post office and they had twin girls, aged five. The house was within walking distance from a tube station, eight stops up the District line from the hospital in which I would spend most of my pre-clinical years. I took the room, paid for a week in advance, and said I would return the following morning with my things.

By now it was well into the afternoon, and I was severely jet-lagged. Wearily, I found a café in central London, had a simple meal and returned to the hostel. I locked myself in my room, drew the curtains and sat on the carpet beside the bed. As I unzipped my luggage, I felt very much alone - and the enormity of what I was embarking upon caught me unawares. I was exhausted, and the adrenaline that had driven me for the past eight weeks deserted me. It was the first time I felt homesick and wondered what the next day would bring. But now at least, I had part of my music collection with me and my small portable Sanyo radio/cassette player. I listened to one of my favourite tapes. The familiar voice of Julie Andrews singing 'The Sound of Music' instilled a calmness and confidence within me, and I fell asleep before it had finished playing.

The London Hospital did indeed have a remarkable history. Founded in 1740, it was wholly financed by private charity, before the advent of antibiotics, when doctors and nurses put their lives at risk for the benefit of their patients. It had survived the cholera epidemics of the nineteenth century, the First World War, the horrors of the blitz and the introduction of the National Health Service. The hospital had been dominated by some of the most distinguished medical and surgical practitioners of the day, as well as such students as Dr Barnardo, who joined the college to train as a medical missionary, Hughlings Jackson, the father of modern neurology, and Langdon Down, who first described 'Mongolism' or Down Syndrome.

It was also in the East End of London, the home of Jack the Ripper, squalor, poverty, ill health and immigrants. When I first saw the London Hospital in Whitechapel a few months earlier I was in awe of its stature. Although I have many vivid childhood memories, including ones of inoculation clinics, school medicals, and a visit to the Emergency Department following a road traffic accident, I had never set foot in a hospital before. It felt very surreal and out of place. A mile from the city, the London Hospital's imposing edifice dominated the flat horizon of Bangladeshi stores and Cockney market stalls.

I had come for an interview with the Dean of the medical school, in the hope of getting a place that year. It was my first trip abroad - a sort of reward from my parents for completing my 'A' levels. Unknown to me, those in the know, government education officials and the like, had warned them that there was no chance I would be offered a place at a British university for medical training. In retrospect, I know that my parents had given me this holiday as a sweetener, in anticipation of the crushing blow that was inevitable - they had been told that in spite of any results I might obtain, it was unlikely that I would be offered a medical school place in the UK. It might be unfair; after all, my parents had sacrificed much to put me through years of an independent schooling system in Hong Kong that was supposed to be akin to the secondary education found in Britain. It was supposed to give students the same educational advantages when it came to sitting GCE examinations and applying for university. It was a system for the expatriate children in Hong Kong. I was not an expatriate. Half Chinese and the other half a mixture of Eurasian heritage, I would be classified as a 'real' overseas applicant, unlike those of other ethnic origins who had studied for and sat their 'A' levels in the UK. Although it was not open knowledge at the time, most medical schools did not accept overseas applicants - their 'overseas' quota was from those who had been schooled in Britain. Of the handful of training establishments that might take applicants like myself, the competition was extraordinary. In fact, there was one successful applicant every two years.

My headmaster summoned me to his office for a friendly chat about my career choice. He advised me in no uncertain terms not to apply for medicine. "Be a nurse instead," he said coolly. I was summoned to see the government's educational officer too, a Chinese woman who was pleasant enough but basically said it would be better to apply for a place at the Hong Kong or Chinese University. In reality, the Hong Kong College of Medicine had existed since 1887, and had trained Dr Sun Yat Sen, the man who later founded the Republic of China. The University of Hong Kong often appears in the lists of the world's top universities. But all my upbringing, and all my years had led me to this point, and I was damned if I was going to let anyone dissuade me from applying to a British university – especially on the grounds of being female and a foreigner. After all, to me, growing up in a colony, London's streets were surely paved with gold.

I had been a qualified medical practitioner for four years

when early one Sunday morning, my bleep went off. I was the duty on-call psychiatrist in a large district general hospital. A couple had arrived in the Accident and Emergency Department, and the casualty sister had said on the telephone, 'this one you've just got to see.' She did not say any more. It was more information than usual; often the referral was 'O/D [overdose] See psych' scribbled on the casualty card by a casualty officer who had not even attempted to assess the patient, apart from his or her immediate physical state. It seemed to be the policy that all 'overdoses' were referred; as were drunks who claimed they wanted to be dried out or threatened some form of self-harm, and those with apparent psychosis who had behaved in a bizarre manner.

I entered the main building. It was often quiet after a hectic Saturday night, and there were only a few patients still waiting to be seen. I remembered my own six-month stint as a hard-pressed casualty officer, but at least it was the only medical job I did which worked shifts; sometimes eight to five, sometimes nine to seven or occasionally a split shift of nine to one followed by five to eleven and then a week of seven nights - from nine to nine. There was none of this seventy-two hours on duty without any sleep nonsense, although I have done my fair share of that as a junior doctor. It was enough to drive even the sanest of us paranoid, as the bleep kept going off constantly, whilst nurses at the other end of the telephone seemed to request the most trivial and routine tasks in the small hours of the morning. I swear, bleeps have a secret life of their own, knowing when their owner is just about to doze off, just about to sit down to a meal or just about to go to the toilet. And bleeps had to be answered immediately, or they would go off again and again and again.

Of course, if it was a crash call, that was altogether different. Then, one would literally have to drop everything and run - it was all hands on deck for a cardiac arrest. That was all right, for the adrenaline would be flowing, and one would have been invigorated by all the running along corridors and upstairs, sometimes whizzing past groups of hospital visitors, staring as we held onto our bulging pockets filled with stethoscope, notebook, tourniquet, ophthalmoscope, torches, tape measures, a collection of butterfly and hypodermic needles and such like. Often it would have been far quicker to get on a skateboard, as these old hospitals seemed to sprawl out in all directions with long corridors between departments.

At times I would be overwhelmed at the thought that all England's hospitals were being covered by me and my contemporaries; we were the first-line doctors in casualty units up and down the country. We assessed patients, whether the 'walking wounded' or an 'ambulance-case', and referred on to the medical or surgical team 'on take' if the need arose. These teams had, as their first point of contact, a newly-qualified doctor, one year our junior, and that one year made all the difference. Consultants were not around at night or over the weekends, although they could be contacted at home or via the air call bleep. Then, it would be left to the most senior of junior doctors to make the call. They never minded, and were actually very supportive, but we felt such contact should be as a last resort. It was frightening, and a huge responsibility. Thank goodness for the nursing staff in casualty. They were highly experienced and taught us a great deal about emergency care and treatment. And they did so with the greatest of humour and an understated air of professional confidence. Now if the casualty sister said, 'This is one you've got to see' it was clearly going to be of interest to a duty psychiatrist.

'Psych? She's in cubicle two, and her husband is waiting outside'.

I picked up the single casualty card. A woman of 44, married with no children. Angry and aggressive. Refuses to go home with husband. No previous psychiatric history. Not a lot to go on, and all was quiet behind the drawn curtain.

I entered the cubicle. Sitting before me was a woman dressed in a white wedding gown. Her face was glowing with an inner energy, and her eyes were very much alive. She looked so beautiful, and so sadly out of place.

It didn't take long to establish a rapport with her, and she started telling me all about her plans to sing in her own operatic production in Milan. She had financed it herself, bought the material and made all the costumes, and had rehearsed the music to perfection. It was to be part of her honeymoon, and now was the time for her to leave. But her plans had not gone smoothly. She had sat and waited all day in the registry office for her fiancé to arrive. He was television's bionic action hero of the 1970s, the 'six-million-dollar man'. She was convinced he would come, but he did not. And then the registry office was closing, and people started telling her she had to leave, and she got more and more angry. Then her real husband, who had apparently followed her to the registry office, and even sat on a bench beside her all day, had brought her here, telling her that there was a special message waiting for her at the hospital.

No, she didn't think she needed to be in hospital. No, she wasn't ill in any way. She was just waiting for this special message.

And luckily, after hours of waiting, she began to believe that I had a special message for her, and she readily agreed to be admitted to hospital under my care. She was elated and full of energy, busily trying to organise the ward when she finally got there. She wasn't actually my patient, but I did see her the next morning when I visited the ward. What a different woman she was then. Her makeup gone, dressed in a pair of jeans and a simple white blouse, she was silent and looked very depressed and withdrawn. Her symptoms had begun when she accidentally discovered her husband having an extra-marital affair. She never told him, but instead it gnawed at her constantly, and she battled with her feelings of anger and betrayal, hurt and depression until they took the form of a mental illness.

8

Sudden death

A chicken ran amok in the kitchen. 'Keep the door shut' was the constant refrain as we circumvented the clucking feathered creature, enjoying its last day of freedom. In under 24 hours it would end up as a cooked offering on a tray in front of our ancestral shrine. Grandmother bought it from the market and carried it back home strung upside down. She allowed it to roam freely in the kitchen, pecking at the cat's food bowl, as she cooked the evening meal, but making it almost nigh impossible for us to bathe that evening. I returned from school the next day to see the bird hanging upside down from a bamboo pole, the last drops of blood dripping from its slit throat, into a small enamel bowl beneath. Soon it would be plucked and cooked, ready for the evening offering and the family feast.

Nothing was wasted; especially food and drink that had been offered for *bei sun* or ancestral worship. The chicken's head and tail would be enjoyed by my mother and grandmother, the feet were considered a delicacy, and the carcass and giblets would be used for stock the next day. My grandmother was a deft hand at wielding the cleaver, a heavy instrument she regularly sharpened on an abrasive stone. She used the same implement for all her cooking; cutting, chopping and mincing meats, slicing fresh vegetables, onions and ginger root, and crushing ginkgo nuts with its robust metal handle. Her chopping board was a three-inch-thick section of a tree, its rim reinforced by wire bound tightly around the circumference two or three times, and its rings giving credence to the fact it was from a tree trunk. We didn't have an oven for many years, and cooking was done on a twin-hob gas stove with a regular delivery of fuel, supplemented by a handy electric rice-cooker. Our cat wandered into the kitchen at whim, unperturbed by the hive of activity that peaked twice a day. When the kettle was boiling on the stove she would sit beside it, sometimes so close it singed her whiskers.

On special occasions, my grandmother made her delicious *har gow* dumplings and *char sui* buns. I was allowed to help fill the dough with diced, glazed barbecue pork before she steamed the buns on a large bamboo steaming tray. *Har gow* was a different matter, and I helped when I was much older as the dumplings took more skill to assemble and wrap. Both are eaten for *dim sum* at restaurants, served as a small bamboo basket of three or four items. But at home, we gorged ourselves until we could hardly move. She was also a dab hand at making steamed turnip cake filled with diced dried shrimps and Chinese pork sausage, *sui mai* (pork and prawn dumpings), sticky glutinous rice parcels and golden coloured steamed sponge cake.

'*Bong ng bong ah?*' was a query often heard in market streets around Hong Kong. The phrase means 'do you want this tied or not'? Purchases were wrapped in old newspaper and tied with string. It's no longer used these days as purchases are carried in paper or plastic bags. When I went to market with my grandmother, I would help carry tied up parcels of food, sometimes one item hanging off each finger. If I was particularly helpful or well behaved, she would offer to let me choose a treat hanging from a wire in a corner street stall – a ten-cent packet of chewy dried soybeans or a small bag of preserved sour plums (*hua mei*) which tantalized the taste buds all at once. A favourite and very popular Chinese snack, it gives a sharp tangy explosive mouthful of sour, sweet and salty sensations that still make me salivate just thinking about it. Or perhaps along the way we would pick up a long stick of juicy fibrous sugar cane from a hawker and take it home to chop into smaller pieces, or sit to enjoy a bowl of smooth sweet *dau fu far* (jellied soya milk with ginger syrup) eaten at a *dai pai dong* (open air street stall). Sometimes I chose a chunk of *char sui*; a full dollar's worth of glazed pork belly, not too dry and not too fat, chosen from a selection of cooked meats hung from metal hooks in open fronted eateries. Occasionally, my grandmother bought a small pot of maltose. I don't think she used it for cooking much, but we happily plunged a heated metal spoon, warmed in hot water, into the thick, sticky syrup and twirled a spoonful of sugar to make our own homemade lollipops.

Playing at home, I spent hours rolling bits of newspaper or tissue into tiny balls, and displaying them in my makeshift market stall. Small sheets of paper were torn into squares and laid beside cups full of different colour, and different sized paper balls. Not many people came to my stall, but I would pretend nevertheless, and proceed to scoop a spoonful or two into an expertly rolled newspaper cone, ask if it needed to be tied, and proceed to do so as I had seen in the local market.

My grandmother was often found to be pedalling away at her sewing machine under the light of a window in the living room. The doors to our little balcony were always kept open unless there was a typhoon, although we would sometimes shut the iron gate. I played a captive prisoner, asking my grandmother to bind me to one of the high-backed blackwood chairs. She wrapped me in a large length of fabric, tying me loosely to the chair. I felt comfortably held but struggled in a feeble attempt to escape. I soon tired of it though, and lost in the soporific rhythm of her pedalling, I would set myself free and curl up under the table, exhausted and adrift on a raft floating in a shark-infested sea. A frightening cry would bring me back to life, the loud, broken voice of a man sounding as if he could cut into me with his raspy cry. A cut-throat pirate. *'Mei laan yeh!'* he would shout. I couldn't make out the words, but I knew he was coming nearer every time I heard him. *'Mei laan yeh!'*, he would shout again. Later I found out it meant he would take away anything unwanted, and for a brief while I was more terrified. He was of course the local rag-and-bone man.

I gobbled and clucked like a chicken, running in circles around my grandmother's friend when she came to visit. She was treated like family, and I called her 'cousin mother'. We never really referred to anyone by name in Cantonese, instead calling them by how they were related to us. Cousin mother was a frequent visitor, having come from the same village in China and living through the horrors of the Occupation with my grandmother. She was my favourite visitor and often arrived with a little packet of sherbet she had picked up from the corner street stall. She was always smiling and I only ever played this game with her. As cousin mother sat on a stool in the middle of the living room, my sister and I ran around her in circles, gingerly closing in as she pretended to be asleep. Suddenly she would reach out in an attempt to snatch one of us, causing much excitement and laughter. If caught, we would be laid on our backs across her lap, our heads dangling as she 'slaughtered the chicken' by slicing through our necks with the side of her hand.

One summer, when I was about eight years old, I remember standing on our balcony trying to cool down in the sweltering heat. It was not so much the heat as the humidity that was stifling. Our ceiling fan was working flat out as my grandmother sat by her sewing machine. In spite of the background noise I could hear the rhythm of her foot pedal: the constant reassurance of the maternal heartbeat. Cotton garments hung motionlessly outside our balcony on long bamboo poles, having been scrubbed clean on the washing board an hour before. Our tabby cat came out to join me on the balcony, licking her lips having devoured another bowl of fresh rice and fish, bought daily from the local market. She meowed slightly and arched her back as she rubbed her fur on my legs.

"Hello there. And what can you see?" I asked, crouching down beside her, hardly aware of the gathering crowds in the street below. The sun was almost directly overhead, and I stood mesmerized by the spectrum of colours as they were diffracted onto the concrete floor. A patrol of ants marched up towards my plastic slipper and I lifted my foot for them to pass under. They declined, and chose a different path. How fragile life can be, I thought to myself. Here one minute, and gone the next. My gaze followed their path through the potted Chinese orchids and tangerine shrubs.

Soporifically, the gentle humming of the sewing machine continued, and soon my gaze drifted onto the massive advertising signboard which hung vertically down one side of our balcony. Large white characters upon a background of sea blue – 'YKK zips' - and the name of the shop next door. We could see the sign from both ends of the street, and whenever we saw it we knew home was near.

The crowd of onlookers below had begun to talk loudly amongst themselves. They were looking up just a little way to my left, so I leant forward over the balcony railings to get a clearer field of vision beyond the signboard. I saw a woman standing on the rooftop of a semi-demolished block of flats. She paced in an agitated manner, up and down a narrow ledge. She was waving her arms about, at times gesticulating to the onlookers below and shouting at them to be quiet, and at other times she threw her arms around her head and talked to herself. Dressed in unremarkable dark trousers and top, the woman looked in her mid-thirties, but I did not recognise her from the neighbourhood. She was clearly distressed, and I watched with disbelief as she sat down on the ledge, dangling her legs over the side of the bamboo scaffolding that partially surrounded the building. One of her brown plastic slippers dropped from her foot onto the ground below. It might have only been three or four floors up, but it was quite a long way down.

A police van arrived, and two officers cleared a path through the crowd. I noticed a red background on one of the officer's silver epaulettes, an indication he was able to converse in English too. Strange what detail comes to mind. Moments later, one of the officers was on the rooftop with her. He seemed to be talking, but I couldn't hear him, and the woman appeared to hardly notice his presence. It all seemed a bit of an anti-climax really after all the curiosity and activity, and I was getting rather bored of it all.

'I've had enough of this' I thought to myself. 'If you're going to do something, do it now, otherwise I'm going back inside'. Magical thinking, or what? Did the woman know what I was thinking? Had she read my mind or heard my inner thoughts, callous if casual? Suddenly, without any fuss, she stood up on the ledge, looked down to the street below, wrapped her arms round her head and jumped, feet first. I looked in disbelief. The next few seconds seemed to go on forever. Her foot caught the scaffolding, and she turned. My whole being plummeted into an abyss of numbed emptiness, and then inflated as if ready to burst in an agonising, guilty, dreadful silence. Nothing seemed real; everything played out before me in slow motion - from that deliberate leap to the fatal dull thud as her head and body hit the street below. But it was real. Her body did not just lie there, still and lifeless as depicted on cinema screens. It bounced like a heavy balloon, and fell back onto the ground. Moments later I saw a trickle of blood seep from her head and pool onto a manhole cover nearby. A fistful of emotions seized the pit of my stomach, and twisted it into a dreadful sickening panic. Was I really so omnipotent that my awful, innocent, secret and darkest thought could be realised? Could this really have happened?

My grandmother came out onto the balcony just in time to see the body being covered with a blanket. She muttered and sighed to herself about a wasted life.

"She just jumped," I tried to explain, but no more words came.

"Come inside now. There is no more for you to see here."

As the end of my first year at medical school approached, so did the MBBS Part I examinations. We either passed first time, or we had to work through the summer break and sit the entire set of examinations again. If one failed the second time, it was the end of one's medical career. In fact, a third of my year did not return after the summer to continue with their studies. Some chose to give up medicine, realising it was not for them. Others were somewhat relieved to have failed, feeling they had been pushed into the career by others, and the rest just did not make the grade. Although pretty devastating at the time, I suppose it was probably better to know earlier rather than later in one's undergraduate career. The sheer volume of work and the pressures we were each under made the traumas of 'A' levels the previous year pale into insignificance.

I worked very hard. I felt I owed it, not only to myself, but also to my family who had given up so much in order to put me through medical school. Over the course of the five years, my parents paid the full tuition fees, my living expenses and, whenever possible, flights home topped up with government travel points my father had somehow accumulated. I didn't know the details, but I was glad of them. But I was driven with an ambition to succeed in anything I chose to do, for in doing so, like the carp's persistence as he forces his way upstream against the rapids, I would bring the ultimate honour to my grandmother, my parents and my ancestors.

Disciplined, focused and organised, I worked to a personally-devised schedule of revision, so that every aspect of work was covered. Each day, I timetabled various subjects, slotting in time to rest and relax too, and at weekends I allowed myself to go out for one complete day without study. Sometimes I worked in the medical college's museum, desks hidden behind cabinets filled with pickled specimens of body parts and bones. In one corner, in a special display cabinet of its own, was the skeleton of John Merrick, better known as the 'Elephant Man' because of his grotesque physical deformities caused by the condition neurofibromatosis. He had lived in Victorian London and was exhibited as a human curiosity, the object of public humiliation, ridicule and fear until Sir Frederick Treves, a surgeon at the London Hospital in the 1880s, rescued him and allowed him to take sanctuary at the hospital. Merrick's grossly-deformed skeleton, a cast of his head and shoulders, the mask he wore, and the model he made of the church nearby were all on display in our museum. Years later, with the release of the film 'Elephant Man', featuring John Hurt and Anthony Hopkins, the medical college museum was besieged with people curious to see his skeleton. Michael Jackson, the pop star, even offered a substantial sum of money to purchase it for his own personal collection. Merrick's skeleton and all the artefacts were taken out of the museum, and I am not sure where they are today. But in my medical student years I often found myself looking at his strangely-deformed bones and thinking what a brutal and ill-fated life he had, yet also marvelling at what I had read of his gentle and creative personality.

I was very proud of the skeleton I owned as a medical student. My parents sent me an extra banker's draft to cover the cost of the purchase, as it had been impressed upon us how helpful it would be to own a skeleton from which we could learn the grooves on each bone and the muscle attachments that went with them. The skull was perfect, and I kept it as a companion on my bedside table. A little macabre, to say the least, but it was my way of confronting the horrors that awaited us during our years of training. I still have the skeleton, in its original box tucked away in the attic.

When not at the museum, I worked in my bedsit, venturing out into the downstairs kitchen from time to time to brew myself a cup of tea. During one such interlude I found my landlady in the kitchen, preparing lunch for her husband. He would be back in an hour or so and I could smell the spices of curry cooking on the hob. As I waited for the kettle to boil we engaged in a superficial conversation. She told me she had a bit of a headache, and asked if it would be appropriate to take tablets from a bottle on the table. It was a bottle of paracetamol tablets from the local chemist. I was sure it would be OK, but reminded her just to take two tablets. It's funny how people talk about their physical ailments when they find out you are a doctor, or worst still, a medical student. She asked what would happen if she took more than two, and I told her it would be dangerous. And yes, it is possible it could be fatal if one takes too many, I confirmed. She said nothing, but smiled and carried on with her cooking as I went back upstairs to my revision.

An hour later I heard the front door open. Presumably her husband had returned for lunch, but I paid scant attention to the background noise that came from a husband and wife's discourse. A short while later, I became aware that it was more than the usual chatter. There were people at the door, and unfamiliar clunking noises. I opened my bedroom door and stepped out onto the landing just in time to see my landlady being strapped into a wheelchair and pushed out by a paramedic. Her husband had gone on ahead.

'What's going on?' I enquired.

The paramedic looked at me. All I can remember was his uniform, and that he was playing with a bottle of tablets in his hand. 'I hope you are satisfied now,' he said to me, and slammed the door behind him.

I was completely stunned. My sense of shock and disbelief slowly gave way to irritation and anger. I realised what must have happened. My landlady had asked me about the tablets because she was planning to take an overdose. 'How dare she involve me!' I thought to myself. That day it began to dawn on me that some patients will cling onto a doctor's every word and that the message that comes across may not be the message that was intended.

9

Climbing the social ladder

My grandmother stood by her dressing table, brushing her long black hair as hairclips hung in readiness upon her lips. Her mirror reflected the sunlight from her window and the lush greenery of the mountains outside. Her room had good *feng shui* indeed. We moved into our spacious fifth floor modern apartment in 1975 after my father had been promoted to a position in the civil service high enough to warrant a subsidised government flat. I was fifteen. The entries in my diary read:

Tuesday 15th April, 1975: Dad received news of housing allowance at last. It has already been approved. Yippee! A few days later, probably this week, we will get the letter and can then sign the lease and move in about May 5th.

Wednesday 23rd April, 1975: Dad got this promotion letter today.

Thursday 24th April, 1975: Dad's signed the lease. Now we have the keys.

Saturday 26th April, 1975: Out nearly the whole day, buying lights for our new place, and also a round coffee table, bed covers and pillows.

Sunday 27th April, 1975: After church - going to use Series III Communion Service, went out again. Bought more lamps, chest, TV stand etc.

Monday 28th April, 1975: Got our new phone number 490013.

It was the first time we'd had a proper bathroom, complete with bathtub, hot and cold running water and a flushing toilet. It was so exciting. My sister and I had a shared bedroom just to ourselves, with bunk beds, our own individual wardrobes, desks and bookshelves. My grandmother had her own bedroom and my parents had a double bedroom with an en suite bathroom. We had a spacious kitchen and a utility area with our first washing machine so that my grandmother no longer had to scrub clothes on a hard washing board, and even a servant's quarters with its own bedroom and a small toilet. All the money we had in our savings accounts went towards furnishing our new home, and we made many visits there before actually moving in.

Saturday 3rd May, 1975: Very tiring day today. Stayed

in the new flat the whole day, signing for furniture delivery. Been very busy. Brought all my treasures up with me today. Fixed my drawers in my desk. Will ask Po Sun to make our book cases.

On one evening visit, I caught a reflection on the highly-polished wooden door leading to the servant's quarters which was to be our guest room cum study. It made me jump, as I was so certain I had seen someone else in the room. But it was only for a fleeting moment, and when I looked again it was gone. I saw it a few more times after that, on different occasions, but my father said it was only the reflection of the suit I was carrying into the room. Even writing this now sends a cold shiver down my spine.

Sunday 4th May, 1975: Moving house today – in the morning. Packers came at 8.30. Moved furniture for about two hours. Arrived at about 10.30 to fix things up. Andy came to fix our television today. Coming tomorrow to fix our doorbell and wiring.

Monday 5th May, 1975: Queen's visit... public holiday. The first reigning monarch to visit HK. Dad saw the Queen today when she went to the City Hall for lunch.

The day of our move was the first visit my grandmother made to the flat. She liked her room, but she was rather quiet. Perhaps it was the enormity of leaving the flat she owned in Western District and the part of Hong Kong she knew so well. Or perhaps it was moving to the steep green hills of Pokfulam, away from the hustle and bustle she thrived on. Pokfulam was gentrified. Its name gave it away. *'Pok fu'* bird in the forest (*lam*). Birdsong did fill the air and camellia and eagles claw flowers clung onto the side of the mountains. On her way to market the next morning, now necessitating at least a 30-minute walk or a bus ride, she lit incense in a burner in the study, and went quietly on her way. It was not until several months later that she told me why.

'Are there really ghosts?' I asked curiously one afternoon, having remembered some newspaper titbit I had read a few days before.

'What, you mean in Wanchai?' my grandmother replied, obviously having heard the news too, or seen it in her weekly Sunday edition of Chinese tabloid.

'You know, the cinema. In Wanchai. It's said to be haunted, isn't it?'

'Oh that. Well, maybe it is. It used to be a graveyard, before they built the cinema there,' my grandmother stated, as if that explained everything. 'I remember hearing about it a long while ago now. A film was screening, and this woman had to go to the toilet. She was washing her hands when all of a sudden, she felt someone tap her shoulder. She looked up in the mirror, so the story goes, and there was no one there. But she felt the tap again. This time she turned round and saw a ghost. Naturally, she ran out of the toilet, screaming. She wasn't the only one to see it either. Lots of women saw it after that. They are not using it as a cinema any more. No one will go there now.'

'Have I ever been to that cinema?' I enquired.

'I expect so. We've all been in that cinema before. But the ghost only appeared in the ladies' toilet. Never anywhere else.'

'It wasn't when we saw that film together, you know, the one with the green ghost ripping the heart out that woman when she was asleep, was it?'

'Which one was that?' my grandmother asked, as she pinned her long hair back into a bun. 'I've seen so many of these ghost films.'

'You know, the one with the net curtain,' I reminded her, an uncomfortable chill creeping upon me. That film had kept me awake all night when we were visiting Seventh Aunt in the New Territories. It was the first time we had been to her farm in Tai Po, and the first time I was expected to sleep with a mosquito net all around me. And I was terrified.

'No, not that one,' my grandmother assured me as a distinct sense of relief warmed my waking terror. 'We saw that in the cinema near here. Remember? We went by tram, with your cousins. That was many years ago now, I'm surprised to still remember it. It was the time I had that accident. I was carrying your sister and helping you board the tram, and before I could get a firm footing the silly driver started to go, and I was flung to the ground. You were very small then. I went into hospital.'

I have vivid memories of that incident. I must have been about five years old. I had already boarded the tram when she fell. I stood there as the tram clanked away, calling out for my grandmother as she lay unconscious on the concrete platform. And I wasn't allowed to visit her in hospital either. Those forty-eight hours are etched in my mind.

'Ah, you remember,' my grandmother continued. 'Your mother told me to complain to the tram company. I never bothered. We went to quite a few movies together, when you were little. Now I remember. I had to sit up with you all night, that time when we stayed over at Seventh Daughter-in-law's farm. I sat up with you, until you eventually fell asleep.'

'Yeah, it was very scary,' I said. 'That ghost was such a horrible green, with those piercing eyes. And when he went into that woman's bedroom, whilst she was asleep, remember? The guards didn't know he was there, did they? And they had lanterns and everything.' I could feel my heartbeat quicken at the memory. 'But he wasn't afraid of anything. Remember how his hand parted the mosquito net, and those long green fingernails? Then he just put his hand right into her body, and ripped out her heart. It was still pumping. And he swallowed it – and all that blood was dripping from his mouth.'

'He returned to take his revenge on her,' my grandmother continued before noticing the irrational fear in my eyes. I was certain she could even feel and hear the thumping of my terror. 'Don't worry, it was only a film. Ghosts and spirits are of a different world. They are not human. I say to myself, they do not eat people. If you do not harm them, they won't harm you.'

My grandmother had many personal experiences to recount and stories to tell. Indeed, she always knew, when she went into a room for the first time, if someone had died there in the past. She also seemed to know if their deaths had been violent, or premature in some way, and she would feel it her duty to call upon a monk or exorcist to placate the restless spirit. She often paid for small altars to be set up for them, so that their souls could rest in peace. The rest of the family did not encourage her sightings and perceptions, so she kept much to herself. They no longer frightened her, but every once in a while she would hint at some experience, years ago.

'You can believe it, or not, that's up to you,' she would

say. 'One day, I will tell you about them. What I saw with my own two eyes.

'I lost my father when I was two years old. He was in Peking [now known as Beijing] and wore his hair in a que. You know, like you see in old pictures. So we were thrown out into the streets, the three of us – my mother, my older sister and I. My sister was sold. I don't know what became of her. I've been thrown out many times, left in the street to die. But I was lucky. I learnt how to cook. I was cooking for the whole household by the time I was eight. When both my parents died, I was taken in by the Wong family. It was my adoptive mother; she was the first wife and she committed suicide – hanged herself because she was so ill-treated by her mother-in-law. Her mother-in-law forced her to make mats, she at one end and her daughter-in-law at the other. Anyway, the poor girl couldn't weave as fast, so her mother-in-law used to scold her and beat her. She was very cruel, with a black and wicked heart. My adoptive mother couldn't take it any more, and saw no way out. She hanged herself. My adoptive father took a second wife, but the first wife's ghost came to haunt him. Every night she'd appear. She would appear and sit on her gravestone when he climbed up the hill for fresh herbs. The ghost would declare her love for him, saying 'if you continue to sleep in my bed you must love me too'. It was quite frightening. He became really ill. Delirious. Started talking all sorts of nonsense. But it wasn't just him. Other people saw her too, and everyone shouted and made as much noise as they could to scare her away.'

My grandmother waved her arms in the air, imitating the villagers as they scurried around the narrow streets and courtyards. '*Aieeyaaa!* Quickly! Worship at the altar and get rid of her!' they shouted.

'But it didn't work. However much she was worshipped, it didn't make a blind bit of difference. So one night, the second wife lit an oil lamp. You know, the little wick you light. It's not like the lamps we have nowadays. They were all oil lamps then. And the ghost came. The flame changed colour, and burned green. Even the husband saw it change. Every time the ghost came, the flame got bigger and brighter and greener. Now that we have electric lights, I don't know any more, but in those days, a green flame meant there was a ghost present.

'Whenever I went with the family to visit the ancestral gravesite during Ching Ming (The Ghost Festival), I was always the one who carried a big lantern – just in case. In those days we were considered quite rich – quite well to do –and we would ask all the village people to come to dinner, and we would distribute food to them. Ching Ming is meant to be a happy occasion, you know, lasting many days and with plenty of food to eat. Ancestors are remembered for happy times too.

'Since the Communists came to power, we have electricity and water pipes in the village, so people don't need lanterns any more. They no longer had to fetch water from the wells or the river. I used to fetch water as a girl. A group of us maidens would run out and scramble down the hill to the river bank. It was littered with many bones – skulls, human skulls too. We used them to scoop water to drink from. After the Communists came the village elders used to joke with me, and said I no longer needed them to fetch water for me. You see, I used to sew clothes for them and their children, and in return they often fetched and carried my water. Now all the children are grown up, of course, but I used to mend their clothes too, when they were torn or needed repair.'

A few weeks after we moved into our new flat, my grandmother discovered that a previous tenant, many years before, had tripped on the concrete steps from the main road leading up to the block of flats, and died. She set up a small makeshift altar on the steps and lit incense for the unfortunate soul. After that, I never saw the reflection on the door again.

Diary: Saturday 14th October, 1978: Grandpa died this morning.

My father wrote to tell me. Grandpa had died, alone, in a hospital in Bangkok. I never really knew him, yet I have unusually warm, if somewhat sketchy, memories of him. I met him only once. It was probably early 1970 and it was his first and only visit to Hong Kong. I recall he stayed at the YMCA over on Kowloon-side, across the harbour, and visited us in our flat. He stayed the day and had dinner with us. He was a gentle man. I remember he gave me a dainty Thai pendant, a black pear drop trimmed in silver and with a silver Thai dancer in the middle. He taught me how to shade my pencil drawings, and following his visit he wrote to me occasionally. His prose was of its time, flowery and elegant, and he ended the letters 'your loving grandpa'. My father later described his father as 'always expecting everything would get better, if only he had a bit of luck. He had an approach to life that some would deem irresponsible, and certainly never bothered giving any of us a decent education. He really should have been born into a well-off family, and would then have been much admired as a kind and talented gentleman, because a gentleman he always was'.

Dad grew up in Burma (now known as Myanmar) during World War Two. He never really spoke of his father, or of his childhood. His mother abandoned him weeks after he was born, and with his father away much of the time fighting with the army against the Japanese who occupied Burma during the war, he lived with aunts, uncles and cousins in Insein before returning to Rangoon (Yangon) after VJ Day. His father's homecoming marked the start of a blissful if short childhood. From what I can piece together, the family had to live off Grandpa's savings, and when that ran out he gambled at cards and lost their beloved family home. They were forced to move into shared premises, taking a quarter of a bamboo house on stilts near the zoo in Rangoon. In later years Dad recalled a tornado ripping off their corrugated iron roof as the whole household tried to shelter under a table, and then the heavens opened and everything they owned got drenched. After that the family took shelter in the main railway station nearby at the slightest hint of a storm approaching.

Grandpa was a talented artist in pencil and completed a number of much-admired large portraits. He was also a gifted mathematician and an expert in English grammar. He walked for miles criss-crossing the city to give private tuition as their only source of income. In time he came home with a lady friend, and they married and started a family. When his first half-siblings were born, Dad recounts that he became the object of beatings from his stepmother. So he spent much of his formative years away from home, loafing around the streets of Rangoon, picking up and selling old used bottles for a few coins, doing odd jobs and whiling away the hours reading in the local library. He never went to school. Instead, he found solace in the local church and soon became lead chorister, until his voice broke. Evensong, late on a Sunday afternoon, was a special time for him. The rehearsals leading up to it and the service itself gave purpose to his week, but it also marked the beginning of a new one where there was nothing much to do.

He soon came to the notice of the choir master and organist, who was instrumental in getting him a church scholarship to attend school for a year. Although Dad enjoyed it, he quickly abandoned the idea, as he was bullied and did not want to be called a 'free boy'. His choir master acted as an *in loco parentis* figure, and in time informally adopted him as a cherished godson. He was a major influence in his life; I don't remember meeting him but I must have done as an infant. Shortly after I was born my birth certificate was changed and I was named after him.

The British returned to Burma towards the end of the Second World War, but the colony quickly moved toward independence. An independent Union of Burma was declared in 1948, but it was a fragile new nation beset by political infighting and civil war involving ethnic minorities and communists backed by China. In the late 1950s, Dad saw uncles, aunts and cousins sail away to foreign shores. With the help of friends, he found enough money to make his own escape. At the age of 18, on the same day that he buried his paternal grandfather, Dad abandoned his birth country to forge a new life for himself, following in the steps of his Godfather who had been posted to Hong Kong. I am not sure when Grandpa managed to get himself to the safety of Thailand, or what became of the rest of the family, but in 1962, the military leader Ne Win seized power and Dad lost contact with his family and friends. It was to be over forty years before he set foot in his homeland again.

10

The Japanese Occupation

In December 1941, Hong Kong fell into Japanese hands. The Japanese troops overran the border from Canton (Guangzhou), bombed the planes at Kai Tak airport and swept through the New Territories' British defences. With the rapid fall of Kowloon, the Japanese troops had taken it for granted that the rest of the colony would be a walkover. Instead, they met unexpected resistance on the island, so they showed no mercy. Historic records state those captured in the neighbourhood of the Repulse Bay Hotel were tied up with ropes and put to death. Some had their arms sliced off; some were decapitated; others were bayonetted or shot over the cliff. On the morning of Christmas Day, wounded soldiers receiving treatment at St Stephen's College were slaughtered, and the bayonets went right through their bodies into the mattresses. Later that day, in the grounds of Victoria Hospital, other captives were put to death by bayonet or fire, with a Japanese corporal reportedly remarking that 'they cried like a lot of pigs'.

After the initial three-day victory carnage for the conquerors, known as 'the sack', when the victors took whatever liberties they pleased with the local civilians, General Sakai wanted to show 'the snooty British that they could be gentlemen too'. The British have since reported finding the '23rd Army's conduct obliging and courteous'. But for the Chinese, unlike the Europeans, the killing went on and they lived in abject terror. The atrocities were public and as far as I know, no one has been held to account for them.

In the summer of 1941, my grandfather died unexpectedly in the streets of Hong Kong, just months before the Occupation. He was in his 60s and left behind a wife and seventeen children. My grandmother was in her early 40s. She had years ahead of her, and wanted to make a life of her own. Now the sole owner of a watch and clock shop, she decided to take over the reins of the family business instead of passing it to her sons. Whatever the motive behind it, I think she was certainly ahead of her time. It caused a rift in the family that gaped into a chasm when her sons decided to flee Hong Kong and return to Guangzhou. They left behind their one sister, aged eight, (my mother) and my grandmother. To this day I am not sure if the decision was related to the business, or to the Japanese repatriation policy during the occupation, fuelled no doubt by a deeply-ingrained patrilineal culture where women were worth nothing and considered a burden, their only role being to bear male heirs. I don't know the details and my mother and grandmother have never spoken of it, but I get the sense that my grandmother was a very strong woman, and had a rightful claim, having borne seventeen children, all male but one. I'd like to think it was because she chose to keep the business running. My grandmother might indeed have encouraged them to find safety in China. I rather suspect my mother thinks otherwise and the abandonment was unforgiveable for half a century.

As the menfolk left, my grandmother remained in Hong Kong, with women from her native village living close by. Their protective maternal instincts were strong, and they did all they could to shield their children from the horrors of the Occupation. Some of her younger sons must have stayed behind, because in later years she told me about her tenth son, a boy with whom she had a very close relationship. He always looked out for her and she was heartbroken when he died at the age of 12. It must have been during the Occupation or just after, as he was buried in a cemetery in Pokfulam.

'It was a very dark time for us', my grandmother recounted. 'Sometimes we had no choice but to defy the curfew. There were bodies everywhere, littering the roads and streets. Mauled and dismembered. Beaten to death, they were. I saw it all. Tortured for nothing. Or attacked by Japanese dogs. So senseless. You won't believe it, but I saw the corpses of women who had been bayoneted through their vaginas.'

Grandmother looked up from her bowl of tea, her hands cupped round the china vessel although the drink was still piping hot. She never spoke about such things as I was growing up. These snippets and anecdotes I gleaned from her as an adult, when I returned home for short visits whilst settled in the UK. But she never gave that much detail, even when probed.

'There was so much hardship in those days. We hid behind barred doors, praying to the gods to save us. We ran from one house to another under the cover of darkness as Japanese soldiers went on the rampage, looking for 'flower girls'. Thousands were raped. They were drunk and lustful. Hammered on the doors. We wore black, and hunched our backs as we walked. Daubed our faces with mud and dirt. We didn't want to attract their attention. One time, I barely managed to escape with my life. I was carrying a child strapped on my back, scrambling over the roof desperate to get away. I was so incensed I wanted to report the soldier to his superiors, but my neighbour talked me out of it. Just as well she did. He wasn't one of the regular Japanese soldiers. He was a Kempeitei - Japanese Gestapo. Like the military police. They did what they liked. They were totally unrestrained.'

From later research into the Japanese Occupation of Hong Kong, I learnt that the Kempeitei were nominally subordinate to the Army, but operated for all practical purposes as a law unto themselves. There was unchecked brutality. Their main task was to ferret out subversion, regardless of where the threat came from. This included clipping the wings of the Triads. Lorries filled with 'dangerous elements' trundled regularly to King's Park in Kowloon, which the Kempeitei designated as their execution ground. At other times, they drove around in special trucks, snatching people off the streets and dropping them off on one of the barren and uninhabited islands to fend for themselves.

'You won't understand such things. Your grandmother has lived through many heartaches and sorrow. Too much to talk about. But they are all in my heart. That is why Mrs Kum and Mrs Chow are so important. We go back a long way. They were there with me. We are like three sisters.'

The Japanese found the colony much less use than they had imagined. It wasn't incorporated into the Japanese-run parts of China, and nothing fruitful came of their occupation. The New Territories became a battleground for bandits. Streets were a mess of corpses and shell holes. Water, electricity and other public services were cut off, normal commerce and industry were at a standstill, the food shortage was acute and there was mass hunger. In fact, Hong Kong couldn't afford to support the Japanese military base as well as the population, so plans were made to trim it from 1.6 million to 500,000. Villages were emptied as many were forcibly expatriated to the mainland.

'There wasn't enough food', my grandmother recounted. She put her hands to her face. 'Our faces were all bloated like this, we had so little to eat. Anything that could be eaten was eaten. There was no fuel. I had to break up our set of blackwood furniture for firewood. Every book was burnt. There was no money. We had ration cards but all we could get was three taels of rice [equivalent to about 120 grams] for one person each day. The Japanese rationed everything - rice, oil, flour, salt, sugar. We journeyed into China whenever we could. The Japanese were actually quite glad when we left the island. It reduced the number of mouths they had to feed. Well, they could hardly feed us anyway'.

Beatings, murders, executions and torture were commonplace. In 1943, seven people were beheaded on the beach for possessing a radio. Local people were used for bayonet practice. Those who managed to avoid the attentions of the Kempeitei death squads seethed at the daily humiliations. The Chinese had to use disinfectant whenever they entered a Japanese building. There was routine slapping of passers-by when the Japanese felt insulted. They apparently suffered daily 'insults' like the Chinese not keeping eyes downcast or forgetting to bow to the Japanese horses. Sometimes the retaliation was worse than slapping.

'The Japanese controlled all trade' my grandmother continued. 'Many shops closed. We had to change all our money into Japanese Military yen. The exchange rate was fixed and we were plunged into poverty. There was hyperinflation. Huge devaluation. Now they are worth nothing. Nothing at all. I have a whole pile of them still. Completely worthless. I took watches into China. Smuggled them in. Watches, watch straps, watch cases, anything that I could use. We bought old watches from China, came back to Hong Kong, changed the faces and resold them.'

I never had much time to be with my family after I left for medical school in 1978, and the brief and infrequent visits home as an adult afforded me brief glimpses of my family's past. 'I was with your mother one time,' my grandmother told me one day when I was visiting Hong Kong during my medical student years. 'The Japanese soldiers found a few watch straps hidden in my umbrella.' I saw the seriousness in her eyes as she clapped her hands together. There was a visible shiver. 'So they searched me. They searched everything. Even my thermos flask. They ordered me to open it, but I couldn't. I just couldn't find the strength in my hands to unscrew it. Luckily, one of the soldiers recognised me from the watch shop. He used to come in. He was all right really. He said he would complete the search. He opened the flask, said there was nothing there and moved us on. He saved me – a Japanese soldier actually saved me.'

'Had you hidden anything there?' I asked, quite astounded by the daring my grandmother had displayed.

'Of course I had. I had hidden them round the sides of the flask. But I can tell you about another time. I was travelling back to Hong Kong by boat. Your mother was with me, I think. Maybe not. She did come with me on many trips, but perhaps not on this occasion. Can't remember now, it was so long ago. But I was on the steamer. Everyone huddled on deck under blankets. It was the middle of the night. Suddenly, without warning, the soldiers started to search everyone. They asked me if I had anything. No, I told them. They shouted at me. No! And then they got their dog, almost as high as me it was. It stood up, with its front paws on my shoulders, facing me. I was petrified. So scared. I'm dead, I thought. No one can help me now. I pleaded with him. 'I haven't got anything, master,' I said. 'Look, I have children with me.' I was pleading with them, begging them. Luckily they didn't find anything.'

'What about under Mao Tse-tung?' I asked. 'Did you have any trouble then?'

'What, you mean when the Communists came to power?

No, we had no trouble then. They killed the rich, but ordinary people like us were OK. I only had those small properties in the village – they're not very grand. Very small really. The size of this room perhaps. Everyone told me to go back to China. The houses were unoccupied, so when other people needed them, they just took them, even though I had the property deeds and everything. It means nothing really. I did go back, once, when your Seventh Uncle got married in the village. But I never went back after that. Not for almost twenty years.'

When I was about 10, I remember my grandmother making the slow return train journey once a year from Hong Kong to Guangzhou and back again, sometimes with a cousin who lived with us, but more often than not alone. The sacks of old clothing would be ready, and she would take as much as she could carry to her family on the other side of the border. No matter the style, any clothes we had outgrown were collected for redistribution. Nothing was wasted. What we could not give away, we tore up to use as cleaning rags or for mopping the kitchen floor. I remember the times I saw my grandmother off at the railway station in Kowloon, close to the Star Ferry Pier. The station has been demolished now, and the railway moved to Hung Hom. The clock tower is all that remains, a poignant reminder amongst a landscaped sea of flowers.

The completion of the Kowloon-Canton Railway in 1911 coincided with the overthrow of the Imperial Chinese Government by Sun Yat Sen's Revolution Army. Decades of political instability followed. With the Japanese invasion the train service was suspended and left to deteriorate. The

British military got it running again after the Occupation, only for China to suspend its end beyond the Shum Chun border as civil war broke out. Although Hong Kong was not directly affected, it put a great deal of pressure on Lo Wu station, Hong Kong's northern end of the line on the Shum Chun River.

I remember the anxiety I felt every time my grandmother made the trip. She would take the single-track locomotive, now diesel-electric rather than steam, that stopped at every station along its rural way, until it reached Lo Wu. Then she would have to disembark, with all her belongings, be searched and checked through immigration and wait for hours in a packed and dingy railway station the size of our living room with little seating. Finally, when the Chinese train arrived, which was haphazard and unscheduled, she would reboard to begin the even longer journey into Guangzhou, some 90 miles away. It felt a dangerous and uncertain journey. Would the Chinese officials allow her to return? I'm not sure if it was a realistic anxiety, but as a child I remember it was something I felt every time she made that trip. It was not until I had left Hong Kong for my golden opportunity of training in Britain that China opened her borders to the outside world. Up until then, it was quite an adventure just to journey to the Lok Ma Chau border in the New Territories and peer into the distance across the paddy fields and marshland, into what was then known as Red China.

A happy whistle heralded my father's return. I'm not sure when it started, but he took to whistling as he ascended the stairs to our flat, giving us ample time to unbar the front door as he turned the final corner to reach our dimly-lit landing, sometimes with the second postal delivery in his hand. After a whole day at work, I remember him sitting at our table after the evening meal, studying late into the night as he worked for his 'O' levels and other examinations from home. I didn't know it at the time, but he was lucky enough to find himself a couple of mentors from the British Council, who gave him tuition and encouragement in those early years. It explains why he felt so indebted to them, and why my parents had such strong attachments to elderly British folk I hardly knew except by name. Even when I visited, or stayed with them during my first trip to Britain, I was not aware of the connection, or how much they had supported my parents, and particularly my father, during those early years.

'Come on, let's take it in,' my father said one day after lunch as grandmother prepared to wash the dishes.

We went out onto the landing. An old signboard, covered in dust, cobwebs and yellowing newspaper tied up with string, was leaning against the railings of the large window overlooking the back courtyard. Pigeons flapped noisily at the intrusion, perhaps hoping for some morsel of food to drop from the heavens. Not a sound came from our upstairs neighbours. I breathed a sigh of relief. It seemed as if the mad woman had not come to her front door to peep out at us. She often did so, opening the door with a half grin on her face, and her hair in disarray. It used to terrify me.

'Let's see if we can get this cleaned up,' my father announced with sudden enthusiasm as we uncovered the bold Chinese characters from beneath the late 1958 newspapers. 'It's the signboard that used to hang outside Grannie's watch shop. We should clean it up and hang it on our wall. Stay here and hold onto it whilst I go in to fetch a bucket of water.'

Reluctant to stay outside on my own, my eyes followed my father's tattered sleeveless vest and boxer shorts, both having seen better days. It wouldn't be long before they joined the plastic carrier bag of rags we would use to polish the living room floor. The hard work applying a layer of polish was amply compensated by the fun we had sliding over the floorboards, rags wrapped around our shoes as we ran and slid from one end of the room to the other. But I certainly didn't like staying out on the landing on my own. As a punishment, when she chose not to beat us with a cane, my mother would lock my sister or me, or at times both of us, out of the flat until we had 'learnt our lesson'. I don't think it was ever for very long, and it probably saved us from some terrible beatings, but at the time it felt like an eternity. And the feeling of being unwanted and abandoned was far worse. Every time it happened, my heart sank to the pit of my stomach as I heard our door being barred from the inside; panic would flood my mind as imagination and fantasy took hold. Madness and danger seeped through the walls around me and darkness descended in an instant.

I knew the bogey man lived downstairs. In all my fifteen years at Bonham Strand I have never met him – 'the man with no nose', my grandmother used to call him. Ignorance was not bliss. I imagined grotesque deformities and a sinister personality to match. During my medical student days, I came across many illustrations in medical textbooks of noses eroded away by disease and malformations at birth. It was probably nothing more than something like congenital syphilis, but during my childhood he was the bogey man, and much to be feared. I couldn't believe it was my misfortune to be sandwiched in a flat between these two neighbours.

My father returned with a plastic basin full of water. He couldn't be bothered to wait for the kettle to heat up, so we dipped our hands eagerly into the cold water, wiping away at the board. With every little scrub we uncovered black and gold and red beneath.

'Hey, come and see! Look at how it's coming along,' my father called out through our open front door.

Grandmother's small frame silhouetted in the doorway.

'Careful!' she admonished us softly. 'Don't scrub too hard. It's gold leaf under there, not paint you know. Just a gentle wipe will do.'

'What does it say?' I asked in Cantonese, referring to the two main characters in the middle.

'*Yau Hing*,' my grandmother replied almost instantaneously, as if anticipating the question. '*Yau* on the right, and *Hing* on the left,' she said.

'But what does it mean?' I asked in English.

'Plentiful,' my mother replied. I hadn't even noticed that she was standing at the doorway too, looking at the family heirloom we were uncovering. 'Plentiful. Means the shop will have plenty – and everything you want. And those smaller characters there, in gold, they are your grandfather's name. The ones in red and gold that make up a square down in that corner, means something like "'your stocks will turn over like a wheel".'

'It's beautiful,' I said in Cantonese. 'Grandmother, this was actually hanging in your shop?'

Grandmother gave a perfunctory nod, and returned to what she had previously been doing, mumbling to herself that we might have inadvertently damaged her signboard and washed away the gold.

11

The old days

My mother taught me a song in Cantonese, to the tune of 'Oh My Darling Clementine'. It was about a flower girl, and I sang it to a very appreciative audience when I visited an old people's home with the cathedral choir fellowship. We regularly organised summer camps, staying in basic accommodation for a few nights, whilst we helped out various charities, doing odd jobs and entertaining their residents. Once a year, we were treated to a launch picnic, and would gather by Queen's Pier on Hong Kong-side, waiting for the large Chinese junk to appear. From the early 1920s, Queen's Pier was the major ceremonial arrival and departure point for visiting dignitaries and successive Governors of Hong Kong, who arrived on the Governor's yacht. There would be a guard of honour and a swearing in ceremony at the City Hall. Sadly, as with so many other iconic landmarks, it closed in 2007 around the same time as the Star Ferry pier, to allow for land reclamation. My older chorister friends arrived with plastic bags full of marinated meats, barbecue forks and charcoal. The junk took us out into the South China Seas, and towards lunchtime we would be on a stretch of fairly isolated beach, sandy and perfect for ball games, paddling and barbecues. Very few of us swam, but we sang *a capella* or with a guitar, played ball games and generally mucked around. By early evening the barbecue would be going, and we tucked into chicken wings and fillets of beef washed down with bottles of 7-Up, Coca Cola or Fanta, before sailing back just as the sun was beginning to set. I counted so many jellyfish on the journey back.

Junks are no longer seen in the harbour, apart from a mock-up tourist one. There are few sampans or wallah wallahs. The boats in Aberdeen have almost all disappeared too. The Boat People, mainly Tanka and Hakka people, were a community of floating boats, but surprisingly most of them didn't know how to swim. They never came ashore, as they had their own markets, schools and clinics. The little boats surrounded a famous floating restaurant frequented by expatriate clientele. I have never eaten there, only ever seeing it from a distance, and depicted on postcards.

When I was a child growing up in a British colony, the National Anthem was played at the beginning of every live concert and theatre performance; the audience rose to its feet and my young heart would swell with pride. When I joined the Brownies, we all had to learn the two verses of the National Anthem and often sang it in full. The noonday gun, immortalised in Noel Coward's song, 'Mad dogs and

Englishman', is still fired every day, but I was never taken to witness it.

The year Hong Kong was handed back to China, the honour of Member of the British Empire was conferred on my father by Prince Charles. It was one of the proudest days of his life. My mother too, had received the same honour sixteen years earlier, for services to the British Council, by the then governor of Hong Kong, Sir Murray MacLehose. I was not present for either, but their achievements allowed us access to the chapel of the British Empire at St Paul's Cathedral, in London, where our children were baptised.

Sitting with a black monocle in her eye, my grandmother scanned the page of Chinese script using the light from the kitchen window. Outside, one of our neighbours was practising his trumpet, and murdering the National Anthem. I could hear the voices from the shop below, callings for workers to come and sit for their early lunch before opening the shop for business.

My grandmother's eyes moved quickly from top to bottom (Chinese writing is read from top to bottom and from right to left). It was a newsletter from the Hong Kong and Kowloon Watch and Clock Association, of which my grandmother had been a founding member back in 1947. Although she had closed her watch business about ten years earlier, she still enjoyed reading about the trade and keeping up with its developments and current practices. She had many friends in the business, men who had been apprentices with her and her husband all those years ago, and associates from the days when she built up the shop alone. Walking through the market streets each day, she would linger awhile as she chatted to old acquaintances and shop owners. She even had some tools from those bygone years, lying in an odd corner of her dressing table drawer.

The shop had been founded in 1893, when my grandfather was sixteen years old. When he died at the age of sixty-four, he had fourteen cents to his name and a number of pawn receipts in the safe. There was no money for his funeral. My third and seventh uncles spent whatever they had on a single tram fare to seek the help of an old family friend who owned an incense shop in Wanchai. He promised to advance all the expenses for the funeral as well as the cost of the burial site, and his kindness has never been forgotten. The money was eventually paid back, with interest. A few months later, war broke out and the Japanese occupied Hong Kong in December 1941. With her sons in Guangzhou, my grandmother continued to run the watch and clock shop on her own, initially single-handedly and later taking on an apprentice she eventually adopted as her godson. My mother only ever recalled his physical chastisement of her; 'he kept knocking my head with his knuckles' she would say. There was unbelievable hardship but after the war, with her limited command of pidgin English, my grandmother was able to attract foreign customers – mainly Japanese and Americans – to her shop in Queens Road, West. She had learnt to greet them in their own language, negotiate and haggle prices, and often chuckled at the thought that others in the small street marvelled at her ability to conduct transactions in this manner. In the days after the Japanese Occupation, she would take a sampan out to sell her wares to the sailors in their ships anchored in Hong Kong Harbour.

'Is that from the Watch Association?' I asked as I gave my grandmother the post I had collected from the mailbox downstairs.

'Yes. The Watch and Clock Association. I don't know why they keep sending me these to read. Of no use to me. It only wastes space.'

'How is it that you don't have your watch shop any more?' I asked.

'No business. Opposite us, they opened a bigger shop, and took all my business away. I couldn't compete any more. I had no choice.'

I must have been too young to pick up any hint of regret or bitterness, but then my grandmother was always very pragmatic in her approach to life. She must have been devastated though, and I learnt several decades later that she was so distraught she became 'deranged'.

'How big was it?'

'What, my shop?' My grandmother put down her monocle. 'Not very big, really. About the size of our living room, I guess. We had a long counter across the floor and then one tall glass cabinet on either side. I've got a photo of it somewhere.'

'You mean the one with you behind the counter? Yes, I've seen it. You gave me a copy of it, remember?'

'Nice, isn't it?' my grandmother smiled. 'That big clock in the background. It's the one we're using now, in the living room.'

'Do you have any other photographs?' I asked.

'No, not any more. I used to have quite a few. A pile of them. But the Japanese burnt them all. Even that nice photo of your grandfather and some of our older sons. I only just managed to save that one. It's damaged though. You can hardly see their faces. And when the communists took over, everything was destroyed. All our ancestral records, everything – back in the village.'

If I could talk to my grandmother now, I would ask so many questions. There is so much I would like to know, about her life, her experiences, her great strength, resilience, courage and wisdom. It seems strange to me that we know so little about our own families, and yet as clinicians and psychiatrists in particular, know so much about other people's lives.

'Did you live in the shop?' I asked, blinkered by my train of thought.

'Of course. Now, the shop was in front, facing the main road, and we lived in the back half. We had a loft up top too.'

'Did you all sleep there, then?'

'Yes, but it wasn't very big, you know. I got a small room for your mother in the next building because there was so little space. We had to climb up some steps. It wasn't a ladder. It was a proper flight of steps. Then there was a kitchen, and we even had a running water tap, although it flooded the whole shop when it was first installed. Before we had the water meter, I got the shop assistants to fetch water for us. You see, when we had water rationing, there was only a few hours supply each day. The older assistant would always send the younger one out. I remember one time he came back having waited in the queue all night long, just for one bucket of water. Once, the two of them had a fight and the older one poured all the water away. The youngster cried because he knew he had to queue all over again. But I solved the problem, I sent the older assistant to fetch the water instead. Later on, when we had a tap, we didn't have to fetch water from outside even when there was a shortage. Your mother should remember this; she was there at the time. People from the neighbourhood used to come to my shop for water. They often flooded the floor so I couldn't do any business.'

'And did you have a toilet?' Strange, the sorts of detail children wish to know.

'No, no toilet. Just like here. But we had chickens running around everywhere.' My grandmother smiled, and leant over to me as if to share a treasured memory. 'And I made your mother catch live cockroaches for them to eat.'

I recoiled in disgust, and a ticklish sensation came over my back as I remembered the time my grandmother squashed a cockroach upon my bare back when I had gone to her one day, complaining of being itchy and asking for a scratch. She then wiped it off me with her pink, coarse tissue paper – wild horse tissue, it was called – and threw it in the shallow pool of disinfectant which covered the bottom of her chamber pot.

'We had two shop assistants and one apprentice, but life was very tough before that. You know, trying to make ends meet. We lived in poverty for many years. There were no watches or clocks to repair. Nothing to sell. Your grandfather only managed to get some business by buying old watch cases from other shops, cleaning them up and making them look like new again. He polished them all with his bare hands: brass, steel, silver. There were no polishing machines around; even if there were we couldn't have afforded one. He was paid just fifteen cents for one new watchcase. Can you imagine how hard life was for us then? But we were lucky, at least we earned enough to put a square meal on the table every day. Whilst your grandfather was polishing, I was busy sewing day and night. Started at five in the morning and didn't stop until one or two the next morning. But we persevered, and life got a little better through all our hard work. By the time your Third Uncle started school I had saved enough money to buy our first sewing machine; it was only a second-hand one, but it made a big difference to us. I even had a friend teach me how to read from Xing Yu Kao (The Book of Complete Sentences) at the cost of a three-cents bowl of goose meat noodles per lesson.'

My grandmother smiled, setting off the dimples on her face and broadening the birthmark that lay across the bridge of her nose. She took out a hairpin, parted the arms with her teeth and repositioned it skilfully in the hair bun at the back of her head.

'You know, when I first came to the watch shop, after I married your grandfather, everyone thought of me as a young girl, even though I was wearing a married woman's hairstyle. You see, after marriage, the hair is worn in a bun; unmarried women wore their hair in a long plait. Anyway, the shop apprentices and employees all liked taking me out to yum char (a breakfast snack or lunch, also known as dim sum, which literally means 'to touch the heart'.)

'I told them I didn't eat much; that I only ate rice. They didn't believe me. Asked if I had a secret illness or something, so they took me out to yum char in order to test out my resolve. I'll tell you why, I told them, when we are sitting in the tea house. Then I told them the story. I used to slaughter a chicken and take it to honour the God of the Earth; I put the offerings down in front of the altar, and every time an elderly woman and her family would come out and eat it all. I saw them eating it. But it was very strange because when I returned from burning joss sticks, the chicken and all the other food I had brought with me was back on the plate – untouched. It was very spooky. Another customer sitting nearby overheard my story and called me a liar, said I made the whole thing up. But it was the truth – and I know, because there was a real living spirit in that temple: the God of the Earth. But let's not talk about that for a moment. Let me tell you about my own family first.'

My rudimentary command of the Cantonese dialect began to fail me desperately as I tried to follow the narrative and the kinships my grandmother began to outline for me. I understood the tale all right, but I never quite knew which relative she was referring to, or indeed whether they were blood relations at all. Chinese kinships are difficult to follow at the best of times as there is specific terminology for maternal and paternal relatives, and hierarchies within the kinship. In fact, following my cousins who lived with us, I called my grandmother 'Ah Ma' which is the term for paternal grandmother, when I should have used 'Ah Pau,' the correct address for a maternal grandmother.

Listening to my grandmother's undulating voice, I could feel her passion and beliefs.

'We had a big house back in the village,' my grandmother continued. 'Passed down by our ancestors. It was your grandfather's Third Uncle, on his mother's side, who owned the first watch and clock business. In fact, he was the one who taught your grandfather the trade when he was a young man. Anyway, because he was well off he was able to buy and build many houses back in the village. This house was very long, and cold. Very unusual in those days to be that big. The flat we are in now would normally house two families; only people with money lived in a whole house. Anyway, it happened like this. A distant relation from the same family clan, called Yee Sing, was a terrible gambler who lived in Guangzhou. He gambled away all his money and possessions, even his home. His wife and son had nowhere to live. What were they to do?'

My grandmother slapped her open palm down on our covered oven hob and raised it towards the sky as if to demonstrate the man's dilemma. The film that had formed around the rim of her teacup shivered from side to side as if it too were awakened by the story. I waited in anticipation, unaware of the darkening storm clouds in the sky above or the silence of the pigeons as they flew away from our tenement rooftop. I noticed the intensity in my beloved grandmother's eyes; they hardly looked as though they had witnessed 70 years of life, yet I sensed the untold wisdom and experiences that lay behind them. For a fleeting moment I tried to envisage Guangzhou, and an old Chinese village in a remote countryside, but all I had to go on were my own childhood experiences, and they bore little resemblance to my grandmother's early life. A life of extreme hardship, poverty, loss and abandonment.

Her voice broke my trance. 'Someone asked me for a house to stay in. Bang on Ah Ping's door, they advised. Ah Ping was your grandfather,' she explained, when I must have looked more confused than usual. 'He was a very generous and kind hearted man, your grandfather. He wrote a letter to number three son, that's your Third Uncle, and gave permission for Yee Sing to live in whichever house he chose. We had six houses back in the village at the time. And of course, Yee Sing chose the best one – the one with the balcony. Well, in China it's considered a mansion, but if it were here, in Hong Kong, it would be considered rubbish! Little more than a hut. Anyway, to cut a long story short, strange things began to happen after Yee Sing and his family moved in. Every night, he and his wife and son would share the big bed, but one night when Yee Sing returned home he found his son missing. How could that be? He was only about four or five months old. He couldn't walk or crawl. Couldn't get anywhere by himself. Do you know what happened?'

Without giving me a chance to answer, my grandmother continued with her tale. 'The Spirits had hidden him under the bed. Yee Sing heard him crying and found him. Carried him out from under the bed. Three nights it happened. Then on the fourth night, Yee Sing returned home a little later than usual. He was looking very unsettled because of all that had happened. As he approached the house, he could sense that something was very strange. He entered and sat down on one of my blackwood chairs. Suddenly, an old man appeared before him, dressed like a fisherman and smoking a bamboo pipe. The old man started talking to him, asking him why he was in the house. *Wah!* Yee Sing was terrified.'

'So who was the old man, grandmother?' I asked. It was a little chilly, I thought.

'The old man? He was my father-in-law. So your great-grandfather.' She sipped from her tea cup and paused for a moment. 'I don't believe that story. I heard it over twenty years later. I returned to the village and someone joked with me, asked me if I was afraid of the dark, because the house was haunted. I said I wasn't afraid, but she said she would keep me company that night, and then she told me the story. In that same house. She said I didn't need to be afraid, because the ghost was my father-in-law, and so he wouldn't harm me. *Wah*! My heart was pounding so fast by then. As if a ghost would discriminate and have any loyalty and emotion!

'You know, some people said to Yee Sing it was because he did not offer incense to my father-in-law when he moved into his house. That was why he was haunted. And you know what, Yee Sing claimed he had no money. Not even enough for incense, but they didn't let him get away with it that easily. If you don't have enough money, you need only burn one joss stick instead of three. So he did, and the old man never appeared again.

'So I lit incense every night, just to be on the safe side, and I never saw his ghost. But it's all very bizarre. There are so many stories to tell you. I never saw him, but I have seen lots of spirits, with my own eyes. Now that I'm used to it, it doesn't bother me. I'm not afraid now, because I know ghosts cannot eat people. What can they do? I believe if you don't harm them, they won't harm you. We all live together.'

Silent for a moment, I pondered how our conversation had drifted from the watch shop to ghosts. Now that the story was finished, the chill had gone and I was unperturbed by what I had just heard, for I had often heard my grandmother speak about spiritual beings. I felt as if she was in some way a conduit between their world and ours;

and not just because she was the matriarch and head of the clan. There was such a sense of calm whenever I watched her lighting incense at my grandfather's shrine in our home. To this day, the smell takes me away into another world – a world where generations are linked together, our elders are remembered and respected and harmony descends.

'What did grandfather do before he had the watch and clock business then?' I asked. My grandmother looked at the small travel clock silently ticking away the hour. It was almost time to prepare for the evening meal.

'Your grandfather did many things before he went into the watch and clock business. You know, he only had two years of schooling, and then he worked as a *ba yim tsai* – you know, the boy who plays the *di* (Chinese flute) at funerals. He did that for a while, and he used to help his grandfather, selling mats. Carried the whole stock on his shoulders, he did; it was physically hard work. He had to walk between Shun Tak village and Kwai Chau in order to sell them. You know, there was very little transport in those days. People had to walk a long way, or if they were lucky, they used a *ma hong chau* [a little sampan pulled by men and rowed with oars].'

I thought back to our recent family outing to Peng Chau, a little outlying island off Hong Kong Island, and remembered the small street ferry and the woman who pulled the ropes to get us from one side of the island to the other. I imagined that it must have been something like that, but my grandmother had already continued.

'When your grandfather got a bit older, he was offered a position as an apprentice in a shop; a scaffolding business. But it didn't last long; it took an enormous toll on his health and so he left and returned to the village to keep ducks. Fortunately, his Third Uncle, the one who had a watch and clock business, offered to take him to Guangzhou to learn the trade. He was good at it, and quite successful. He was recommended to work in a much larger watch and clock firm, called Lee On. He became a senior staff member there, and very expert at repairing watches and clocks. Two years later he established his own business in partnership with a friend. They called it Yau Hing. Later, when your grandfather became the sole owner of the shop, he renamed it Yau Hing Peng Kee. That's the signboard that now hangs in the front room.

'When your grandfather first went to Guangzhou he could not even afford the ferry fare. He tried to borrow it from Shui Sam, who was the boss of Yue Shing Cheong, a very large business shop nearby. Not only was your grandfather refused, Shui Sam said he wouldn't lend him the money even though he had plenty. Don't ask me why. Your grandfather was so upset. He remembered it always. Carried it in his heart.

'Yau Hing was established in 1898, at No 28 Queen's Road West and later moved to No 36. Very close to here really. I've shown you before, remember?'

I remembered it well, a prime site along the main route now frequented by red London buses and Chinese minivans, rickshaws, bicycles, cars, lorries and lots of people. Little wonder my grandmother knew so many shop owners and traders in the area.

'So when did you give up the business, then?' I continued.

'1958. I had to sell it. To the Changs. In fact, it was

Dragon Boat Festival. I had settled the sale that day, and they forced us to leave that very evening. Didn't even let us finish our festival dinner. We were all sitting around the table eating together when they came to take possession. It was a very sad day.'

'Why were they so heartless?' I was puzzled.

'Well, I think they were angry with your mother. Don't tell her I told you, but she had been going out with their son for a number of years, and then she refused to marry him.'

12

A Chinese New Year

Sunlight streamed through our balcony railings in Bonham Strand, casting a mosaic of shadows on the large, round rattan trays propped up between stools in the living room. Layers of taro and sweet potato, shredded and sliced the night before, were strewn in delicate disorder, drying out in the warmth of the late January sun. Marmalade, our cat, having had a lucky escape a few days earlier when she had disappeared down a hole in the floorboards, groomed herself in their cool shade. Nonchalantly she stretched and arched, not bothering to peer up at the unusual sagging roof above her head. She had been to investigate much earlier, in fact when they had first appeared, and must have thought better of it after all the scolding she received from my grandmother. After all, they could hardly be as tantalising as the isolated salty fish my grandmother bought from the market from time to time. Marmalade extended her feline body into a long relaxing stretch, and prepared for another lazy afternoon.

Having just returned from school, my sister and I happily chatted with our grandmother about our day, exchanging details of how the hours had passed and wondering what she had bought for dinner. School offered not only physical space and a degree of freedom but exposure to Western ideology and culture, and interactions and friendships with expatriate children. It was so divorced from the realities of home. I remember one morning, in school assembly, we were told in no uncertain terms not to ask a young boy anything about a film he had just completed. It had not yet been released, but there would be quite a stir when it was. We were told not to treat him differently from any other child at school. His name was Mark Lester, and he had just finished filming the musical 'Oliver'. He was a year or two above me, and I don't think he was at my school for long but I do remember walking behind him up the main stairs into the school building, and he was indeed just another kid in the playground.

The world we shared with our grandmother was seeped in Chinese traditions, myths and practices; spirits and ancestral worship, festivals rich in symbolism and rituals affirming the delicate harmony between Heaven and Earth and the continuity of life after death. I don't remember much physical contact, apart from when I was very young and carried on my grandmother's back. There were no warm hugs or cuddles, that wasn't the way - but she constantly showed us love by her constant and unquestioning care, the food she cooked and the giving of herself. Using the Cantonese dialect with my grandmother reinforced that special relationship, and kept it separate from the bubbled Western world I inhabited whilst at school.

Being the family elder, my grandmother always made it her duty to see that we had new outfits for the 'coming of the year', for it would bring us luck and good health. Amongst the other preparations, she took time out to sew us a pair of trousers, for the Cantonese word for trousers (*fu*) is a pun on the word meaning 'good luck'. In later years, when as teenagers we abandoned home-tailored cotton pants for more fashionable attire, she gave us the money to buy a pair of Texwood denim jeans. They were all the rage then. She also took time to create for us young girls the most luxurious padded jacket (*meen lap*) from the finest silk brocade she could afford. I couldn't wait for the Lunar New Year's Day. I had helped choose the material myself, a delicate motif of pretty blossoms upon a sea of green, and I had watched my grandmother create the jacket out of almost nothing, a tailor's triangular chalk to one side, her large dressmaking scissors at the ready, bits of newspaper cut out as a pattern and pinned together, and a small saucer of gluey flour to hold smaller fragments in place. After the body of the jacket had been put together, every detail and finishing touch would be hand sewn with expert precision. This particular year, I was going to have a traditional maiden's jacket, which fastened in a gentle curve down the right side. No child's design for me that year. I had tried it on for size a few nights before, and swooned in its cool soft luxury. I felt held by love. It was so light and warm and comfortable. It was very special and when not in use my treasure was stored in a wooden chest under my grandmother's bed.

'Have you finished eating now?' my grandmother asked as my sister and I shoved the last crumbs of wafer into our mouths. 'I need to go out, to buy things for the New Year sweet box. Are you two coming with me?'

I volunteered instantly. 'Have we got lots to buy?' I asked eagerly.

'Well, probably not that much really. All this we'll be frying tonight,' my grandmother answered, waving her arms in the general direction of the baskets by the balcony. 'The usual. Candied fruits, lotus seeds, coconut triangles, that sort of thing. Oh, and red melon seeds, white pumpkin seeds. So, are you coming?'

That evening, after dinner, the main preparations for the New Year began. Earlier in the afternoon, my grandmother had kneaded a large quantity of soft smooth dough, from two catties of glutinous rice flour and slabs of jaggery sugar. It was now time for the whole family to work together, cooking traditional sweetmeats for the festival. There was no way we would complete the task in one evening, but spread out over three, it was just about manageable, especially if the adults were prepared to work well into the night. Having consulted her Chinese almanac, my grandmother had chosen the most auspicious day to start the serious preparations, as well as the appropriate days to close the old year, and later, open the new. They would be a day or two apart, sometimes three, but everyone would be there. Even the cousin who had moved out into a bedsit of his own near the harbour would return to take his place at the dinner table.

With flour-covered fingertips, my sister and I sat in the living room, wrapping dumplings filled with mashed sweet red bean, carefully pinching our thumbs and fingers together to seal the seam in a delicate pattern. We never quite got it right, but it was great fun trying. Our father stayed out of the kitchen with us, but declined to get involved in the fiddly details. Instead, his main task was to knead a hard mixture of popcorn and peanuts into solid balls, wrap each in a coat of thinly rolled out dough, finished with a sprinkling of sesame seeds in readiness for a deep fry.

In the kitchen, my grandmother, mother and older female cousin were already standing over a deep wok, dipping long-handled wire scoops into the fiercely-bubbling oil. Each scoop had been individually filled with a generous portion of shredded taro, mixed with sesame seeds and coriander. When cooked, they popped out of their caged confines with ease, filling the kitchen and soon the rest of the flat with the most delicious aroma. Seeing the speckled golden clusters floating in abundance on the surface of the large wok was enough to send the taste buds crazy. Happy chatter ascended the rafters as the hot oil spluttered and popped, each successful batch of taro clusters fuelling the growing excitement. In spite of all the noise, and the apparent chaos, everyone seemed to know what to do and when to do it. No one took any notice of the time, and the minutes ticked away into the early hours of the morning until each individual's ascribed task had been completed.

By day, we went about our routines as usual. My parents were at work and my sister and I at school, while a cousin already on her Chinese New Year holidays was able to help at home with the extra domestic chores and festival preparations. After the evening meal though, our little flat would be transformed into a workshop of bustling activity. It was exhausting work, but when we woke the next morning, it was as if the elves had come in to lend a helping hand. Every cupboard would be filled with large jars of taro crisps, sweet potato flakes and freshly-roasted peanuts, all mixed together and ready to eat with a little salt and oil. Steel cauldrons were piled high with clusters of golden shredded taro, which crumbled in a delicious heap at the slightest pressure, and pans full of fat dumplings stood on stools in the already overcrowded passageway. A covered steamer balanced rather precariously on a small surface between the kitchen cupboard and a stack of newspapers, filled with dainty crispy puffs, their shapes carefully moulded to resemble moneyboxes and gold nuggets.

No sooner had the cooking finished than the cleaning started. Two days before the New Year, it was time to clean the flat from top to bottom, cleansing it of all bad, in readiness to welcome in only good fortune. After all, there would be no housework on New Year's Day itself, in case good luck was swept away too. All brooms, brushes, dustpans and other cleaning equipment would be put safely out of harm's way, as well as any sharp implement. And there was a knack to sweeping the floor too, for sweeping dirt over the threshold meant sweeping one's family away. To sweep dirt out of the front door is to sweep away the family's good fortune. Dust and rubbish had to be collected inwards and then carried out, by the back door if possible, so no harm would follow.

Grandmother still had a few other special foods to prepare, and busied herself with a large turnip cake she was steaming in her wok.

On New Year's Eve, my sister and I returned from school, one of the few in the colony not to have two weeks off for the festive season. But then, I suppose, we did have the two-week Christmas break and now the three public holiday days in which to celebrate, feast and greet our many Chinese visitors.

'Shall I prepare the *laisee* packets for you?' I volunteered as my grandmother was scrubbing the stove, most of the special dinner now either prepared or already cooked.

'Have you the time?' she asked me, peering up from behind her thin rimmed spectacles.

'Oh, yes. I can easily do it for you. There's no homework set for today. I'll get the stapler and begin if you tell me what you want done.'

My grandmother washed her hands and went to her room. She brought out bagsful of dollar coins, and a bundle of five-dollar bills.

'Here,' she said, placing a box of empty red envelopes on her bed. 'Just do as many as you can. And fill some with two dollars too'.

Sitting cross-legged on the mat upon my grandmother's bed, I prepared myself for one of my favourite tasks. I fingered the red envelopes in front of me, studying their designs and debating with myself whether to choose the envelopes with the large Chinese characters or the ones with the pictures of the two children in padded jackets and Chinese hats greeting one another. Or perhaps I could use the old man of longevity, with his characteristic staff in one hand and the peach in the other. Pondering for a while, I wondered which design my grandmother would choose for me when she gave me her special *laisee* on New Year's Day. I knew that she paid scant attention to the motif on the packet itself, but I humoured myself, fantasising the choices she might make and reasons why things might be so. These red packets were the only ones my grandmother prepared herself.

'Come on! Come and offer prayers to your grandfather!' grandmother shouted out to us as she placed three bowls of steaming rice on a tray in front of the ancestral altar. The smell of burning incense sticks wafted through the air, as if guiding the spiritual essence of the offerings to the world beyond. Two plates of oranges stood guard on either side of a brass incense burner, all three under the mantle of the red tablet, bearing in bold black calligraphy, the family lineage:

> *You have toiled and laboured in the fields;*
> *May your family reap its harvest.*

I watched keenly as the three incense sticks smouldered, hoping Grandfather would enjoy the feast before him. Spread out on a tray were dishes of roast suckling pig and a whole steamed chicken freshly slaughtered in our kitchen that day (the creature had been running amok in there for the past few days, scaring the cat no end and making it even more inconvenient to have our daily bath). There was also grandmother's special *jai*, a vegetarian dish made of root and fibrous vegetables, each ingredient chosen for its symbolic meaning. 'Buddha's Delight' it is sometimes called. It included lotus seeds to symbolise many male offspring, ginkgo nuts to represent silver, black moss seaweed as a homonym for exceeding in wealth, bamboo shoots which sounds similar to 'wishing everyone well' and my favourite ingredient of all, dried bean curd for fulfilment of wealth and happiness. Fresh bean curd is never used on special occasions, for white is an unlucky colour and signifies death and misfortune.

Towards the front of the tray, facing the altar, were three sets of chopsticks, three dainty cups filled with Chinese wine bought specially for the occasion and three bowls of rice. A selection of fresh Chinese greens, still uncooked and tied together in a length of red ribbon, lay across the tray. Pressing my palms together in front of me, I offered my prayers in silence – a mixture of English and Cantonese thoughts and whispers. I kowtowed three times and poured a little wine from each cup; a rather awkward business when done with both hands on such a small vessel, but to use one hand for such an offering would have been the most inconceivable sign of disrespect.

When the last of the household had worshipped before the ancestral altar, my grandmother knelt down and hit her forehead on the wooden floorboards, kowtowing to the living spirit of her husband, in continual obedience and respect. She uttered verses with each bow, calling upon his vital energy not to waste away in the grave but to continue to protect his descendants; that though his body had returned to the earth, that his spirit lives on in his home and continues to share in the lives of his posterity. On behalf of the family, she renewed and strengthened all the sentiments of kinship, and called upon him to join in the Closing of the Year feast. I stood to one side, watching my grandmother's every movement. She was in another dimension and I sensed her inner spirit was far away.

By nine o'clock that evening the special feast had been consumed, and every dish had been washed and put away. Soon it would be time to go to the nearby flower market, open all night on this most special of occasions. Hung up on our walls and doors were posters of the important deities: the God of Wealth, the God of Happiness, the two Door Gods each in full military regalia, keeping out evil spirits, and the Kitchen God whose job it was to report back to Heaven on the family's deeds throughout the past year. On the dining table, a round black sweet box stood in readiness, each section filled with a selection of candied fruits, lotus nuts, coconut and melon seeds. To complete it, the only thing left to do was for my grandmother to bless it with a lucky red *laisee* first thing on New Year's Day.

It was such a shame we only had three days of holiday for this festival, for there were more social gatherings and visits than any of the Christian festivals we observed. And it was far more exciting and colourful. Living in the same household as the family elder meant we received many visitors, but rarely made visits ourselves. Apart from an overnight stay at Seventh Aunt's little farm miles away in the New Territories, I only recall one other visit as a young child. This was to call on my grandmother's friend and her adult daughter, the one who took great delight in pinching my cheeks hard and exclaiming how much I had grown every time she saw me. At least she didn't say '*waah, yum fai ya!*' which was often a welcome Chinese comment meaning 'wow, so fat,' meant to indicate that the household was well off and the family well-fed. I suppose it must have grown from the real experiences of famine and poverty. I do remember my grandmother saying 'but don't be too fat!' These friends lived in a tin shack in a shanty town on the hillside near Shaukeiwan. Our flat was palatial by comparison. These dwellings were often destroyed by mudslides in heavy rain, or by fires, often due to illegal electricity supplies. I remember the shack, but apart from taking tea there, my most vivid memory is of climbing up the hillside with this daughter, my mother and sister, picking Chinese mountain blueberries and gorging ourselves along the way. I have never come across fruits so delicious. There was a slight grittiness to them which is always triggered in my mind when I eat fresh figs, but they were also juicy and sweet.

I looked forward to the constant round of guests who would be coming through our doors throughout the fifteen days of the New Year, each arriving in order of kinship hierarchy to pay respects to my dear grandmother as the family elder. Unusually for Hong Kong, all the shops would be closed, yet the streets would be full of families, all with their children, carrying bags full of gifts and pockets full of *laisee* packets. I enjoyed pouring out tea for our guests, and offering the sweet box only to replenish it once they had left. Some would take a single piece of fruit, others would take sweets, but every adult was obliged to dip into the small red compartment in the middle filled with red melon seeds, and they would leave a small *laisee* in the box to bring luck to the household. Even more than at Christmas, our tiny flat would soon be bursting with noise and people and every gesture of goodwill and affection. As children, we also knew one thing for certain – we had to take care not to use 'bad' or 'unlucky' words in conversation. Particularly the Cantonese word for four could never be mentioned, for it sounds like the word for death and therefore was taboo during the festival. Children's bad behaviour was more tolerated and not admonished or punished, for crying on New Year's Day would bring to the family a year of crying. All debts had to be settled by the close of the year and references to the past year are also avoided. Everything turned towards a new year and a new beginning.

On the day itself we would not be allowed to wash our hair, in case we inadvertently washed away good luck. Bright happy colours were worn to bring a bright and sunny future and to set the tone for the rest of the year. I had my new trousers and padded silk jacket and I couldn't wait to put them on. And then I would offer tea to my grandmother, reaffirming my obedience and devotion.

Out on the balcony, I could see the crowds making their way to the all-night flower market, the cries of young children almost lost in the noisy background hum. Soon we would be amongst them, jostling and pushing, going from stall to stall in search of our New Year blossoms. It was too dark to see much of the market from where I stood, but I could make out the speckles of light coming from the naked lightbulbs which lit the market streets. All the familiar daytime shops and stores were closed, and in their place were pavements littered with flower sellers, displaying a host of colourful blooms upon beds of green. Once out in the streets I could hardly see past the backs of people pressed close up to my nose. I dodged this way and that, trying to keep up with my grandmother and mother as they disappeared in the crowds, feeling completely safe in my home territory despite the excitement and confusion and apparent disarray. Leafy bamboo stalks stood as tall as my head in tubs of water, only to be dwarfed by row upon row of peach tree blossoms, towering above.

The night was filled with the noise of adults haggling, trying to get the best bargain for their purchases. Intermittently, a whole family would push by, the man carrying their prized tree, wrapped in crimson paper, high above the head of the crowds. Legend tells of the God of Longevity emerging from the fruit of the peach blossom, and everyone had a tree displayed proudly in their homes and businesses. It would be a sign of good luck and fortune, should the tree flower on New Year's Day and bear fruit during the festive season.

Pots of kumquats, a Cantonese pun for gold, added even more colour to the splendour of the night, their yellowish orange fruits symbolising wealth and good fortune. Swaying in the breeze beside them was a host of chrysanthemums as far as the eye could see, a variety of shapes and colours: powder pink to remind one of peaches, round heads to symbolise happiness, golden shades representing the phoenix or the tassels of a lion's mane, and a spectrum of reds for luck. I didn't know the names of everything, but I loved the electrifying atmosphere of it all. It was a carnival of colour and noise, excitement and tradition. It was just amazing to me, how my little home streets could be transformed into such a magnetic place to which the whole world seemed to be drawn.

An hour later, with our flowers and peach tree blossom set up in our tall antique Chinese vases brought down to Hong Kong by my grandfather, my grandmother announced she was going to the temple. She made the journey once a year, when she offered prayers to Kuan Yin (*Kwoon Yum* in Cantonese), the Goddess of Mercy. Originally a male deity, she took on a female form when 'canonised' and is found in both Buddhist and Taoist temples. It was this deity, my grandmother believed, who had heard her desperate pleas many years ago when my mother, her only daughter, was taken seriously ill. I do not know the detail, and certainly none of the clinical facts, but as with all good stories, it changed a little with each telling. My mother had apparently been ill for many days, and was deteriorating rapidly. Grandmother described it as seeing her only daughter dissolving away in a pool of water. She had already lost a son in childhood a few years before, and she could not bear to lose her only daughter as well. No medicines or Chinese physicians could help. Out of desperation and despair, she went to this temple close to her shop, and prayed to Kuan Yin to help her. Her cries must have reached the Goddess of Mercy, whom it is believed has the power to heal all human suffering and pain. When grandmother returned from the temple that afternoon, my mother began to recover. Ever since that day, my grandmother has made a pilgrimage to the same temple each year, no matter where we were living, to offer her thanks and worship.

As a child I never went with her, and I remember many years when she went alone. One year in my teens, I accompanied her to the temple. It was a cool night. No stars could be seen in the eastern sky. After the uproar of the night flower market, a peaceful silence filled the air as we climbed the steep hill as if towards the heavens. Hidden away in a narrow street, and now tucked behind a residential block of flats, were the gentle green slopes of a temple roof. Gazing down onto the quiet empty street, a ceramic carp stood guard, its tail fanned out and poised towards the sky. It was as if it were swimming against the current; a symbol of perseverance. Lanterns, with long tassels, hung outside the red brick walls like isolated sentinels, pointing the way as we ascended the short flight of steps to reach the main worshipping hall. Huge coils of incense hung down from hooks overhead, completely covering the ceiling with spiralling circles of smoldering incense. Bright red slips of paper dangled in the centre of each, bearing the name of its donor. Groups of women, deep in prayer, were offering incense to effigies of the female deity placed around the temple. The humming of whispered prayers echoed in the small scented hall, adding to the hallowed ambience. In this most sacred, gentle place no one could fail to be moved by its spiritual essence.

An old Buddhist monk noticed us slipping in, and came to greet my grandmother by name. She stayed only a few minutes, lit a handful of incense sticks and made arrangements with the monk to light an incense coil to honour her husband's ancestral spirit. And then we slipped quietly back into the night.

13

Exodus

In 1981 I visited Hong Kong briefly, to introduce my boyfriend to my family and to a heritage he knew very little about. It afforded us a one-day guided visit, by train, to Shenzhen (Shum Chun), China's first Special Economic Zone under Deng Xiao Ping, the nation's window to the outside world. It was very different from the prosperous, bustling, hectic, commercial pace of Hong Kong, but we came away thinking it must have been what Hong Kong was like in the 1930s, pre-Second World War. Today Shenzhen is almost indistinguishable from any Westernized city, with its high-rise buildings, five-star hotels, traffic and tourism.

I have very sketchy memories of meeting a young man, introduced to me in the late 1960s, as my cousin's betrothed. She was the eldest daughter of my Third Uncle; my Third

Aunt, two daughters and two sons lived in rather squalid conditions in the Kowloon peninsula of Hong Kong whilst the rest of the family remained in China. Then, Shenzhen was a small fishing village, and the most popular escape route for refugees fleeing the poverty and starvation of rural Communist China, for a better life in the British colony. The 35-kilometer land border had been closed in 1951, patrolled by the police force and Gurkha troops on the Hong Kong side of the border in an attempt to limit the mass exodus that had begun during the Chinese Civil War (between the Communist and Nationalist Party). This reached its height in 1962, following the failure of Mao's Great Leap Forward, which resulted in devastating famine ravishing the mainland. Nobody knew at the time exactly what triggered the exodus, but for nearly four weeks, the Chinese authorities made no attempt to try to stop it. I think it was during this time that my uncles sent some of their children to live with us, for once the exodus started many tried to escape. Many died on the way, or were caught and sent straight back. Illegal immigration was not unusual in Hong Kong, but the mass influx in 1962 was. Most were illiterate peasant farmers, the majority in their twenties and thirties. An estimated 2 million entered Hong Kong as illegal immigrants back then. Most were repatriated, transported by truck to the Lo Wu Railway Bridge where they walked back into China with no penalties; those who were accepted ended up in shanty towns and refugee camps, none of which exist today. It is now recognised that this influx provided many domestic workers and supplied the manpower which helped Hong Kong to become one of the world's leading manufacturing centres today.

This young man I was introduced to was quiet, reserved and spoke no English. He was in his late 20s. He had abandoned his family, successfully making his escape, on his second attempt, by swimming from the Shekou area of Shenzhen to Hong Kong. The waters of Dapeng and Shenzhen Bays were deep and dirty. The four-kilometer swim was often fatal, thanks to drownings, shark attacks or shootings by the People's Liberation Army soldiers. His first attempt failed as he tried to cross over the land border; he was deported back to China. The second time, although unable to swim, he held onto a makeshift raft for three days, kicking his legs through stretches of shark-infested waters and avoiding barbed wire fences secreted beneath the surface. Finally, arriving on one of the small outlying islands in the archipelago, he was hidden by fisher folk until it was deemed safe to cross over to Victoria Island. His two companions were not so lucky. The more popular route was to swim to Yuen Long in the northwest area of the New Territories. Details of his escape to one of the outlying islands were kept secret, but were used by others in the months that followed.

He worked hard all hours of the day and night in a small and dingy tailoring workshop, until he took up a position in a shop located in one of the backstreets of Causeway Bay. He eventually married my cousin and set up his own small tailoring business. My father commissioned his first tailor-made suits from him when in 1970 he was offered and accepted an exciting opportunity to go on a 10-week educational visit to the United States of America, to learn about the world of libraries and museums.

Over the years, four cousins have lived with us in our

little overcrowded flat in Sheung Wan. A brother and sister were sent to my grandmother by her eighth son; I regard them more as my older siblings as they lived with us from as early as I can remember. The boy went to school during the day, while the girl helped my grandmother and attended evening classes. She often walked my sister and me home from primary school until we were old enough to return unaccompanied, and would scare us with stories of a haunted public toilet we walked past every day. A few years later, my Seventh Uncle also sent his older son and daughter to live with us for a while, but they soon moved, with their mother, to a small farm in the New Territories, north of Kowloon. The New Territories was a different world, with mountain ranges, fish ponds, rice fields, water buffalo and squat toilets.

Our sleeping arrangements in the flat were more problematic when the weather was humid and the heat stifling. As we only had one ceiling fan, in the living room, there was a jostle to sleep under it in the living room if such conditions prevailed. At times there might be nine of us. We would unroll straw mats onto the wooden floor, light a slow-burning mosquito coil and find a space to settle down, careful not to sleep with our feet pointing to the door, as to the Chinese this is deemed the route one takes to one's funeral.

Thunder broke the sky, and soon I could hear a ferocious downpour. '*Aieeyaa*! It's falling rain. Quick, bring the washing in,' my grandmother called.

Bamboo poles threaded with heavy wet clothing were carried through our small flat into the kitchen, where each was lifted with the aid of an iron pronged pole and hung into makeshift loops high above our heads.

'Is there anything I can do to help?' I offered rather sheepishly, knowing I was not tall enough and would probably get in the way. Certainly the cat was nowhere to be seen. She had sensed the rude intrusion as she was curled up next to the gas hob, and immediately darted out of the way to hide under my grandmother's bed.

'No, it's all right,' my grandmother answered as the last transfer was completed. 'One monk can carry water on a shoulder pole by himself, two monks may carry water between them on a pole, but three monks go thirsty.'

In spite of the heavy rains, the downpour afforded very little relief to an otherwise humid and sultry day. I had hoped for a typhoon. At least that would clear the weather.

One morning in late August, the crackling of my parents' pocket transistor radio woke me from my sleep. A special weather bulletin was being broadcast in the melodic intonations of the Cantonese presenter. A typhoon which had been hovering over the South China Sea had moved quickly overnight, and was heading towards Hong Kong. The number five tropical storm signal had been hoisted in the early hours of the morning, whilst we were all asleep, and only minutes before the bulletin, it had been upgraded to number eight. I knew that meant everything in the colony would come to a complete standstill. No work. No transport. Shops closed. What a pity schools were still out on their summer break. It would have been an extra day off, had the number three signal been hoisted during term time.

'Mother!' my mother called out. 'Number eight typhoon

signal. No need to go to work today. We do not have to get up so early now!'

Ironic really. It was welcome news to the adults in one respect, but it also meant a lot of anxious waiting around, listening out for weather bulletins all day long in case the typhoon changed course and the normal working day resumed. Luckily, my parents were both working on the island at the time. Had the typhoon signal been hoisted whilst they were at work on Kowloon-side, they would have been stranded on the other side of the harbour, unable to get home. Lower typhoon signals allowed plenty of time to prepare for the storm; hundreds of sampans would make their way into the safety of the harbour from the open waters. Those who lived in shanty towns and tin shacks on the mountainsides would find refuge in a temporary government site, fearful of the ubiquitous landslides and torrential floods.

'Come on!' my father called, suddenly wide awake. 'Let's make sure everything's secured.'

The household was galvanised into action. Unlocking the iron gate, we gathered what was left of the previous day's laundry from the poles hanging outside the balcony. Then we quickly tied together the six bamboo poles and secured them to the iron railings.

My mother cast a critical eye on our work. 'Tie them properly. We don't want anything to get blown away,' she warned. 'And we had better bring those flower pots indoors – and this tangerine peel,' she said, taking hold of the dried remnants threaded on a length of cord. My grandmother had kept them to flavour the delicious hot breakfast of congee (rice gruel) she sometimes treated us to, accompanied by fried dough sticks freshly purchased from the local market.

The street below was unusually deserted, even for so early in the morning. Neighbours were securing their own property and taking precautionary measures for the potential calamity ahead. The sky loomed menacingly above, dark and grey, as if clamping down on the world. So deadly and still; all so calm.

I wondered how many signboards in our neighbourhood would survive the high winds, and whether or not there would be a direct hit on Hong Kong. Typhoons are severe tropical cyclones from the West Pacific Ocean or South China Seas. The islands of the Philippines often bore the brunt of them, and some of the deadliest have struck Southern China. I have vague recollections of the violence of Typhoon Wanda. She was the most intense tropical cyclone on record in Hong Kong, and made a direct hit on 2nd September 1962. The devastation she caused was intensified because she moved ashore during the daily high tide, causing storm surges 5 meters high and massive flooding. Sustained winds of 90 miles per hour and gusts of up to 160 miles per hour whipped up signboards, scaffolding and trees and blew fishing vessels from the water into the streets. Thousands of squatter huts were destroyed, tens of thousands were left homeless, hundreds were killed, and there was severe damage. When it rained, it rained. Really wet rain, that would drench your whole being. During typhoons, it rained in biblical proportions.

We worked hard, slotting wooden shutters into place and battening them down to protect our exposed windows and balcony door from the battering we would undoubtedly receive. When they were in place, our little flat was engulfed in darkness, with barely a glimmer of daylight coming through the cracks.

Grandmother mentally checked the supplies we had in store. There would be enough food for a while, she convinced herself, even though she often went out to the market twice a day. Preparing fresh food for her family was her number one priority, and the cuisine she produced with her wok and a handful of ingredients never passed unappreciated. Indeed, the Chinese pride themselves in their gourmand tastes and skills; food is not just for eating, there is a whole ritual and conversation about food, from its price in the market stall to its freshness and flavour, right through to the way it is prepared, cooked and digested. It wasn't so much Shakespeare's music being the food of love, but food being the music of love.

I saw my grandmother check the small jar of pickled bean curd we had in the larder and the tin of preserved lettuce we had in the refrigerator, sitting rather obtrusively in our living room next to the torn plastic sofa. She checked behind the kitchen door; we still had the flat duck (*larp arp*), salty fish and Chinese dried pork sausages (*larp cheung*), all available to be steamed over rice. Our earthen rice pot under the stone sink was three quarters full, so there would be plenty for a few meals, to say the least. She decided to use to a sliver of pork belly from the fridge. She could steam it, minced and mixed with salty egg. That was always one of my favourite dishes.

By the time we sat down to lunch, the typhoon had made her way closer to the little archipelago of islands, once the haunt of marauding pirates and bandits. Any glimmer of daylight quickly vanished. The calm before the storm broke with torrential rain beating upon the wooden shutters, rudely demanding to be let in. Harsh, incessant demands. The raindrops rapped ceaselessly, growing in strength and anger with each deluge. Ferocious winds howled round the tenement block, wiping up litter off the streets and plastering them wildly against the closed shop fronts. I could hear the sound of signboards creaking at their hinges. Something crashed only a few feet away. The smashing of glass. Water began seeping into our flat from the shuttered balcony.

'Quick! Get the floor cloths!' my mother shouted as the tide of dirty rainwater spread across our polished wooden floor. Within seconds we were all on our hands and knees, mopping as fast as we could, wringing rags into plastic buckets, unable to keep pace with the world outside rushing in.

An hour later, the rains had subsided and we waited with bated breath for the next onslaught. For the moment, we were keen to just take things a little slower. My parents settled down into their bed for a short afternoon siesta. My sister and I joined them, but we had no intention of going to sleep. The bed was our raft, drifting aimlessly in a vast ocean of dangerous and shark-infested waters. Pirates sailed the South China Seas, and we had two adults to look after, collapsed from severe dehydration and sunstroke. Driftwood from our shipwreck floated around us, but we knew that if we looked hard enough, we would see land on the horizon.

14

The Dragon's Gate

Cheung Po Tsai was a notorious Chinese pirate of the 19th century who harassed the Guangdong (Canton) coastal area during the Qing Dynasty. At his height he had a fleet of over 600 ships. His pirates though were well disciplined, shared the booty equally, and were forbidden to injure or kill women. There are tales of legendary treasure, the most famous hoard involving a cave on Cheung Chau Island, a few miles from Hong Kong Island.

Going to these 'outlying islands' was a real treat when I was a young child. The ferry was more expensive than the frequent Star Ferry which crossed the harbour from Hong Kong to Kowloon for a few cents. It had an air-conditioned upper deck, with a refreshment counter selling the usual snacks as well as bowls of instant noodles. They were a real novelty and a special treat. One weekend, when my father was away, my mother suggested we go on a day trip to Cheung Chau to explore the dumb-bell shaped island. Cheung Chau at the time received few Western visitors. It was small and primitive, and a window to what old Chinese village life must have been like. Front doors opened freely into the main street, allowing anyone to wander in. Dogs and cats lay lazily in the shade, totally uninterested in strangers walking by.

After meandering through the winding cobbled lanes, too narrow for cars, we visited Cheung Po Tsai cave. Armed with a torch and in mounting excitement, we squeezed our way in. It was dark, very small and difficult to crawl into, and after all the effort there was actually nothing to see. At least nothing memorable to a small child. I have vivid memories of my petite grandmother waiting for us at the mouth of the cave, a rope at the ready, to haul us out should we need a helping hand.

Hong Kong ('*Heung Gong*' in Cantonese) means 'fragrant harbour', and relates to the production of incense in the region over a century ago. The incense tree was introduced from North Vietnam; wood would be collected from growers, assembled in Tsim Sha Tsui on Kowloon-side, shipped by junk to Aberdeen in Hong Kong island and loaded onto large vessels sailing into and out of China. The industry has long gone, having reached its height during the Ming Dynasty. My Hong Kong, in the 1960s, had a population of around 3.7million, 98% of whom were Chinese. It covered an area of 400 square miles, and was very much a British colony, as Hong Kong Island and Kowloon were ceded to the British Crown in perpetuity by the Treaty of

Nanking. The New Territories, on the mainland, and Lantau Island, by far the largest island in the territory, were leased to Great Britain until 1997. The remaining 230-plus islands were mostly uninhabited. I do however, remember visiting the leper colony on Hey Ling Chau (the 'island of happy healing'), and the rough boat journey we had there. It left from Queen's Pier in Central District, now demolished, and must have taken about an hour to sail. The swell felt more intense as we sat in the little cabin below deck, having been invited to the island by the superintendent, who was the parent of a school friend. At its height the colony had over 500 inhabitants, but it closed in 1974 and relocated to Lai Chi Kok, which I also visited when I returned to Hong Kong as a medical student.

I walked alongside rickshaws, street pedlars, hawkers and beggars. Once I even rode a rickshaw. We were out to choose a roll of linoleum for the floor to the 'loft' we were having constructed, and it was so heavy we were unable to carry it home. My parents hailed a rickshaw, and I sat in it with my sister beside me, our purchase balanced upright between us whilst the adults walked alongside, all the way from Central District to home. The rickshaw puller, in shorts and a sleeveless vest, with a towel draped across his neck, trotted at quite a pace as we passed the many familiar landmarks. *Lou tai gai* ('staircase street') was one I knew well, being a stone's throw away from our flat. This very early street in the colony's history still makes an iconic picture featured in many postcards. It was built for sedan chairs, the only mode of transport long before I was born. Elegant ladies in *cheong sams* would transfer from their rickshaws at the foot of the steps to sedan chairs, in order to be carried higher. The street is still lined with a cornucopia of stalls selling everything from flowers to haberdasher's supplies.

We went everywhere on what my father referred to as 'the number 11 bus', meaning we would be walking. On the rare occasion when we were taken to visit the Po Lin (precious lotus) Monastery, before the new temples opened in 1970, the journey involved a ferry to Silvermine Bay on Lantau Island, a bus ride to what I can only describe as some deserted cattle shed half way up the mountain, a long, exhausting, hot and thirsty trek up a narrow mountain trail. What a relief it was when we came upon the monastery grounds and were treated to a vegetarian feast washed down with tea or a cooled bottle of soda. The only snack that kept us going was a small packet of sour plums or a segment of orange. We had no water with us, my father saying that the sooner we got on with it, the sooner we could have a drink.

An embarrassing moment came one afternoon when we were returning from an outing organised by the church. It was something we did very occasionally, often being attracted to join in if it was to a destination which otherwise would have been difficult to get to under our own steam. At the end of the day the coach returned us, exhausted, to the Star Ferry pier on Kowloon-side. I had felt a little queasy with a belly ache I couldn't quite understand, but the tension eased when I wet myself, just a fraction – enough to wet my knickers. It felt so much better, and I was convinced no one would notice because I was wearing my favourite dark blue cotton shorts. But as we approached the pier my parents pointed out that I had blood running down my legs.

It was before my 12th birthday, and I had started menstruating.

Quickly I got myself into the public toilets, cleaned myself up, stuffed a wad of toilet paper between my legs and went to join the rest of the family. It was slightly embarrassing sitting on the ferry with such dampness. My father asked if we should take some transport back – a tram, perhaps – but my mother decided there was no need and we would walk the two miles home. I was so glad to be back. A cousin nipped out to buy an elastic sanitary belt and a packet of sanitary pads for me from the lane of shops behind our building. Such products are very different from what is available today; thick and bulky, the pads would move and ride up, particularly if they had not been properly secured to the belt. My mother warned me, saying she had seen a soiled sanitary pad fall onto the pavement when she had walked behind some unfortunate woman. My grandmother referred to the menstrual cycle as a time for riding the horse.

One of the happiest memories of my childhood is the lunchtimes we spent on Victoria Peak. At the end of the primary school term, my mother would take time off work to meet my sister and me at the school gates, with a lovely picnic basket in her hand laden with homemade bacon and egg sandwiches, ham and marmite sandwiches, a selection of fresh fruit and little cartons of Dairy Farm milk. We would catch the Peak Tram, a funicular railway, from May Road station, to avoid having to walk down to the terminal just outside St John's Cathedral. Ascending to the peak was an extraordinary sensation; the 27-degree gradient was tough on the neck, but we always got a seat. Once we reached the upper terminal, we sauntered past the peak café, not daring to even peek in, as we knew it was well beyond our means. We always found the most exciting trails off the main path of Harlech and Lugard Roads, as they wound around the mountain. There was greenery everywhere, including clumps of touch-me-nots which just invited the opposite, interesting insects, colourful butterflies and birds that seemed to sing all day long. The waterfall, amidst the banyan trees, was a favourite place to stop, and there was often a cool breeze which blew across my sweaty forehead as I sat cross-legged on the picnic mat, waiting for my food and drink.

In my grandmother's day it must have been quite something to be up on the Peak. For a start, the area was out of bounds to the Chinese, unless they were domestic staff working in the large expatriate residences, or carrying produce or *gweilos* in their sedan chairs. There were many establishments in Hong Kong that reflected the territory's colonial history – the Repulse Bay Hotel, the Hong Kong Club, the Ladies Recreational Club, the Country Club. The list goes on. To most of my friends at school they must have been part of their social lives; their parents were members, they made use of what must have been extensive facilities and often entertained in such establishments, but to me they were of a different world; a world in which I did not belong.

Often rising before dawn, my grandmother's first thought would be to boil several kettles of water over our gas stove. She would pour one into a flask sprinkled with fresh

Chinese Bo Lai tea leaves, and fill another with water to satisfy my father's penchant for instant Nescafé coffee. The next lot of boiled water she poured into glass bottles that had been rinsed out and left them to cool for our daily consumption. A couple of bottles were destined for our little refrigerator which sat in the living room next to our tropical fish tank, filled with guppies. Next, she would brush her teeth with salt in the kitchen sink, splash water on her face and then wake up the rest of the family. We did not have a bathroom. Personal hygiene tasks were performed in the kitchen, over our big rectangular stone sink. Our toilet was a small enamel chamber pot, which lived under my grandmother's dressing table, covered with a wooden lid. When it was full, the last person to use it would take it into the kitchen either to sluice it out or to transfer the contents into a large bucket which lived under the kitchen sink. There would be times, mainly at night, when the stench was so awful my mother would call out *'chung chui fong,'* meaning 'wash out the kitchen', and often my grandmother or a cousin would rise to chuck water and disinfectant down the sluice. It became a running joke in the family, as the phrase bore some resemblance to my grandmother's name, 'Cheung Chui Fong'. Once or twice a week, the large red plastic soil bucket into which we threw all our human excrement would be carried from the kitchen, through the little flat, into the front room and out onto the landing, waiting for the night soil woman to empty it in the early hours of the morning.

Bathing for us as youngsters was in the kitchen sink, but for the adults it was a rather unenviable task. As a teenager, I remember bathing every day in the kitchen, before my grandmother began cooking the evening meal. We used a tin tub, filled it with cold water from the kitchen tap, put it on the tiled floor and doused ourselves with a ladle, taking care not to make too much of a splash, nor to wet the pile of newspapers sitting against the wall which served as a makeshift tabletop or handy seating area. It was cool and refreshing after a long day at school. Unfortunately, the last person to bathe also had the task of mopping the kitchen floor, leaving it dry enough for my grandmother to start preparing the evening meal.

Our one luxury was a small black and white television set, bought when I was about ten years old. At first we had one English-language and one Chinese-language channel, on subscription, and broadcast for several hours each day, the English channel for a much shorter length of time. Eventually we exchanged it for a new television set that allowed us to receive the free TVB Jade and Pearl channels too. One of my favourite television series at the time was the Japanese animation 'Marine Boy'. Marine Boy was a slim, attractive youngster who dressed in a red bulletproof diving suit and saved the oceans of the world riding on a dolphin. Oxy-chewing gum gave him the ability to stay underwater for long periods of time, but for some reason he was easily knocked out and needed saving too. The tune was catchy and it became a very popular series. 'Batfink' was another favourite; a small grey creature in a yellow costume and red gauntlets, who used his supersonic radar and bulletproof wings to fight crime. Batfink teamed up with a rather oafish and clueless aide, Karate, who, though a martial arts expert, seemed to always make the situation worse. The main villain, Hugo A-Go-Go, 'the world's maddest scientist' was often fun with his wacky inventions and fiendish ability to catch Batfink. Towards the end of each episode, Batfink would invariably be tied up and about to meet his doom. The action would freeze, and the narrator would ask 'is this the end of Batfink – and Karate?' Each episode was only about five minutes long, but I loved them.

If there were no visitors, my grandmother would enjoy a film in the afternoon, often just finishing when we returned from school. Sometimes it would be a Peking Opera, with all the high pitched wailing and period costumes that went with it. I was often amazed at how many of the songs my grandmother actually knew. The stories of course, were well-known classics, and grandmother had many favourites. They were all fairly similar though. The one I remember was about a woman and her children who had been thrown out into the streets when her husband died. They ended up being taken in by a nasty landlord. Those who lived on his land were abused and maltreated, beaten and starved by this heartless man who had cheated his way through life, taken from the poor and lived on the fruits of their labour. In a desperate attempt to stop the misery and hardship which had befallen his family, the eldest son bade farewell to his mother and journeyed far away to sit the series of open, competitive imperial civil service examinations. If he passed, it would allow him to rise above his social status. Regardless of birth, background, age or appearance, a man could leap from rags to riches overnight if he was successful. Children of mandarins did not automatically inherit their fathers' titles. They had to sit the exams like any ordinary peasant or labourer. Education was the only way forward.

And this peasant had worked hard at his books, studying the four Confucian Classics.

During this young man's absence, his mother and sister had been thrown out of their humble shack, and had been left to roam the streets, begging for their keep. I remember the tears in my grandmother's eyes as she empathised with the peasant woman, reliving her grief and misery.

'You'll never know,' she whispered to me during the film. 'Your grandmother has so many sorrows and heartaches, buried deep inside. You are too young to understand.'

And I did struggle to understand. I was frustrated by my limited mastery of the Cantonese dialect. All I could have with my grandmother was a child's conversation. I did not know the words or the language to comfort her; physical displays of affection were not customary. My educational career, rooted in the British school and university system, took me away from my Chinese roots, and I never acquired the language to say what I wanted to say, even as an adult. But intuitively I felt for my grandmother, and our relationship was deep and profound and unquestioned, but it was never verbalised. After all, it was she who looked after me as a child when my mother returned to full-time work when I was two weeks old. It was she who comforted me when I was in pain; who nursed me through illness. It was she who clothed and fed me, and who was there at home when I returned from school. I can see now how it must have hurt my mother to witness such a relationship and perhaps to feel her position somehow usurped, as a daughter and as a parent.

On the television screen, a peasant woman who was about to be stoned by villagers for some petty crime made a dash towards an official sedan chair being carried through the streets. She was crying out, begging for mercy and justice. A man stepped out from behind the plain curtains that shielded his world from the outside. He was robed in a fine satin gown, with cloth slippers on his feet and a thick ornate belt hanging loosely round his waist: the Hoop of Office. He had the authority to preside over decisions; he had the power over life and death. He turned to the woman, collapsed in a pleading heap before his path, and gently he helped her to her feet, asking her to tell him what she was crying about. As his gaze fell upon her he recognised her sallow features.

'Mother!' he called. In a spontaneous display of filial piety, he dropped to his knees and kowtowed before her, his fine robes soiled in the muddy tracks.

The story continued with him sitting in court, judging the wicked landlord for his deeds and passing sentence over his family's worst oppressor, the wings of his black gauze hat protruding like the arms of the law. He had honoured his mother in the ultimate manner. He had succeeded in his imperial examinations, swimming with the persistence of a carp, forcing his way upstream against the rapids, until he had achieved the status of a dragon. He had made that transformational leap and passed through the Dragon's Gate. His ancestors would indeed smile upon him.

Aged two, with my younger sister

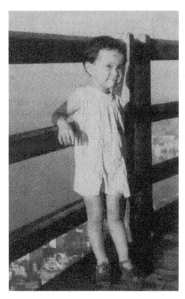

At Victoria Peak, aged three

My grandmother at Victoria Peak
in the 1930s

Grandmother at 50

Grandmother in her watch shop

The sign on the watch shop

Ancestral village, 2001

Mum and Dad with my great-godfather JJ, 1959.

Cathedral choir, 1970s

Mum's MBE, 1981

Dad's MBE, 1997

Above and below - my home streets as they were in the 1980s

Ancestral village street, 1993

Bonham Strand, 2005

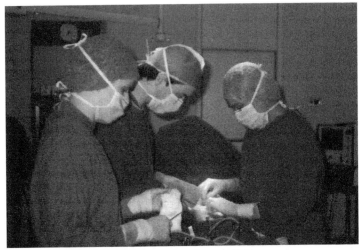

In the operating theatre, 1984

At grandmother's requiem mass, 1988

With Julie Andrews, 1986

15

London adventure

One day in late July 1978, I boarded the British Airways Boeing 747 at Kai Tak Airport that would fly me away from Hong Kong for the first time in my life. Although unspoken, I knew it was a special treat and sweetener for the inevitable rejection that was to come from my applications to medical schools in Great Britain. My grandmother, father, mother and sister saw me off at the departure lounge. It was to be my adventure of a lifetime. My school career and 'A' levels behind me, I was facing six weeks of touring the land of golden opportunity. I had set up my own travel itinerary, having written to friends, distant family and my mother's fellow workers at the British Council offices. I had planned roughly where I wanted to be across the nation, and soon I had most of my accommodation needs sorted. I would stay half the time with complete strangers, affiliated to the British Council, who had generously offered to put me up in their homes. With one suitcase of luggage, a shoulder bag and a new camera not yet loaded with film, I waved goodbye to all those who were dear to me and faced the world alone. I was 18, and had never been out of Hong Kong. In fact, apart from a one-week residential school trip to an outlying island off the shores of Tai Po in the New Territories, and a handful of church choir retreats, I had never been away from home. I was acutely aware of a door opening before me. How strange, to suddenly have all this freedom thrust upon me – and for it to happen 6000 miles from home.

It is a memorable experience flying into and out of Kai Tak airport. It was considered one of the most dangerous and harrowing airports in the world, not just because of its single short runway jutting into Victoria Harbour but because the surrounding area in Kowloon was so densely populated, and with mountain ranges a few miles to the north, northeast and east of the airport.

The plane taxied up the short runway. Within seconds of the thunderous jet engines exploding into an acceleration of increasing energy, we were off the ground and the skyscrapers and residential tenements of my little homeland loomed so close beside me I could see into the flats and almost touch their walls. Their bamboo poles, hung with the daily laundry, waved us goodbye as traffic queued towards the cross-harbour tunnel. In those days one was not allowed to fly into Chinese air space, and the route was a rather tortuous one. The plane had to land twice for refuelling, once at Bombay's Dum Dum airport and again at

Bahrain. Passengers were required to disembark into the transit lounge, and had to return after being shepherded into little cubicles with curtains on either side, as we were frisked by customs and immigration officials. Before we could be airborne again, the plane was sprayed to kill off foreign bugs, as though we were travelling aliens from some strange land.

My first glimpse of London from the air as we began our descent into Heathrow International Airport was a sight I shall never forget. I could not believe the greenery; the patchwork quilt of meadows and farms, the trees, open spaces, expanses of land and woods and forests, individual houses so low on the ground. Everything was large and spacious, and very, very, English.

My brief diary entries during this time went like this:

Tuesday 18th July 1978: leave for London BA022 at 22.15

Wednesday 19th July 1978: arrive London 09.40. Staying with Sara.

Saturday 22nd July 1978: Stay in Colchester for Nick's 21st

Monday 24th July 1978: Stay with Aunty Mary and Uncle Arthur in Croydon.

Tuesday 1st August 1978: Letter from Dean of LHMC.

'with reference to your recent telephone call, the Dean can see you on Wednesday next, 2nd August, at 2.30pm in his room in the Medical College'

Wednesday 2nd August 1978: interview with John Ellis

Thursday 3ʳᵈ August 1978: leave for Newcastle-upon-Tyne. Victoria Coach Station 9.30am;

Saturday 5ᵗʰ August 1978: leave for Edinburgh

Thursday 10ᵗʰ August 1978: Oban and Western Highlands trip instead of Glasgow

Friday 11ᵗʰ August 1978: leave for Liverpool

Sunday 13ᵗʰ August 1978: Return to London – stay with Westcotts in Catford.

Tuesday 15ᵗʰ August 1978: Depart for Cardiff

Saturday 19ᵗʰ August 1978: return to London

Sunday 20ᵗʰ August 1978: received my A Level results today by cable. Went to the Tate Gallery and St James' Park.

Monday 21ˢᵗ August 1978: meeting Sara tonight for a celebratory dinner.

Tuesday 22ⁿᵈ August 1978: visit to Cambridge.

Wednesday 23ʳᵈ August 1978: leave for Southampton. Staying with Aunty Dock.

Thursday 24ᵗʰ August 1978: lunch in the New Forest; dinner in Lymington.

Friday 25ᵗʰ August 1978: went to Bournemouth.

Saturday 26ᵗʰ August 1978: return to London.

Cable and Wireless telegram: 30ᵗʰ August 1978 (sent to Hong Kong):

URGENT

A VACANCY HAS ARISEN IN MEDICAL SCHOOL FOR OCTOBER 1978 PLEASE ADVISE IMMEDIATELY IF YOU WOULD LIKE TO ACCEPT THIS PLACE DEAN LONDON HOSPITAL MEDICAL COLLEGE

It was relayed back to me in London, presumably by telegram.

Saturday 2nd September 1978: saw 'The Sound of Music' in Croydon.

Monday 4th September 1978: Westcotts coming at 2pm to pick me up and take me to Heathrow. Plane for Hong Kong BA 021 17.00hours.

Tuesday 5th September 1978: arrive HK 17.45.

Sunday 17th September 1978: Moon Festival celebrations

Saturday 23rd September 1978: 7.30 dinner party – farewell and Dad's birthday.

Wednesday 27th September 1978: collect visa, passport and air ticket. BA020 20.00hrs

Thursday 28th September 1978: arrive Heathrow 08.25

Monday 2nd October 1978: report to the London Hospital 10.00am.

'It must have been such a culture shock for you,' my friends have often said when they learnt of my journey. But to be honest, I did not feel it was so at the time. My formative years had been such a rich tapestry of different experiences, cultures and expectations. My parents struggled to afford to send my sister and me to an English school, where the entry requirement was that one's mother tongue had to be English. I am told that my father sat with me every evening when he returned from work, teaching me English words so I would qualify. The whole family was united in this effort, and as a result I never really learnt to speak Cantonese fluently, or to read and write the language. When I was at school, I was a true British subject – learning about the British Empire, reading the history and geography of countries thousands of miles away. I learnt French as a second language, and was indistinguishable from my fellow classmates who came from expatriate families, or well-to-do business classes from other Asian and Far Eastern countries. I went to church, sang in the choir, helped out at the Oxfam shop on a Saturday morning, enrolled on the Duke of Edinburgh Award scheme and joined the brownies. I even passed a badge which required me to make a bed; I had to guess what was required, as I had never made a bed with a mattress and bedsheets before, much less slept in one. I studied piano and ballet. As the years went by my parents became more successful in their careers and in their financial status, but it is only in retrospect that I can appreciate how much they and my grandmother must have sacrificed to put my sister and me through such an education.

When I was at home, I spoke with my grandmother in my fluent but rather limited Cantonese. I ate Chinese food, observed and celebrated Chinese festivals, and played my part in ancestral worship and offerings to various Buddhist and Taoist gods. I lived in very modest circumstances, with a shelf of toys and books and one drawer of clothes to my name, most handmade by my grandmother. We sat on a red plastic sofa, which had been scratched so badly by the cat it had to be covered by a rather unsightly length of lace. My cousins often caught cockroaches the size of an adult thumb, or used them for shot pellet practice as they came out of the floorboards or crevices. When the atmosphere is heavy, cockroaches fly. They were a common cohabitant with us, so we had to take care to put food away and keep everything clean. One year I remember my younger sister being heartbroken when she discovered her prized collection of soft furry toys had to be thrown away; she must have played with them with sweet sticky fingers, for ants had left a trail of destruction on her shelf of prized possessions.

As a school project, I bred cockroaches. We were meant to watch a caterpillar on a leaf, or something like that, but my cousin had caught a cockroach in his hands and challenged me, on a whim, if I wanted it. I said yes, just to show I wasn't a wimp, and rushed into the kitchen to fetch an empty Robertson's jam jar, with the label already soaked off. We soaked and peeled them off with care as we could exchange them for the little Golly badges, which were iconic and still very popular in the 1960s despite growing criticism. My mother even made me a black rag doll with big white eyes, as we couldn't afford the real ones selling in shops. With the lid firmly screwed on, and the cockroach in it, I used a screwdriver and a handy weight to pierce a few air holes through the lid. Within hours my cousin had added a few other cockroaches to the collection, and before long there was an egg capsule. I was fascinated and convinced myself I wanted to see it hatch, but as the days went by it gradually dawned on me I would soon have a whole jar full of young cockroaches, perhaps 30 or 40 of them. Disgusted by the thought, I threw the whole thing out. Someone else's problem!

Friends who visited were all Chinese; most were treated as kin even though they were not strictly blood relations. I do remember a handful of occasions when we received other visitors. The most vivid was one afternoon when I heard whistling outside our flat. It was so persistent I couldn't ignore it. I looked through the peep hole in our front door and thought I saw a fair-haired boy. I rushed into our kitchen as the whistling continued, and there he was again, this time holding onto the fence which surrounded the back courtyard. How he managed to climb in, I didn't know. He must have accessed it from the landing window, by the madwoman's front door. He was a boy from my class at primary school. It turned out he had taken a fancy to me. Somehow he had got hold of my address and came to find me all on his own. Or maybe he followed me after school one day, I don't recall. I was only 10. Naturally, we invited him in and gave him a cold drink. I think he only stayed for a little while before leaving. It was the talk of my family at the time.

On my eleventh birthday, he invited me out to dinner. His mother had made a reservation for us at a French/Italian restaurant in Wan Chai, and came along to chaperone and of course pay the bill. I remember they paid for a taxi to take me home too, but I don't remember how I got there – just how excited and nervous I was that evening. It was a very special occasion. He was gorgeous and so handsome, with his mother's relaxed and engaging manner (she was a television presenter) and his father's good looks (he was in the Canadian Mounted Police). He gave me a birthday present – a golden musical jewellery box. It played 'Für Elise', and in the months and years after when I watched the little ballerina twirling on the glass top as the music played, it filled my heart with such joy.

The waiter came round with a basket of roses. His mother indicated it would be for her son to give to me a single red rose. It was such a perfect evening, and he gave me a little peck on the cheek when we parted. Sadly, he left Hong Kong soon after we transitioned into secondary school.

So it didn't feel much of a culture shock after all. I feel, and I know, that I am both - a fusion of East meets West. I remember listening to a visiting American professor of psychoanalysis many years ago, who spoke about the psychodynamics of working with people from different cultures and backgrounds. He compared a person such as myself with a wooden chess piece. He said this is how he explains it to friends.

'When I hold up this block of wood, what is it to you? It is a block of wood. But when I carve this block of wood into a chess piece, what it is to you now? It is a chess piece. But it is still a block of wood, is it not? It does not have to be one or the other. It can be both.'

16

Cultural differences

'You Filipino?' a woman enquired, running up to me and my sister as we waited to cross the road near the bronze lions of the Hong Kong and Shanghai Bank in Central District.

'No' I answered, looking at this complete stranger in ankle-length trousers and flip-flops.

'You Filipino,' she stated, nodding knowingly at my sister. 'You definitely Filipino. You look Filipino. You must be Filipino.' My sister was so annoyed. It happened frequently, sometimes ending in an embarrassed chuckle, and at other times almost indignation and unacceptance from the stranger.

Chinese amahs, who had long served expatriate families and did everything from cooking and cleaning to childcare, had slowly started to give way to an influx of women from the Philippines. Nowadays, on their days off, usually Sunday, these maids congregate in swarms around pavements and walkways in Central District, picnicking on mats and newspapers, buying and selling clothes from large plastic carrier bags, their music blaring as their chatter rises above the noise of traffic and usual passers-by. Walking past them can be a real assault on the senses, and one to be avoided where possible. But back when I was growing up, it was an unusual sight – and these Filipino maids were keen to make contact with their own.

The gardens and water fountains of Statue Square and the air-conditioned luxury of Princes Building were never that busy, but it was the thoroughfare between the tramline and the Star Ferry concourse and City Hall area. The cenotaph stood proudly, if poignantly, at the northern end of the square, a memorial to those who died in World War II.

I scrubbed for theatre. First on the list was a dilatation and curettage. The team was busy and fellow students had assembled in a small silent crowd. I must have been late. The consultant beckoned us medical students to come to take a closer look before he removed the vaginal speculum. I peered in; a healthy cervix and well-perfused tissue. When we were all done, the surgical team began to remove the theatre greens and to take the patient's legs down from the stirrups. I remember being taken aback. The woman was a deep mahogany colour. It really struck home at that moment that colour is only skin deep. Inside the body, devoid of the skin's melanin pigment, we are all the same.

Of course, intellectually I knew this was the case, but it was a defining moment in my medical student experience.

The net curtains that shielded the middle-class residents of Winchmore Hill, North London, twitched as we walked down the leafy suburb from the railway station. It was a crisp Easter Sunday morning, and I was going to meet my boyfriend's family for the first time, and to join them for a traditional English Sunday lunch. It was 1980. I wore my best frock, bought the weekend before, at Petticoat Lane market in the East End of London, for about five pounds. It was the only dress I owned. My boyfriend met me at the station, and walked excitedly down his local streets, oblivious to the twitching curtains and reserved, subtle British stares of passers-by. During our courtship, I was always aware of the looks people gave us. It didn't matter to me, but I was aware of them – and of the prejudice in some people's ignorance. I can still feel the coldness when I walked into a bakery in the middle of Essex as a medical student on placement at the local district hospital. The sudden hushed silence could be spliced with a scalpel. The stares – curious, unwelcoming, judgmental, discriminatory. Instead of avoiding the bakery, I would make a point of going to the same establishment again, and asking in my most English of accents for an iced bun or a jam doughnut. I spoke the Queen's English – and that shocked a lot of people.

'So, you don't mind that your son is going out with a girl who is, well, not English?' my future in-laws were asked time and time again by well-meaning family and friends.

It was not an issue for my in-laws, and I did not

understand why it should be. After all, my grandmother had let my mother marry someone who was not Chinese. When grandmother first met my father, she thought him strange and awkward in his manner. He had been invited home for a Chinese meal, and whilst chewing on a mouthful of fish, he did not know what to do with the fishbone he encountered. To my father, it would have been exceedingly rude to spit the bones out of his mouth, so he swallowed them. My grandmother told me she could not believe what she saw.

'And his handkerchief!' she told me years later. 'Such a disgusting habit. So filthy. He blew his nose on his handkerchief, and then folded it up and put it back in his pocket.'

The concept of 'face' in Asian cultures is difficult to explain; there is no Western equivalent. It is not simply pride or ego. It is a complex ingrained notion that embodies a person's identity and human worthiness; it is not particularly related to social status. Behaviour that may cause a person to 'lose face' is frowned upon; it is unforgiveable if it is perceived to cause a major loss of face. Deference to one's elders is also paramount. When I was growing up, for example, it was unacceptable for a student to disagree with a teacher, even though she or he may have made a mistake; nor was it considered proper to ask a difficult question in front of the class in case the teacher was unable to answer it satisfactorily. It was therefore completely foreign, and rather challenging for me, when in my first year at secondary school I had an American teacher who encouraged debate and questions and was more interested in what I had to say than how I said it. She was very fond of a quote from Henry David Thoreau which hung as a poster on her wall. She gave it to me when she left Hong Kong.

If a man does not keep pace with his companions,
Perhaps it is because he hears a different drummer.
Let him keep step to the music which he hears,
However measured or far away.

Chinese parenting is paradoxical, and affection and love are often displayed by rebuke. Criticism, reprimand and harsh words were the prerogative of parents and grandparents, showing they cared enough to want one to improve. There is no loss of face in such circumstances, but such interaction from others may cause considerable insult and offence. I see this at times when working in multi-cultural environments, and often marvel at the tolerance of the affected and the apparent lack of awareness of the transgressor. Knowing doesn't make me immune, and I can recall two occasions in my career when, unknown to me at the time, it caused spectacular upset that is difficult to understand or explain, when seen through a Western lens. On one occasion I was the culprit; the other the recipient.

Politeness and the small rules of etiquette are deeply ingrained in every Chinese household. I'd never heard of 'going Dutch' before I came to the UK. It was such an alien concept, as it would suggest that the person who made arrangements to go out, for example, couldn't afford to pay. So, despite my denial of culture shock, there were and are narrow social attitudes and practices I sometimes find prickly, although I am aware of this and certainly understand them. Often casual and rather insignificant, they serve to remind me that in everyday discourse we tend to ignore, or are unaware of, cultural differences.

A frequent common example is an invitation to a meal. Chinese families do not extend casual invitations. Nor is it customary to invite guests to one's home, where family members are entertained. So when an invitation is extended, either to the home or more likely elsewhere, it is considered an honour to be asked – and unless there is an extremely good reason, it is accepted graciously, saving face for the host. But all too often in Western society there is either no response, or invitations are declined, sometimes because one doesn't feel bothered. At times I am guilty of this too.

The giving and receiving of gifts is another example. It's considered impolite not to remember family and friends when one returns from abroad, so souvenirs and gifts are bought and shared, but this is rarely reciprocated. I've heard people interpret this as a need to show evidence of having been away. The gesture of passing an object, whether it be a gift or a cup of tea, is done by using both hands and is considered rude and disrespectful not to do so, unless it is being passed to someone of a younger generation. If the gift is substantial, or given as part of a celebration, the recipient returns some of the good luck the giver has brought by way of a small *laisee* (red money packet). The intention of the giver is what matters most and not what is given. To reflect this, and to avoid being seen as greedy, the gift is not opened in front of the giver but put to one side until much later. Very different from Western culture.

I also remember not so long ago offering to pay for

drinks at a team Christmas party. It was well meaning when it was suggested I could perhaps pick up the tab with a colleague, but for a split second I had to remind myself this was the Western way of doing things and not said to imply I couldn't afford it.

Food is a matter of extreme importance, and normal greetings take the form of enquiring if someone has eaten. Food etiquette is ingrained, as is respect for one's elders. They are always invited to eat first and the table will wait until the eldest has lifted his or her pair of chopsticks to begin the meal. The concept of 'time is money' did not exist either; there was always time to have a chat and to deliberate on a matter.

Chinese tradition is filled with symbolism. I remember my sister and me saving to buy our grandmother a special present when she reached her 70th birthday. We were so excited, and went out shopping to big department stores on our own; stores such as Diamaru in Causeway Bay (which was a fairly long tram ride away), or Wing On near the waterfront close to where we lived. We even had the courage to go into Lane Crawford, the premier department store on Queen's Road Central. Eventually, we decided on a gold-plated carriage clock; a handsome item which was aesthetically pleasing and elegant to the senses. We were thrilled with our purchase, and gave it to our grandmother on the morning of her birthday, filled with such pride and achievement. I was only 10 years old, and did not realise that the Cantonese word for clock has a homophone which means 'to go to a funeral'. Mother scolded us and said that giving a clock as a gift was a bad omen – especially on such a special birthday. I was absolutely mortified. But my grandmother accepted it graciously, with a smile on her face and a generous heart.

'Don't worry,' she said to my mother. 'They are only young. Anyway, what does it matter?' and she placed the carriage clock in pride of place on her dressing table. It was still there the day she died, almost twenty years later.

17

A big birthday

There was much bustle and excitement early one morning. Everyone, it seemed, was up that weekend, and the straw mats and bedding had been put away – thrown up into their storage place in a built-in cupboard above our wrought-iron door. Floorboards, shining in their splendid polished beeswax hue, smelt strong and healthy, every groove and corner cleanly swept of dust. Even finger smudges, which ordinarily graced the glass panes of our tall built-in bookcase, were wiped away the evening before. An effigy of Buddha, its delicate colours complementing his gleaming porcelain belly, sat silently in the middle of the shelf, a wide grin covering his face and earlobes hanging pendulously on either side. The rest of the furniture was dusted, and a white linen antimacassar stretched the length of the small sofa, obscuring the cat's clawed handiwork upon our red plastic seat.

'Come out here and sit down,' my sister and I called out in near uncontainable excitement as we led our grandmother by the hand into the living room.

Rays of sunlight, not yet bestowed with its awesome radiance, streamed gently through the open balcony, as if unrolling a carpet of gold before a throne. A high, upright, rather austere chair, made of solid Chinese blackwood, one of two left which had survived the Japanese occupation, stood majestically at one end, its back flanked by the expanse of the room's pale blue partition. A makeshift throne amongst the heavens. We placed a red silk cushion on the floor in front of it.

'Come sit down here,' we motioned as our grandmother sat, still wearing her usual black silk trousers and cotton blouse, buttoned up to the neck. 'We all want to offer you tea.'

It was Grandmother's seventieth birthday, a *dai saan yat* (big birthday), and being the family elder, each one of us was going to offer her a cup of tea, in a traditional tea ceremony; an observance of filial piety. Throughout the day, other grandchildren, family members, and even some close friends, would do the same – either in the privacy of our flat or in the public arena of the local restaurant we had booked for the day's celebration.

I watched my mother offering tea first, and my grandmother imparting words of wisdom I did not understand. Then it was my father's turn. His large hands gripped the small bowl of tea rather awkwardly as he knelt before her. Excitedly, I went into the kitchen and replenished the bowl of tea after my grandmother had taken a sip or two.

Carefully I carried it out with both hands, willing it not to spill, and blowing gently over its surface so that it would not be too hot to drink. Kneeling down in front of my grandmother sitting perched on her throne, I hardly noticed that her feet were not touching the floor, or that her simple pair of black slippers was dangling carefree from her feet.

I looked up at my grandmother's wizened face; the birthmark spread across the bridge of her nose, her dancing eyes and her row of perfect, false teeth. I studied the prominent veins on the back of her hands and her nimble thin fingers, and prayed she would never leave me. Although I knew my grandmother would be angry with me if I voiced my deepest wish, I knew I could not imagine a world without her.

'Grandmother,' I began, offering the bowl of tea with both arms stretched out in front of me. 'Please accept this tea. Wishing you birthday happiness. May year after year have today, and every age see this morning.' I had learnt the traditional Chinese greeting off pat, and to my young ears it sounded just fine for the grand occasion.

She took the bowl from my hands and sipped it twice, making a great show of the pleasure it gave her. 'You are a good girl,' she told me gently, before continuing in a more formal Chinese verse. 'Your grandmother knows that you are truly pious.'

I felt a warm glow flush over my face, and my young heart skipped with joy. Grandmother reached into her pocket, fumbled around a little, and fished out a thin red envelope, decorated with a gold motif of a dragon, its head raised free and its claws in majestic repose.

'Here, a *laisee* for you, because you gave your grandmother a cup of tea.'

I got up from the cushion, receiving the red packet of good fortune in both hands, but I knew better than to finger it, despite my curiosity at how much money it might contain. It was the only red packet I was allowed to keep and spend; the other much bigger *laisee* I received later in the day would have to be deposited into my bank account. Although it was Grandmother's birthday, she made a point of giving everyone in the flat a *laisee*. It was her way of sharing her happy occasion with us. For a traditional Chinese elder, the giving of such a *laisee*, regardless of how much money it contained, was the most delicate gesture of affection.

In Chinese culture, a child's birthday is not celebrated past its first month, when it is regarded as one year old. The next birthday would be celebrated after the completion of a whole life cycle, when the lunar cycle of twelve animals had come round five times, covering the five elements. That was the big birthday, at sixty, and each year after was considered a bonus and a long life.

This year was particularly special, as it was the first time my parents could afford to celebrate my grandmother's birthday in style. We had made arrangements to host a dinner party at a nearby restaurant along the tramway, and many of Grandmother's friends and relatives would be gathering for the occasion. Mum and Dad even had a surprise parcel too, wrapped in glittering red and gold paper, the auspicious colours of luck and good fortune.

I had never witnessed such a sparkle in my grandmother's eyes, as she put her spectacles on to begin negotiating the sticky tape that held the parcel together.

'Ah, ginseng,' Grandmother mumbled with approval. She fingered the prized root, examining it with surprising expertise and enjoying its subtle aroma. 'You shouldn't have spent so much money on me,' she said to my parents with obvious delight.

'What's it for?' I asked, sniffing the dry roots packed tightly in a plastic box and expecting them to smell really exotic and expensive.

'Oh, it's very good for you,' my grandmother enthused as she began to pack her gift away, for it would be improper to be too enthusiastic. 'It's good for general weakness, to vitalise the organs and to make one feel young and healthy. You've seen me chew a thin slice every now and again, haven't you? A little helps calm the nerves and stops palpitations.'

Shortly after ten o'clock in the morning, familiar voices accompanied by plodding footsteps came to a gradual crescendo outside our front door.

'Grandmother!' I shouted as I peeped through the key hole. 'I think they are here!' I lifted the heavy bar away from its bracket and opened the door a split second before the bell rang.

'*Jo-sun*, Mrs Chow. *Jo-sun*, Mrs Kum. Please come in and sit down. Grandmother is in the kitchen. *Lei sek-joh faan mei-a?* Have you eaten rice yet?' I knew they couldn't possibly have had their meal so early in the morning, especially as they had travelled quite far from the Kowloon area to be with us. But the greeting is a customary one, much as one would ask 'how are you?' and not expect a tirade of honesty.

Mrs Chow nodded and smiled, revealing a mouth full of

wired teeth. Her slim figure, very tall for a Chinese lady, was dressed in a pair of black tailored trousers and a fashionable flowered blouse. She hardly spoke, but made her way quickly to the back of our flat to greet her life-long friend.

Grandmother's voice rose in the distance. 'Hey, you. What is the meaning of this, arriving so late?' she admonished playfully in a deliberately exasperated tone, which actually meant 'you're very welcome. You could have arrived earlier if you had wanted to; it would not have inconvenienced me, but this is fine'. 'Had *yum char* before you came, did you?' she continued.

'Of course not,' Mrs Kum retorted in glee. 'We were waiting for you. Come on, are you ready to go?' she said in pretence, knowing full well my grandmother would not have been able to accept her invitation that morning anyway, as there was much to do.

Mrs Kum was a regular visitor, but she seemed to dress in the same *sam fu* every time I saw her. Her husband worked on the ferry going from Hong Kong to Macau, a small Portuguese colony across the Pearl River estuary. Every year he returned from one of his trips with a bamboo basket full of large live crabs, and I remember my grandmother keeping them for a day or so before cooking them as a special treat. I watched her turn them onto their shells and use a screwdriver to pierce their underbelly. On one occasion, Mr Kum came over with two terrapins for us, and they lived for many years as pets on the kitchen floor.

Mrs Kum was much more child-friendly than Mrs Chow, and plumper. She stroked my face, muttering, 'So big now. Your face has become more beautiful since I last saw you.'

It was no wonder I liked her. 'There is good colour in your cheeks. I can see your grandmother looks after you well. Now, let me go and greet my big sister.'

The women were not really sisters, but they had known each other for a lifetime and had lived through the Japanese Occupation together, so they felt closer than blood relations. Grandmother, being the oldest, was big sister to the other two, and the three sisters often met together. Minutes later, Third Aunt, who was married to my Third Uncle, arrived to make up the foursome that would be needed for their first game of mahjong; in Cantonese '*da ma cheuk*', which literally means 'playing the sparrows'. It was lucky we had managed to hire the table and a set of ivory tiles from the corner shop, and had collected it only minutes before.

Our little flat was filled from floor board to rafters with the noisy bantering of seasoned players as the hired ivory *ma cheuk* slabs crashed onto the square table set up in the cramped confines of grandmother's bedroom. Everyone knew Mrs Chow meant business, for she had settled herself into the most comfortable position, a cushioned seat on the old wooden chest that held up one side of the bed. Her thin-rimmed glasses perched on the bridge of her rather beaked nose, and her cigarette hung from pencilled lips. It was such a contrast to the cheerful, benign features of Mrs Kum, who beamed from ear to ear as she sat on grandmother's bed, a bowl of tea on the dressing table beside her. Third Aunt checked her purse, counting out her change and looking around for the birthday lady to join them.

Four pairs of hands reached into the centre of the table, shuffling the thick green and white rectangular playing tiles in a furore of noise, slamming each piece down to hide the engraved surface beneath. To the unknowing child, it had an atmosphere of contained chaos and dangerousness as each player became absorbed in their 'big business gambling', playing fast, furiously and seriously. Exclamations of '*Heh!*' and '*Aieeyaa!*' would be punctuated with a deathly hush, a silent whisper, a slamming of tiles and a sudden explosion of conversation, laughter and exchange of coins. I listened out for the latter, because it was my cue to come around offering refills of tea, or bowls of monkey-nuts. They never played for big stakes, but if Grandmother won we would soon know about it, as my sister and I would each be a dollar or two richer.

My imagination ran wild. What I could do with one whole dollar! It would be worth a large bagful of small plastic Cowboys and Red Indians on horseback; I had loved playing with those ever since a friend who visited my parents from Scotland took me to the cinema to see an American Western film called 'Broken Arrow'. Or I could buy ten notebooks with their colourful flowery covers and thick wads of drawing paper. I could easily afford ten ice-lollies from the street peddler on his bicycle, or two Mr Softy ice creams as I crossed the harbour on the Star Ferry. Or perhaps packets of sour plums, preserved lemon and ginger, tubes of Haw Haw flakes made from the fruit of the Chinese Hawthorn – the latter were thin circles of sweet and sour delight, with which I could emulate the grownups receiving Holy Communion during the Sunday church services.

Grandmother and her guests played a full four rounds of *mah jong* before stopping briefly for a simple lunch of steamed rice and chicken, which my mother had prepared.

It was one of the few times she turned her hand to Chinese cooking, as it was grandmother's domain and expertise. However, she did occasionally cook Western dishes – pork chops, sausages and roast turkey with stuffing for Christmas.

We left the four to have their meal together, and I overheard them talking about long-lost friends, and members of the family who had finally managed, after waiting many years for sponsorship, to emigrate to American shores, dreaming of making their future in the land of golden opportunity. The women ate heartily, their chopsticks hardly resting as they reached for morsels of juicy meats and vegetables to accompany a shovel of steaming hot rice. When they laid their chopsticks down, it was only to slurp noisily from a bowl of soup.

Our cat came out from under Grandmother's bed to investigate what all the noise was about. We hadn't seen her for several days. She had disappeared under the bed, and much as we tried to entice her out of her hiding place, she refused to come. My grandmother stored a battered trunk, filled with winter clothes, under her bed, as well as Chinese quilts she had made, boxes of shoes and a bottle of baby mice wine, brought back by a relative from China and given to her as a special health tonic. All we could do was shine a torch between these bulky items, catching sight of her ear or a bit of fur and convincing ourselves that all was well.

Marmalade stretched her feline body under the mahjong table and peeped out between the women's legs. She licked her lips and went into the kitchen in search of her food bowl. She was well fed, and at times we feared she might end up as dinner. Cantonese people in Hong Kong were partial to cat and dog meat; the latter was even to be found on the menu on the slow boat to China. One time, Marmalade went missing for days. She never responded when my grandmother cooked her food, placed it in her bowl and hit the side with a pair of chopsticks, calling *'miew miew'*. Ordinarily she would have raced into the kitchen almost immediately, but on this occasion there was no response. We feared the worst, until about a week later when we heard a faint meow from outside the flat. We found her hurt, frightened and rather scrawny, under the floorboards. and had to prise her out with a crowbar. How she ended up trapped there we did not know. There was no way we could afford to have her checked out by a vet; in fact, the thought never even entered our minds. She made a quick recovery once home.

I followed her into the kitchen. Our terrapin was scratching inside her food bowl, gnawing on the fish that had been left out for the cat, her streamlined nostrils poking out from above the rim. Marmalade strode up to her shiny metal bowl and peered inside, seemingly unimpressed by the antics of the reptile, which could hardly negotiate its way around such a confined space. She sniffed the hard shell, and decided instead to have a drink. I ran to the fridge and got out a carton of milk, hoping it would be received as a special treat after her days away. Marmalade meowed, and raised her tail.

'You've had enough, Mr Terrapin,' I said as I lifted him out of the bowl, put him into the stone sink and let the tap drip slowly. 'It's Marmalade's turn now.'

I turned back into the passageway, just in time to see

three blind kittens stumble out from under the bed. No wonder she was so fat! I hoped that this time we would be able to keep at least one of the kittens instead of giving them all away.

After resuming a few more rounds of *ma cheuk,* the foursome agreed it was time to move onto the restaurant for a more serious game. It was already three o'clock, and other guests would be arriving and setting up mah jong tables of their own before the evening meal. Almost as quickly as they had arrived, the three women departed, leaving Grandmother to put away her long pink envelops – each containing a banker's cheque from her friends. She unwrapped the parcels of oranges and mangoes, a tin of All-Butter Cookies and a tin of Fry's Golden Cups chocolates, extolling the generosity of her friends and remarking on how much money they had unnecessarily lavished upon her.

In the relative silence that followed, our doorbell rang unexpectedly. It was Third Aunt's son-in-law. He had closed his tailoring business early that day to join in the celebrations, and to try his luck at mah jong. It was serious business, especially as the game was banned in China when the Communists first came to power. I always thought he was very shabbily dressed, especially for a tailor. His trousers never seemed to be pressed, his shirt never quite matched, and his sandals always seemed a little too big for him as if he thought he might grow into them. I tried to imagine what it must have been like for him, as he arrived in Hong Kong unnoticed and undetected by officials. I remember the first time I saw him a few years earlier. I liked his young features, his rather shy manner, his downcast eyes and the strange way he puckered his lips.

'*Ah, Ah Pui! Lek sek-joh faan mei-a*? Have you eaten yet?' my grandmother enquired as she sauntered towards the kitchen.

'Yes, thank you, grandmother,' Ah Pui answered with his usual shyness.

'Oh, you don't need to stand on ceremony here, you know,' grandmother continued, hanging a plastic basin back behind the door. 'We are all the same family now. Come, have something to eat. I can always reheat it in the rice cooker.'

Ah Pui declined politely, and offered his birthday gift with both hands and a little bow.

'Heh! There's no need,' grandmother exclaimed, in her usual tone of 'I knew you would, but I was not really expecting anything'. 'How is your wife? Where is she? Is she coming? How's the pregnancy going?'

'She's fine. She'll be here later,' Ah Pui assured her.

By now Grandmother had returned to her bedroom and was sorting through a pile of red packets, bunching them together in elastic bands in preparation for the evening.

'Here,' she said, pressing a *laisee* into her grandson-in-law's hand. It was customary for the host to return a little of the good fortune a guest had brought in with him. 'In return for buying me something,' she said.

Ah Pui didn't stay long when he realised that the action was to be found in the restaurant. He stopped just long enough to offer tea to his grandmother before heading off to join the others. An hour or so later, Grandmother was dressed in a simple but newly-tailored *cheong sam* she had made for herself for the occasion. She searched her wardrobe for a suitable cardigan.

'Must take this with me,' she explained. 'There's going to be air conditioning in the restaurant, you know. Oh, and I mustn't forget my supply of money,' she chuckled.

I laughed, knowing what she meant. We both reached out for a wad of pink tissue paper. I helped my grandmother fold them up and stuffed them into her beaded purse. Minutes later, she left for the restaurant with my mother at her side; the only two who knew how to play mah jong were going to join the other guests.

'Don't forget to buy some more monkey nuts,' my mother called as she disappeared around the corner of the staircase and away from view. 'And the bottles of brandy are in the plastic carrier by the fridge. I'll buy the oranges on the way.'

It was seven o'clock when my father, my sister and I made our way to the restaurant. My cousin had already gone on ahead, and the other was making his own way there after a football match. I acknowledged the familiar faces along the journey as we walked through the dark alleyway, lined on either side by tin shacks. Some were still open, with plastic bags of colourful sponges selling at ten cents for two. Printing machines were still working overtime, pressing business cards in a rhythmic piston action which never failed to fascinate me. I was mesmerised by its ingenuity. With a natural, unobtrusive sense of timing, the middle-aged proprietor collected the printed cards without even looking, fingertips stained with tobacco and permanent dry-fast ink. Seemingly unaware of the approaching dusk, he fitted the cards into a small plastic box, gave it a quick polish and started collecting once again. Next door, another, older man was hand-engraving pictures and characters onto ivory or bone *ma cheuk* tiles: green bamboo, circles, red and black characters, flowers, girls, dragons and sparrows.

We turned left onto the tramway, stopping at the stationers to buy a packet of playing cards so we could kill the two hours before dinner. After all, there would be little for children to do. The grownups would be engrossed in their *ma cheuk* games, and those who were not would be chatting away about grownup matters, drinking tea and cracking open monkey nuts with their teeth.

Green and white trams chugged their way along the tramline beside us, their windows wide open and their sides displaying advertisements for Marlboro and Salem cigarettes, or VSOP cognac. They afforded a wonderful view of the busy streets during the day, and magical night markets at dusk. Although high up, they never quite reached the fresh flower-edged placards that hung in perfumed splendour overhead. I wondered if Grandmother's name would be up there, indicating that a party was being held in her honour. And then I saw it, my grandmother's name inscribed in beautiful black calligraphy, as we approached the restaurant. It would be very special indeed.

The cool air-conditioning was luxurious in the sultry August evening. Almost half the restaurant floor had been set aside for the celebration, but I never really noticed the rest as it was well partitioned. Attentive waiters greeted guests as they stepped out of the lift, offering steaming hot flannels, individually wrapped in clear plastic, and glasses of refreshing soft drinks or cups of Chinese tea. They piled all the gifts onto one sideboard, cleared away plates of monkey nut shells, refilled drinks and set up additional *ma cheuk* tables as required. An atmosphere of chatter and party noise filled the air; a sign that everyone was busily enjoying themselves. Young children were running around, hiding behind chairs and between tables, stuffing their pockets with handfuls of nuts and sweets. Sweets and chocolates were a luxury for us, only to be bought for special occasions. The colourful, individually foil-wrapped chocolates from the cake shop in the ground floor arcade of Gloucester Building near the Mandarin Hotel, were very special treats at Christmas, but we always shared them with our neighbours. I remember what a coup it was when my sister won a jar of sweets in a competition run by a children's television programme. It was the size one might find on a shelf in a sweet shop. She was invited on set to collect her prize, and I remember standing in the wings. We never got to see it on screen when it was aired, as I have vague memories that it was a live programme, but in any case we did not have a television set able to receive the transmission.

A few guests pressed a bundle of fifty-dollar bills into grandmother's hands as they greeted her, their faces full of smiles and birthday blessings. Others came with tins of biscuits, chocolates and candy – very handy for keeping knick-knacks and bits of haberdashery when emptied. Grandmother's *ma cheuk* game would be interrupted, as she received each new arrival and sipped on numerous cups of tea.

I looked at my watch as I heard my tummy rumbling again. It was almost nine o'clock. The waiters swiftly and expertly cleared the *ma cheuk* tables away. The guests did not seem to mind at all. They all got up, instinctively standing together in groupings of twelve, ready to sit at one of the three round dining tables already set out with silver chopstick rests, spoons, bowls and glasses. The head table was placed between two red pillars, the enormous golden figures of a dragon on one side and the phoenix on the other, both breathing down upon the hostess and her honoured guests. Everyone knew their place in the hierarchy of family kinship. Immediate family members sat together, extended family at the second table and friends at the third.

We had a saucer of boiled peanuts and a dish of preserved duck eggs (known as 100-year-old eggs), served with pickled sliced root ginger. Everyone agreed how fresh the eggs were, even though they had been preserved in lime, salt and ground charcoal for 100 days, the egg white being black jelly and the yolk greyish green when cut open. Then the serious business of eating began, washed down with tumblers of diluted cognac. It was time for the first of twelve pre-selected dishes to arrive, including the obligatory melon soup with lotus seeds (the emblem of redemption), shark's fin soup, fish and chicken. There was much excitement as each platter was brought out in turn, its delicate aromas filling eager nostrils and tantalising every primed palate. Guests spoke like connoisseurs, marvelling at the succulence of the meats and the harmonious balance of all the well-chosen ingredients, not only for the eye and stomach, but for their symbolic meaning. It was a fine art, to be enjoyed and savoured, in splendid poetic order.

I loved watching the excitement and the waves of enthusiasm that caught each table infectiously. When the garoupa (sea bass fish) was brought out, I wondered which guest would have the honour of eating its head, or sucking on its eyeballs. For the Cantonese word for fish (yu) is a pun on the word meaning plenty, or surplus. The fish also signifies freedom from restraint, and hence of high symbolic importance. The decibels increased when the chicken made its appearance, and I laughed as I watched the waiter rotating the silver platter above his head. I wasn't sure why I was laughing so much; was it because of the comical antics or was it because of nervousness that I might be chosen to eat the chicken's head? Spurred on by the happy guests, the waiter turned the platter a further three hundred and sixty degrees, and brought the chicken's head down to Ah Pui. At birthdays and opening festivals, the chicken's beak pointed to the luckiest person, but on Chinese New Year's Eve, it pointed to the person who was to lose his job.

During the meal, guests would come up to Grandmother, toasting and drinking her health, and she reciprocated in kind with her glass of tea. At designated intervals, the entire table of guests appeared at the head table, and everyone rose to their feet, cheering everyone else on and thanking each other for coming. It was the part of the traditional dinners I loved the best. It was such a tangibly joyous atmosphere; everyone standing, honouring one another, and most of all, paying respect and giving face to my beloved grandmother.

Dishes of fried rice and noodles were brought out at the end of the meal, for anyone who had not yet had their fill. In spite of all the eating that had gone on in the two hours since we had come round the table, there was always a little room left to sample a new dish. By the time the red bean soup and lotus paste buns arrived, the table cloth was splattered with soups and sauces; a good sign that the meal had been most appetising. Grandmother did not have time to enjoy the desserts though, or the juicy orange segments and cups of tea that arrived to refresh the palate. It was time to bid farewell to her guests. One by one, they said their thanks and farewell and left; and suddenly the whole restaurant felt strangely empty.

At last Grandmother was able to sit down, in a little peace and quiet, to reflect on her special celebration. It was the waiters' turn to approach her. They offered her more tea before presenting her with a hefty bill for the evening. After my parents had settled everything, the team of waiters wished her a happy birthday, and presented my grandmother with a glass-covered box. Cushioned in red satin were a rice bowl, a soup spoon and a pair of ivory chopsticks.

18

Too little knowledge

One of my first clinical attachments as a third-year medical student was at St Andrew's Hospital, in the East End of London. It was apparently built along architectural lines favoured by Florence Nightingale, and opened in 1873 as the Poplar and Stepney Sick Asylum. It became St Andrew's in 1921, had a school of nursing and as with hospitals at the time, transferred into the National Health Service when it was formed in 1948. The hospital site was closed in the mid-1980s, but I remember it having one of the longest corridors leading to the accident and emergency department. It was a favoured fantasy of us juniors that the crash team (the team of doctors who would respond to an emergency bleep in case of a cardiac arrest) could get on roller skates at one end of the corridor, and skate down it to the patient at the other.

I don't recall much about my attachment, or any of the patients I met there. But I remember the hospital, its large curved columns and its massive wards; of particular note to me were the scuff marks on the walls and pillars which had been made by passing gurneys. This was where I spent long periods in the library, reading and searching the literature for information on gliomas and other brain tumours.

My grandmother had been rushed into hospital in Hong Kong with an unremitting and extremely painful headache. The doctors and nurses had done all they could do, but without a brain scan they could not investigate any further. My parents were called in, and they immediately gave financial authorization for the CAT scan to go ahead. It concluded that my grandmother had a brain tumour, and the treatment recommended was surgery.

The anguish, worry and fear I felt was exacerbated by being so far away from home, and made worse by the information I had found myself reading in the medical library. Instead of being reassured, this overwhelming exposure to every possible complication and risk, however small, ate away inside me – and being so new to the world of clinical medicine, I found it almost impossible to make much sense of what I was reading. My tutor was completely unmoved by my predicament. He did not understand why I was so worried, nor why I needed to know as much as I could. I realised then that there was very little in the way of pastoral care, support and understanding from within the medical profession. You either survived or you didn't.

When my grandmother refused to have surgery, the hospital discharged her, saying they needed the bed for someone else who wanted treatment. She went home and prepared for her fate. But the doctors were wrong. Years later, when I accompanied her to one of her routine medical checkups, I asked what had become of the results. I discovered there was no brain tumour. It had been a misdiagnosis. I shudder to think what would have happened had my grandmother consented to surgery.

Dr Tsoi was a long-standing family friend who had known my grandmother and her husband. He had a private practice, as most doctors in Hong Kong did, and performed a role akin to that of a general practitioner. Apparently he was influential in advising my grandmother not to support my mother's ambition to train as a nurse, even though she had been offered a place. My mother told me years later that this was because he did not think she had the right temperament for it. I only ever met him when I accompanied my grandmother for her health reviews when in later years she was on beta-blockers for hypertension. I don't remember him that well, but I do remember him advising very regular appointments, all paid of course, so that he would be in a position to issue the necessary paperwork when she died, without recourse to a post mortem. I am not sure how well-meaning that was.

In our final year at medical school, we were all encouraged to do a two-month elective in a different country, to widen our experience and to see medical practice from a different perspective. I wanted to return to Hong Kong, to see for myself how healthcare was being provided at home. I wanted, in particular, to see what psychiatric services were like, as I had often thought of our neighbour who lived upstairs and her regular admissions to the mental institution at Castle Peak. Queen Mary's Hospital was the flagship teaching hospital in Hong Kong, so I wrote to them, but its medical school declined my request, on the grounds that psychiatric services were so basic it would not be beneficial to my training. Instead, they offered me consecutive attachments at their Obstetrics and Gynaecology and General Medicine departments.

The campus at Queen Mary's Hospital in Pok Fu Lam was not very far from where my parents and grandmother were living, and it allowed me to return to live at home for the entire two months.

Medical student life was very different in Hong Kong; the student canteen was an incredible mosaic of noise and colour and smells, and a far cry from the student union building in the East End opposite the outpatient block at the London Hospital in Whitechapel. The choice of hot dishes was quite staggering. The young medics filled their trays with gastronomic delights whilst calling out to one another and squeezing around tables to join their friends and colleagues in an orgy of Cantonese chatter and Chinglish. Their lecture theatres were fully equipped too, and one could not hide amongst the 200-plus throng of students gathered to witness a clinical demonstration, or hear an eminent professor speak. Microphones on extended arms allowed every student who did not raise their hand to be the subject of humiliation when asked a question they could not answer. Medical training was a bit like that really – a mixture of humbling and emotional experiences, coupled with utter humiliation in front of fellow students, patients, doctors and nurses on consultant ward rounds, and years of hurdles, hoops and other obstacles to negotiate.

It seemed to me that my Chinese counterparts were extremely knowledgeable and academically superior. They were able to distinguish much more than the two sounds of the heartbeat on auscultation of the chest; they knew their applied anatomy and physiology backwards, and they seemed to know even the smallest minutiae of an uncommon or rare disease. I was quite in awe of their grasp, and wondered if I would ever pass my final examinations. But when it came to the art of patient consultation, to bedside manner, to speaking and treating patients, I felt the training I had in London served the practice of care and compassion in clinical medicine better. I have always believed that what one does not know, one can look up – but being a medical practitioner is an art, as well as a vocation.

I was amazed at the crowds of people waiting outside the clinic doors for a session to begin. The numbers of students in those government clinics was like a mini-theatre, with two to four rows of seats, whilst the patient and the doctor sat in front of the audience. The gynaecology clinic was like a cattle market; women were herded into a row of thinly-partitioned cubicles, and a curtain screened the doorway through which the patient would enter, undress from the waist down and lie in wait with her feet pointing to a drawn curtain directly opposite. We medics walked down the corridor, drew back the curtain, checked out the pre-screened history and proceeded with an intimate internal examination. We then closed the curtain and left. I don't remember giving the patient any results; that must have occurred in another part of the clinic experience. To be fair though, it was very similar to the practice I witnessed as a medical student in Britain, only there were fewer cubicles.

The wealth of clinical material I saw on my elective was astounding; tuberculosis was rife, as was leprosy. We visited the 600-bedded Ruttanjee Sanatorium in Wanchai, one of the main institutions treating tuberculosis before outpatient chemotherapy was available, and the leper community in Lai Chi Kok. Leprosy thrived in the poor socio-economic environment of post-war Hong Kong, and those afflicted were compulsorily admitted for isolation and treatment. I shall never forget the men and women I met who had been blinded because of the loss of feeling they had in their eyes, which had allowed injury to go unnoticed and infection to spread; nor the lepromatous skin lesions in their faces and ears, and the nerve damage that came with the later stages of the disease. The stigma of leprosy was strong, but these people had been resettled from the isolated island of Hei Ling Chau (subsequently turned into a drug rehabilitation centre) into a relatively integrated community, although they still lived together. With the introduction of the World Health Organisation Multi-Drug Treatment regime, the successful elimination of leprosy in Hong Kong was officially declared in the mid-1980s, although there is still a population with an inactive form of the condition.

19

Hong Kong, 1984

'Come and take my pulse for me,' my grandmother invited me, holding her arm out towards me. 'How is it?'

Happy to put my newly-acquired medical training on show, I placed two fingers over her radial artery to feel the pulsating beats beneath my fingertips. After all, I was a fully-qualified doctor (*'yi sheung'* which means 'healer of life') looking after a full clinical caseload back in England.

'It is strong and regular,' I told my grandmother, satisfied that I had not found anything untoward.

'Is that all you can say?' she asked me in a rather disappointed tone of voice. 'If you had trained in Chinese medicine, you would have been able to tell me everything about my health. You would be able to tell me about my flow of *chi* and whether it is obstructed or imbalanced. There are at least twenty-eight different pulses, you know. But I guess they do not believe that in Western medicine.'

I wished then that I had learned more about the traditional Chinese art of healing; about the balance of *yin* and *yang* forces and the five elements my grandmother so often talked about. Throughout my childhood, she sought to give us a proper diet, supplementing it from time to time with a Chinese medicinal brew, saying there was too much heat in what we had eaten the previous day. In creating her meals, she endeavoured to restore the flow of *chi* and the harmony that keeps a person healthy, in body, mind and spirit. I don't recall seeing a doctor when ill; I remember when I was very young being taken to a child health clinic where all the children were lying on a bench with their bottoms exposed in order for the nurse to get a rectal temperature. Sometimes that and a brief conversation would be it; other times it ended with a vaccination, the most painful being the BCG for tuberculosis. My only encounters with a Western doctor were the required health checks with the school doctor. He looked rather elderly, had an engaging smile and large warm hands. He reminded me of the American TV character, Marcus Welby MD, though that might be more fantasy than reality. I remember going once, and standing in front of him with my cotton top up to my armpits and my knickers down at my ankles.

I watched as my grandmother prepared an infusion of chrysanthemum flowerheads to apply to her tired eyes. In forty-eight hours, I was to be married, and we were relaxing and anticipating the exhaustion of the occasion ahead. My fiancé and I had flown back to Hong Kong, so that my grandmother could be at the wedding, and so that I could be married in the cathedral church where I had grown up.

'How come you let Mum marry someone who is not Chinese?' I asked, thinking about my own forthcoming union with an Englishman whom I had met on the first day of medical school. 'It must have been very unusual in those days, wasn't it? Especially in your generation, when you had arranged marriages and everything.'

I reminded my grandmother about the tall tailor who had lived and worked in a shop opposite our little flat ten years before. Grandmother had adopted him as a godson (a 'kai' son) after his parents' death, and he often popped round to the flat to seek her advice and counsel. Taking on a 'kai' child is a very popular custom amongst the Chinese people. It can be a casual affair, with nothing more than a feeling of kinship between the child and 'kai' parent, or it can be a formal arrangement with a degree of ceremony, privilege and obligation. That particular day I remember well, as her godson was very agitated and unable to settle. His thirty years sat heavily on his lean features, and his eyes darted from one corner to another as he pleaded and implored my grandmother to arrange his marriage to a woman he had seen at a dinner party the week before.

'Your mother's brothers, your uncles, wrote to me from Guangzhou when they found out. Scolding me, saying your grandfather would never have had any of it, had he been alive. They were very much against it. But I didn't listen to them. After all, I wasn't the one getting married. It was your mother's life,' my grandmother recounted as she pressed the warm flower heads onto her closed eyelids.

'But yours was an arranged marriage, wasn't it?' I persisted.

'Yeah, it was. We weren't meant to know our future husbands. But in my case, it was a bit different. You see, we used to live near your grandfather, in the next hamlet. Once we even talked to each other, on our way to Hong Kong by steamer. He already had his watch shop over here, and was travelling from Guangzhou to Hong Kong on business.'

'Did you know him well?'

'Not at all. But at least he wasn't a complete stranger to me. He was a lot older than I was. I didn't know how old he was then; he looked quite young to me. I was only fifteen when I married him. Everyone warned him not to marry me. They told him I was a stubborn, bad-tempered girl.'

It was difficult to imagine my grandmother being stubborn and bad-tempered. Sure, she had her fiery moments, and she must have had such strength and determination. Perhaps they were not the qualities one wished for in a typical, subordinate wife, but those same qualities led her to learn to read and write from the boys living across the alleyway late at night, when other women around her remained illiterate. Even in her 80s, my grandmother was keen to learn and asked me to teach her the English alphabet.

'I desperately wanted to go to school and learn how to read and write, to learn everything I could, but in those days people didn't educate girls that way. Not only that, but I was a foster-daughter and really treated like a servant. But my foster-brother, Ah So, was about the same age as me, and he taught me how to read. I always listened to him whenever he did his studies, his homework, so I could learn as much as I could. I managed to buy three books when I was a girl. I remember them well; *Liang Shan Bai* and *Chuk Ying Tai* (The Love Story), *Mou Yue Shue* (Wooden Fish book) and *Xing Yue Kao* (The Book of Complete Sentences.)

'And grandfather didn't mind?' I asked.

'No, he was very good to me. You can tell from his photograph. He was a decent man. He always told me not to work so hard. I helped with the shop, and looked after the children, and when the staff weren't there, I did the cooking as well. And then, at night, when everyone else was asleep, I would sit up by the sewing machine, sewing padded silk jackets. I worked from morning to night; helped earn quite a lot of money that way. Your grandfather would always say, it's dark now. Get some sleep. Do not work so hard, you must have your rest. It was so hard in those days. But we survived. I even saved up enough money to buy myself some gold bangles, the first pieces of jewellery I ever owned.'

'Have I seen them?' I asked. My grandmother shook her head. 'What happened to them?'

'I pawned them, to pay for your Second Uncle's wedding. You know he was my stepson right, from your grandfather's first marriage, but I didn't want anyone to think that stepmothers treated their stepchildren badly, so I wanted him to have the best wedding I could afford. I pawned the bangles, and we had a really grand wedding back in the village. It was 1928. But I was never able to redeem them from the pawn shop. We went badly into debt at the end of the Chinese New Year; our creditors took back all our goods and business started to slip again. Perhaps I should have chosen to buy a new sewing machine instead, but I felt so strongly that I should give Second Son a good wedding.'

'So, when was your first child born?'

'Your Third Uncle? Oh, let me see.' Grandmother thought for a moment. 'It must have been when I was about seventeen. It went on for days. And after that, my breasts were so sore. No one said anything about breast milk, you see. Our breasts were always bound, so men couldn't see them wobbling about. Not like nowadays. It was all very decent and proper. After the birth, mine were still bound and they started to swell and got very painful.'

'What did you do then?' I asked, remembering the acute mastitis I had seen in women during my medical student training, their breast tissue red, hot and extremely painful.

'Well,' my grandmother continued, straightening up from her treatment, wet petals in therapeutic disarray around her eyes. 'Luckily, one of the elderly women in the village saw me crying, and said you'll have to undo all this binding and release the swelling. And then she stuck a big needle into them and all the blood and milk came out. After that, I felt much better.'

I recoiled at the thought of such barbaric treatment, probably with no thought to antiseptics or infection. 'And what about when you had your other children?'

My grandmother smiled, and said in a very matter-of-fact way, 'Oh, I knew after that. It never happened again. But you know, don't have children too early. In my day we had no choice, but you do now. I induced five abortions. Drank a potion to get rid of them. I couldn't carry so many. Don't get pregnant too soon. Don't be in a hurry to have children. Live your life.'

20

My first delivery

As a second-year clinical student, one of my attachments was with an Obstetrics and Gynaecology firm at a district general hospital. Students liked being placed away from the main London teaching hospitals, for they often got more hands-on experience. In large teaching hospitals, filled to the brim with consultants and multiple tiers of junior doctors and trainees, lowly medical students barely got a look in, let alone the chance to assist with an operation or suture a woman's episiotomy cut, or perform an invasive procedure. Ward sisters were more like traditional matrons – barking at students if they came on the ward at an inconvenient moment, and making them feel totally unwelcome and complete idiots. Coupled with the humiliation one often received from consultants during ward rounds, it was a relief to be sent to an outlying district hospital. But it also meant hard work, and many hours at night shadowing the junior doctors on call, as they rushed from one job to another, their list of things to do piling up after each intrusive bleep.

On the antenatal ward, we were allocated to a patient and expected to follow the birth through from start to finish. Sometimes, the finish meant a normal delivery by the midwife; at other times it meant an assisted delivery by the medical obstetric team using forceps or a ventouse (suction cup to the baby's head), and occasionally it led to an emergency caesarean section, often performed by the consultant, who was called in from home.

'She's 10 centimetres,' the midwife proclaimed. 'Get her in now.'

I was hovering about, not quite knowing what to do or what to expect. It was my first delivery, and I was hoping to witness this event in the reassuring knowledge that an experienced midwife would be present to deliver the newborn. But the midwife was called away and she sent me in – alone. The next few minutes were filled with terror, but I mustered enough common sense to tell the woman to concentrate on her breathing, panting, and pushing. She was in agony, having refused all forms of pain relief. She asked me how many babies I had delivered before.

'Oh, not that many,' I lied.

'Don't worry,' she said, sweat painted over her forehead. 'This is my fourth. It'll be all right.'

And it was. By the time the midwife returned, the baby was born and I was retrieving the placenta, one hand firmly placed on the woman's lower abdomen and other holding onto the cut umbilical cord. I hope such a terrifying experience is not a common occurrence for students these days, but it certainly was the bread and butter of our junior doctor years.

The asylum was on the outskirts of London. A porter's lodge marked the start of a long driveway through avenues of historic trees and extensive lands. There was a calmness and tranquillity about the place, despite the imposing listed red brick building which dominated the landscape. An abundance of corridors, long and straight, with paint peeling off the walls, seemed incongruous to the majesty of the building and the acres of landscaped greenery outside. People were milling about everywhere; men and women who seemed to have aged prematurely due to a lifetime of potent drugs, their gait stiff and their features mask-like, their odd mannerisms accepted as the norm. The first-time visitor, however, would have noticed the 'kangaroo-lady' skipping along the corridor, making whooping noises as she went by, or patients wringing their hands together, licking the walls and talking to themselves.

When I first arrived at the hospital at the start of my psychiatric training, I wasn't given any advice about personal safety as trainees are now. There were hidden corners everywhere in the hospital, and no panic buttons or alarms I can recall. I remember we had to campaign for months before we got staff to agree to stay in the room with us as we assessed a new patient in the middle of the night who had presented to the hospital distressed, psychotic and in need of an acute admission. More often than not they were brought in by police, for behaving bizarrely in a public place. Over lunch one day, a senior nurse told me how a female patient had attacked a male consultant with a knife a few years earlier, so severely that he still carried the scar on his forehead. Apparently he had been interviewing this patient and had scratched his forehead whilst talking to her. She interpreted this as him attacking her and playing with her clitoris, so she lashed out at him. Not sure where she got the knife from though; must have had it on her. Ever since, I have always been very aware of my non-verbal cues and body language when assessing acutely mentally-unwell patients.

The first consultant I worked with during my psychiatric training only ever appeared for ward rounds, when he heard about the patients under his care from his team of junior doctors and ward nurses. He never held his own clinic and very rarely set foot on the ward at other times, but it was obvious he trusted his ward sister completely. I don't remember observing him interviewing a patient or conducting a mental state examination. One medical secretary commented at the time that he gave us so much rope we could have hung ourselves.

It was not surprising, therefore, that my first psychiatric outpatient clinic was fraught with anxiety, as I was so inexperienced. I often wonder how those patients would have fared were I to see them now; I remember being totally out of my depth, and left to handle every psychiatric emergency and complex case with the help of a junior colleague who was only slightly more experienced than myself. In those days it really was a question of 'see one, do one, teach one'.

A woman in her early thirties came to clinic. She sat in

the chair in front of me, much lower than I was, and launched into a detailed history of her schizophrenic illness. She had come for a routine review of her medication – a potent, powerful, major tranquilliser given by regular injections. She supplemented this with tablets, in order to control her symptoms. But before I could say anything about her medication, she pleaded with me not to take her symptoms away. Cliff Richard was the voice speaking to her, through her arm. He was the only company she had. Without him she felt she had nothing, and she did not want him taken away.

One evening, a woman in her 50s was admitted onto the ward, and as the duty psychiatrist I was called to clerk her in. She had been seen by my consultant, either in clinic or on a home visit, diagnosed with severe depression and sent into hospital for treatment, which was often medication and sometimes electroconvulsive therapy (ECT). Apparently her symptoms had started several weeks before, shortly after she discovered her husband's infidelity. I was chatting with the charge nurse when she came into the room. Rather unkempt, and with signs of self-neglect, she wore a cardigan partially buttoned, although the buttons were misaligned. She looked much older than her age. As I chatted with her I noticed some mild dyspraxia; when I examined her eyes with an ophthalmoscope, I thought I saw swelling of the optic nerve, which is a sign of increased intra-cranial pressure. There were no other doctors around, I was in a psychiatric hospital far away from physicians and the nurses working with me were mental health nurses. Thankfully, I had only recently left my casualty officer post, so I was pretty clued up with physical healthcare. I phoned the local hospital and asked to speak with the registrar for neurology. Luckily, I had worked with him as a surgical houseman and we got on well together. He was a senior registrar in neurosurgery, and has since gone on to have a very illustrious career. We arranged to transfer her urgently, and she had a head scan that night, an investigation that was very difficult to get for psychiatric patients at the time. We discovered a 10-centimetre tumour in her frontal lobe, which luckily was benign and operable, and she made a good recovery.

I also remember assessing a young woman who had head injuries. I think she was found severely bruised and with multiple superficial lacerations, but it was unclear what had happened. There was nothing untoward in her behaviour whilst recovering on the ward, so I don't recall in what capacity I was asked to see her. However, when I chatted with her she disclosed, for the first time, that she had been hearing voices for years, and that they had increased in intensity and frequency. She had not told anyone, but had been so distressed by them she was hitting and banging her head against a brick wall in an attempt to get rid of them. It struck me then how stigmatizing and isolating severe mental illness can be, and often we are oblivious to the suffering. I didn't have anything to do with her aftercare, so this must have been a one-off assessment, but the encounter has stuck with me and shaped my clinical interactions.

As medical students, we were taught to take a comprehensive history when assessing someone for a possible mental health disorder, although it wasn't the same when assessing for a physical health condition. Psychiatric history taking followed a prescribed format: history of presenting complaint; past medical history including hospital admissions, major illnesses and risk factors, key questions targeting the major systems of the body; past psychiatric history including hospital admissions and treatments; family history including relationships with significant others, mental illness or mental handicap (now known as intellectual disabilities); personal history including developmental milestones and schooling; psychosexual history; treatment history and current medication including allergies; use of tobacco, alcohol and illicit/other substances; contact with the police and social history including living circumstances, employment and relationships. We also asked them to describe themselves and their usual personality before the onset of their presenting complaint. These questions all preceded any physical or mental state examination. With experience these questions become more targeted and nuanced.

When I was working in a district general hospital, on my liaison psychiatry placement, I was asked to see a man who had been admitted onto a medical ward. He had become confused and staff were seeking a psychiatric assessment and advice on managing his delirium. It's a common presentation, but when I saw him things didn't quite fit. After speaking with him I did a neurological examination, including testing his cranial nerves and asking him to get out of the hospital bed to walk for me. He was ataxic (poorly coordinated), with a high-stepping gait that had been missed by the medical team who had just seen him in bed. I suspected tertiary syphilis, which turned to be the cause of his presentation.

At its peak, Claybury Hospital in Woodford Green on the outskirts of London was home to 4000 mental health inpatients. It had listed buildings and extensive land: 50 acres of ancient woodland and 95 acres of open parkland, ponds, pasture and historic gardens. I spent my early psychiatric training there, and was very aware of the asylum it offered to acutely unwell patients, as well as the segregated and protected institutionalised care for those with more chronic mental health problems who had lived there for years. The hospital has long been closed with the move to 'care in the community'. I lived there in the doctors' quarters when doing my nights on call, and remember a very supportive environment when I was the junior doctor assessing people brought in by the police, as well as covering the whole hospital and admission wards at night. Early in my psychiatric career I came across a woman on one of the wards. She was the exuberant star of the inpatient group I ran every morning with the senior nurse, where patients were encouraged to discuss how things were going, and to have the chance to bring up issues with staff. This small woman, with short-cropped hair and a rather stout frame, stood centre stage as if gracing us with her presence. With arms outstretched she proclaimed her special powers and divine spirituality. After the group, she would make a beeline for me, demanding why certain things had not yet been done and angered by the slightest comment. I was terrified of her, and she knew it. She stood in the main corridor of the ward, waiting for me, rosary beads in hand and talking to herself, whilst directing staff and other patients to do her will. She had been a very respected nun at her local convent and had been admitted only a few days before. In the weeks preceding her admission the other nuns had revered her, believing she had been truly touched by the Lord. She had spoken of visions and special blessings and genuinely appeared to them to be in receipt of something divine. During mass she often stood up and took over the service, and the nuns came to regard her as a holy woman. However, as the weeks went by her utterances became more bizarre; she began to leave her excrement out for the birds, believing the Lord wanted her to feed them with her body. It was at this stage that the nuns sought psychiatric help for her. She was diagnosed as suffering from mania, a condition characterised by grandiose ideas, hyperactivity and elation. Once her acute episode was treated, she turned out to be one of the loveliest, gentlest and warmest women I have ever met. As her mood stabilized I enjoyed chatting with her on the ward – she was an amazing woman.

On one occasion I was almost smothered by a patient who came over to where I was sitting, grabbed my head and held it to her breasts, her huge arms enveloped round me. I could hardly breathe. She wanted some of my hair, she said, so she could do something positive with it – in fact, she wanted to keep a part of me with her, always.

Halfway through my core psychiatric training, which lasted three years, I was lucky enough to work with a consultant psychiatrist who was also a psychoanalyst. His ward rounds were often challenging for patients and difficult for us to manage as he would confront them and say things that often resulted in raw emotions, explosive anger and physical aggression. He always sat at the opposite end of the room from the patient, with a whole staff team between them. One day, I witnessed him confront a man about his most bizarre symptoms. Then and there the patient suddenly exploded; his anger and stress totally transformed him. His face was bright red, his hair was literally on end and with his right arm flexed against his chest, he blew hot air like a steam engine. It was piercingly accurate. I did not believe it possible that a man's face could mimic a steam engine in this way. On another occasion, I was convinced the patient was suffering from a physical illness we had yet to uncover and treat, as her physical symptoms and signs were so distressing and obvious. I kept thinking about other tests we could do, and referrals to a host of physicians. My consultant allowed me to pursue this but he also said that they were all psychologically driven. He was right. I learnt a great deal about mental distress and its physical manifestations on that training placement.

My consultant was one of the few practitioners using psychoanalysis and psychoanalytic frameworks in his everyday clinical practice, even amongst those with acute psychotic illness. He introduced me to the work of Wilfred Bion and Melanie Klein, and whenever he spoke it made sense to me why someone's mental state might fluctuate from psychosis to depression, and the problems with a diagnostic label. He told me something I remember to this day. He told me it was very important for the sane part of us to stand up to the insane part within our patients. They desperately need to see that there is sanity around them.

Of course, implicit in that sound advice is the notion that there is both sanity and insanity within us all. Not only within us, by within the organisations in which we work and within the world in which we live.

21

———

The joys of music and dance

'Feed the body food and drink, it will survive the day,
Feed the soul art and music, it will live forever.'

As already mentioned, I fell in love with the Rodgers and
Hammerstein's film 'The Sound of Music' from the moment
I saw it, at the impressionable age of five. I remember
sitting in the darkened auditorium, asking my father
whether it was really possible to sing so loudly on a public
bus when one is trying to find confidence and reassurance.
I remember my mother saying this was the way I should
wear my hair, as it was short and practical for the humid
Hong Kong weather. I remember in the film watching Maria
sitting on a pinecone as she joined the Von Trapp family for
her first evening meal. I was so confused; I had never seen
a pinecone before and could not, for the life of me, fathom
out what the little creature was that rolled on Maria's seat
and caused such a stir at the dinner table. The grandeur of

the Captain's home was something I could only realise in my dreams. It took my breath away, and I gasped with the audience. We could only afford to see the film once on its first general release, but the soundtrack played over and over again on our old gramophone player. My sister clearly identified with the children. She happily sang Liesl's part in 'I am sixteen going on seventeen,' and 'Edelweiss' and Gretl's part in 'So Long, Farewell'. But for me, I only ever sang Maria's part – and I loved it. I loved the music, the songs, the scenery, the storyline, and most of all, Julie Andrews' portrayal of Maria von Trapp. For me, it was the most magical film. It was the first time anything had touched my soul.

At the age of 12, over the Chinese New Year break and with a few days off from school, I was able to enjoy a new television series called 'The Julie Andrews Hour'. It was a revelation to watch the woman who had been the Maria of my childhood fantasies singing and dancing as herself. I discovered to my joy that a copy of an unauthorised biography was held at the main City Hall library. I borrowed it, and kept renewing it continuously until I finally obtained my own copy, many years later, from the rare books department of Hatchards in Piccadilly, London. Its 'rarity' made it all the more precious. I was fascinated by the interplay of her public persona and private life, the fickleness of the general public's adulation, the power of the media and the phenomenal talent of Julie Andrews.

As I was walking up Battery Path on the way to choir practice one evening, the cover of MacCalls, a glossy imported American magazine, caught my eye. It bore a picture of Julie Andrews, and I knew I had to have it. In those days I was given regular pocket money - a grand total of four Hong Kong dollars a month. The exchange rate was something like sixteen dollars to a British pound. The magazine cost almost eight dollars, but because I did not have enough money, the newsagent kindly agreed to keep a copy aside for me until I did. I saved my pocket money for two months, and the magazine was the first tangible thing I ever bought for myself. The cover was scratched and a little torn when I got it, but I still have it, tucked away amongst my collection of memorabilia.

Music became a big part of my childhood, and remains so. My favourite teacher at primary school, Mrs Edwards, gave the most enjoyable music lessons. At school assemblies, she taught us many lovely hymns such as 'Morning has broken', 'All things bright and beautiful' and 'Hills of the north rejoice'. I still find myself humming and singing hymns when I'm driving or doing housework, much to my children's annoyance! Mrs Edwards also led the school choir through many school festivals and competitions, as we sang our way to first place on most occasions. One year, she asked me to sing a solo for the school's nativity play. I remember almost every detail of that performance, the school hall filled with expectant parents anxious to see their child, chosen to perform on stage. I remember the calmness I felt before the performance, and the chatter of the audience on the other side of the curtains. I can still see and hear Mrs Edwards, sitting at her piano at the side of the stage, accompanying me as I sang to my little doll of the infant Jesus. I can feel the hand of my classmate, Adrian, who played Joseph, as he touched my shoulder whilst I sang. Everything came together, and it was magical.

Mrs Edwards tutored me in breathing technique when she entered me for a solo singing competition. I remember the song, and her tremendous encouragement.

'Have you seen the cobwebs on a misty, misty morn?
Spun upon the hedges of a leafy, leafy lane.
Gleaming bright with silver light, the mirrors of the dawn,
Touched by every tiny drop of rain.'

Soon after leaving primary school I joined the Cathedral Choir, rehearsing every Friday evening and singing at two services on a Sunday morning, with the occasional wedding or funeral on a Saturday afternoon. Marriages for officers in the British Hong Kong Garrison usually meant a service with full honours. Royal visits to Hong Kong almost always included a stop at the Cathedral, and a full choir was expected. I have so many fond memories of my years there: singing my favourite anthem, Stanford's Te Deum in B Flat; the annual procession for Remembrance Sunday, not only in the Cathedral but to and around the Cenotaph in Statue Square; the Christmas invitation to the Governor's House where we sang for him and his guests before indulging in a wonderful selection of mince pies, hors d'oeuvres and drinks. The residence was a short walk from the Cathedral, but carrying the heavy lantern became a memorable challenge. The occasion I remember most of all was the special service to mark the Queen's Silver Jubilee in 1977. The guest of honour was Princess Alexandra, with her husband, Angus Ogilvy. We rehearsed for weeks leading up to the service, with trumpets and a military band joining us just days before. Naturally the Cathedral was packed with the elite of Hong Kong society, but as the choir we had pride of place. I was so excited at seeing my first ever Royal Princess and walking past her, just a few feet away, as I processed down the nave. I was blown away on hearing the military band play Walton's 'Crown Imperial' for the first time, and their majestic introduction to the National Anthem.

Dance also played an important part in my life. At the age of about seven or eight, my parents enrolled my sister and me for ballet classes. Initially on a Saturday afternoon at the City Hall dance studios, it soon moved across the harbour to Star House in Tsim Sha Shui. My grandmother offered to accompany us on the journey, as it took a good hour with the two-mile walk from our home to the ferry concourse, as well as the short Star Ferry ride across the waters. She socialised with the other adults sitting silently on the bench at one side of the studio, and enjoyed watching us dancing, often losing herself in the music. In fact, whenever we practised at the piano at home, it was my grandmother who would put down her kitchen towel or apron for a few moments to come into the living room to hear us play. After my grandmother's death, I discovered that she had been sold to her 'foster' family, at the age of seven, after her own mother had died. This family owned a business making musical instruments. I'd like to think that in some small way, my daily practice on the piano spoke to her in ways I never could.

I was lucky enough to be chosen for a few dance roles on television well before my teens, although I never got to see any of them, apart from a brief excerpt when staff in the watch shop below our flat saw it screened and shouted out to us from the back courtyard. On one occasion a small group of us danced through the opening credits of a Mandarin film; I remember dancing in a red frock through artificial snowflakes and having to do numerous takes. We were in the film studio for the whole day, just for that one scene, and I did enjoy watching the film crew and sharing in a hot lunch on set. My Seventh Aunt saw the film in New York quite by chance. She had recently emigrated to the United States, and was so excited when she recognised us that she wrote to my grandmother about it. Again it was a film we never saw, and I don't even know its title.

When we were old enough my teacher suggested my sister and I should join the Hong Kong Ballet. I am so glad we did, because shortly after, its patron, Dame Margot Fonteyn, came over to Hong Kong. She was the epitome of the Royal Ballet and its most famous classical ballet dancer, and of course her partnership with Nureyev was legendary. Much was made of her early connection with China, and with a ballet school in Hong Kong near the lower Peak Tram station, as well as her devotion to her quadriplegic husband following an unsuccessful assassination attempt on his life by a rival Panamanian politician. Dame Margot was to perform at the City Hall, I think, but in amongst her busy schedule she had agreed to attend a tea party the Hong Kong Ballet were hosting in her honour. My sister and I were on the selected guest list and I still have a newspaper cutting from that special afternoon. I remember being struck by her petiteness, seeing her small frame as she graced us with her presence; that broad elegant smile, those eyes and her gentle touch on my shoulder. She stopped by our table and spoke to us all individually. I asked her if she ever thought about teaching dance, but she replied she did not feel she would have the patience it required. Dame Margot invited our table of young dancers to join her at rehearsals the next day, to watch the company before the evening performance. I kick myself now, but at the time I was firmly convinced my parents would never agree to let me skip school for such a frivolous and non-academic pursuit, so I never asked them and they never knew.

We did have tickets to a performance, and watching Dame Margot dance on stage was the best education a ballerina could have. I learnt more about poise, grace and technique in watching that one performance than I did in a whole year at dance class. Her skills and flair and sheer brilliance outshone the other dancers on stage with her. It is sad to know that she died so alone, and with such little ceremony and recognition.

'I never had my feet bound,' my grandmother told me when I was a child. 'It was out of fashion by then. But I can remember my foster mother did. I told her once they smelt like dead mice. I unbound them for her, slowly, a little at a time. My mother had taught me; she had bound feet. Such tiny feet. She could hardly walk, let alone go down the stairs on them. It was tragic. She died when I was seven, maybe eight. She was so young, only thirty-one. That was when I had to cook for everyone – all by myself. And my father, he was an official in the Manchu government. Cheung Zui Zhu was his name. He was a scholar; an excellent calligrapher with a fine brush stroke. You know, he was an official in the Chinese Court of Justice and earned a good income. He had one of those long pigtails at the back, like you sometimes see on television. It was considered treason if a man didn't have one. I can remember the day when all the men cut their tails off. Their queues. But my father was killed in Peking, when I was two years old.

'No mother and no father. His youngest brother wanted to sell my mother and us two girls, as slaves. So we ran away. We had nothing, just ourselves, but we ran. We were very poor. I have been dead three times, you know. Taken for dead. Thrown away with the rubbish. My mother threw me away. But a woman picked me up, and three times gave me life. I tried to find her again, when I was first married. I went back to her village to look for her, but she had died in the floods.'

22

Learning from early clinical encounters

I have been fortunate in my life to have met so many good role-models and mentors who have shown me the way through their counsel and example, and given me such wonderful opportunities to learn. It is a never-ending process of education and reflection and personal development. Many of my patients have been through indescribable emotional, psychological and physical traumas, yet they have a humility about them and the human strength to continue to laugh and love. They have been the source of my real development as a clinician. It is not something taught from text books, or in the classroom.

One tragic case I remember from my first job as a surgical houseman was a man in his forties who had an oesophageal cancer. He could not afford to wait for his operation on the NHS, and decided to have it done under a private health insurance. I clerked him in; I chatted with him, took his medical and social history and gave him the required examinations and blood tests before his operation. Despite the gravity of his condition, he was relaxed and cheerful and spoke with such a sense of purpose and inner calm. He showed positive optimism as he took control of his life and decisions. He had a young family, and wanted to get the operation over and done with so he could spend as much time as he could with them. I knew he was in good hands – the very best. My consultant was an experienced and dedicated man, with such a good surgical technique that there was hardly ever any blood in his operations. None of the gory scenes one normally associates with surgery. His work was neat, meticulous and sound. He was an expert in his field, a highly-regarded tutor, and had an unusually good bedside manner – for a surgeon. His training job was the most sought after amongst newly-qualified doctors and more senior trainees alike, and I was lucky enough to have landed it.

It was a private operating list, performed separately from his NHS work. I was asked to assist him in the four-hour long operation, as he opened the patient's abdomen and proceeded to pull the stomach up through the chest cavity after he had resected the cancerous part away. His surgical glove was covered in blood, right up to his elbow, but the operation seemed to go well and afterwards he went to speak to the man's wife.

That night, whilst in intensive care, the man started to bleed from his internal wounds. My consultant came back into the hospital, and again the same surgical team went to work to stop the bleeding. The tissue was so friable it had burst apart at the sutures and almost the whole procedure had to be done again. I was exhausted, but adrenaline kept me going. I was rooting for this man; he just had to make it.

The following afternoon, we had to take him back to theatre again – and this time, he died on the operating table. I was shocked by the whole experience. I felt for his wife. I felt for his family. He didn't deserve to die. The irony was he had paid for the operation outside the NHS; the operation that killed him. In the months that followed his surgical bill was settled. I was given a nominal amount for my assistance, but it felt so wrong to take it.

In those days there were moral dilemmas and clinical decisions we were expected to take as junior doctors, without involvement or advice from others. Thankfully it doesn't, or shouldn't, happen now but looking back at the diaries I have kept over the years I found this entry from 1984. I had been in clinical practice for 7 months.

He came to us through A&E
A query MI at seventy-three
'Look at those changes on his ECG,
He's had a massive coronary.'
The vice-like pain across his chest
Went down his left arm,
For ten minutes he lay in agony
Before he raised the alarm.
Breathless, sweating and with irregular beats

He called out his wife's name,
She reached out for his angina pills
But the pain was still the same.
He came to us through A&E
A query MI at seventy-three
'Look at those changes on his ECG,
He's had a massive coronary.'
In haste we slapped leads on his chest
And wired him to the screen,
Whilst another got venous access
And administered diamorphine.
His pupils constricted, his pain eased
His pulse a regular seventy-three.
His BP dropped to half his norm,
But he remained symptom free.
I spoke to his wife explaining his state,
And painted a picture of gloom,
She sat and listened, smiled and laughed
As though not in the same room.
He came to us through A&E
A query MI at seventy-three
'Look at those changes on his ECG,
He's had a massive coronary.'
Before him lies the critical time
These seventy-two hours ahead,
His rhythm is good but his heart's not strong,
We're monitoring him in bed.

Into cardiogenic shock he went that night
His blood pressure continued to fall.
We set up a dobutamine drip

It didn't pick up at all.
I spoke to his wife again the next day
She seemed not to hear.
Then suddenly I was called away;
I knew his end was near.
His breathing laboured, his eyes glazed
He was sweaty, really quite blue.
Should I resuscitate this man?
My judgement was torn in two.
I knew it would be to no avail,
Yet could I deny one last try?
'Doctor, should we put out the arrest call?'
I stopped... In peace I would let him die.
So instead of the panic and heroic deeds,
I let his life slip away.
His wife sat with him till the end.
I think... I would make that choice again.

Inadvertent deaths caused by overdoses was another aspect of my clinical work I found difficult. My first encounter was during my medical house job, the year after qualifying. Those years as a junior doctor are something of a hazy memory, as we all struggled to cope with the physical and emotional demands of our workload. Thirty-two hour shifts during the week with 80 hour shifts to cover a weekend, no protected rest periods and a pittance of a salary which was often misquoted by the media when they fought for nurses' and teachers' pay. Working outside the Monday to Friday 9-5 resulted in payments for units of medical time (UMTs). Rather than attracting a premium, it was paid at less than a third of the normal rate. The National Health Service in

England was a monopoly employer and this allowed hospitals to exploit the working conditions of junior doctors who needed to be in accredited training posts. However, such long hours, with no protected breaks and little opportunity to get proper food, were considered a rite of passage, allowing us to gain invaluable hands-on experience in clinical practice and autonomous decision making. Such intense conditions engendered a deep sense of camaraderie, and the knowledge of working together as medical or surgical teams with ward staff gave a real sense of collective responsibility and continuity in the delivery of clinical care. We wouldn't let our colleagues down, even if we felt ill ourselves.

Although in the early days of my training hospitals still had a doctors' dining area, complete with tablecloths, this soon disappeared. On call, we were lucky if we managed to get a sandwich or chocolate bar from a vending machine, as the canteen would invariably be closed. In my early years after qualifying, the doctors' mess and the doctors' bar allowed some relaxation, and alcohol could be bought and consumed when on duty. Both have disappeared. The on-call room, with its single bed, basin and telephone, was barely used. Sometimes it would be a sparsely-furnished room in the nurses' home, far from the hospital wards and casualty department; on one occasion it was at the other end of the hospital grounds beside the mortuary.

Certifying a death was one of the duties of the junior doctor. The call often came in the early hours of the morning. In the beginning I would respond as quickly as I could to the nurses' request to come onto the ward when a patient passed away where a decision had been made earlier not to call out the resuscitation team in the event of a cardiac arrest. We had to check for and certify the absence of vital signs of life and note time of death. But after being so shaken by agonal (death) breaths on one occasion in the first few months as a junior, I made a point of waiting for a while before doing so.

Perhaps the chronic tiredness we felt was inbuilt as a means of detaching from the traumas we faced in everyday clinical practice. Rarely did we have the time to think about our patients as people as we coped with life-threatening conditions and overwhelming experiences. Weekends when we were not on call were spent getting away from it all; a good friend often invited me round to her little attic flat on the edge of Hampstead Heath. Before singing with her choir at Evensong we would walk her dog on the heath, enjoying the restorative beauty of the natural world around us, and talk. I remember confiding in her about how difficult and conflicted the practice of medicine could be; how I tried my best to not let patients, especially dying patients, feel alone and to endeavour to keep them pain free, sometimes knowing the levels of painkillers prescribed might lead to an earlier death. Such young people were dying of cancer, while others who were unable to look after themselves somehow managed to survive the most horrendous operations.

'Well, maybe they've done what they came here to do,' she suggested. It was so simple, so full of faith, that I felt very comforted. She became my dearest and closest friend.

One weekend, when I had taken over from the previous on-call junior doctor, I was doing my obligatory round of all the medical wards, checking to see if things needed to be seen to in order to avoid any trivial calls later in the day. Tasks like re-siting drips that had tissued, writing up medication for patients to take home as they prepared for discharge; checking through the mountain of blood test results which flowed onto the ward each day; writing up fluid charts, checking in with the nursing station and just being visible on the wards so patients knew a doctor was about in case they needed one.

I stopped by the end of a hospital bed. An Asian family were sitting around, engaged in jovial conversation, whilst a young teenage girl was lying in bed, oblivious to the goings-on around her. I had made a particular point of visiting her, as her treating clinical team had said she was suspected of having taken a large overdose of paracetamol tablets after an argument at home. They had advised that it had been too late to give her an antidote by the time she presented to them. When they assessed her she clearly had no wish to die, but had taken the tablets out of frustration and desperation to escape her situation. She had no awareness of how dangerous her actions had been. I greeted the family with a nodding smile and went to review the observation charts at the end of her bed. The nurses on the ward had taken regular recordings of her temperature, blood pressure and pulse. The last entry read: Pulse = 0, BP = unobtainable. I looked at the pretty teenager lying in the bed in front of me, so still and quiet, and had no choice but to draw the curtains and put out a call for the crash team.

I felt so angry at being put in such a position, and guilty that had I checked on her earlier in the day perhaps her fate, or at least what the family witnessed and experienced, could have been avoided. There were so many 'whys' and 'what ifs'. Why hadn't the nurse called the crash team when she couldn't obtain a pulse and blood pressure? Why hadn't the girl or her family sought help sooner after she had taken the overdose? I remember her coroner's inquest, but I don't know what happened to the nurse involved.

On another occasion, as a young psychiatric trainee, I was summoned to attend a coroner's inquest. By then the consultant who was in charge of the case had emigrated to another country, and left his junior staff team to account for the decisions made. Six months after the suicide, the three of us met again for the first time outside the court room, having previously gone our separate ways when our six-month placement had finished. It was strange meeting; I was glad to have the company of colleagues who had been with me at the time of the ordeal. In the weeks leading up to the inquest, I had met with experts from the medical defence unions, gone through my statement with them and considered whether or not there were any grounds for malpractice on my part. Thankfully there were none, and I felt at least confidence that should the inquest proceedings take a nasty turn, legal representation would be made on my behalf. The hospital was not there to support us as they often are these days.

The deceased was a young mother. We had admitted her into the mother-and-baby unit at her local district general hospital. She had been suffering from post-natal depression and had suicidal thoughts but was otherwise relating fairly well to her new baby. There were no homicidal thoughts she admitted to, and she was able to look after the infant with some prompting and support from staff on the ward. Placid by nature, the baby quite happily slept in his cot beside his mother's bed whilst she joined in with ward activities, group therapy and individual work. She was an articulate woman, gentle, easy to talk to and eager to understand her illness. I visited her daily on the ward, reviewing her mental state, depression and suicidality. I liked her husband too: a tall, lanky man with a full beard. He looked like an artist, and I could imagine the creative and intelligent upbringing the little boy had in front of him. They were a devoted couple and supportive of one another. I felt a sense of relief that the baby did not need to be removed from his mother during her illness, and that mother and baby were able to bond with each other in spite of everything.

She made good progress on the ward over the weeks of her inpatient admission, and was looking forward to a brief period of leave over a weekend. Before I left on my annual leave, as we had to take two and a half weeks in each six-month placement, I had a ward round with my consultant. He was a young, up-and-coming academic psychiatrist who seemed more interested in getting his name in print than he was in clinical practice. He had a detached manner about him, and his harsh, croaky voice did not fit well into his short, slim frame. The stubble of a moustache only accentuated this awkwardness. The clinical team did not know him well, as he was appointed to fill in for a more senior consultant who had taken a year's sabbatical overseas.

It was during this ward round, when we had finished discussing all the patients admitted under his care, that he told me the ward was due to be refurbished and the psychiatric liaison ward would be dismantled. Patients were to be dispersed around the hospital, in general medical wards, or discharged home. There would be no mother and baby facility on site for the foreseeable future. I was dismayed for our patients. Whilst some could be transferred to the large psychiatric institution a few miles away, it was difficult to see how those with additional medical problems could leave the general hospital. I advocated for this mother to be given a large side room at the general hospital, as I knew she was not ready for discharge and admission into the psychiatric unit, which was unable to admit her baby with her, would be detrimental.

On returning from leave I found that a small number of patients had indeed been dispersed around the hospital, but she was not amongst them. She had been discharged after one successful visit home, and would be returning to receive outpatient treatment instead. A few days later we were informed that she had died, having hanged herself in the family kitchen.

My heart went out to her husband, sitting there in the coroner's court. He blamed everyone who had treated his wife, but most of all he blamed me – and I could not understand why. We had developed a good working relationship; he had been kept fully informed and consulted at every stage of his wife's treatment; he seemed genuinely to appreciate all the support she had been receiving. Perhaps it was because I had gone away. Accusations flew in the heat of the inquest and stung me, but I knew I had not done anything wrong. If only I could have spoken with him one to one, if only my consultant had been there to

THROUGH THE DRAGON'S GATE

answer the questions leading up to her discharge from hospital - if only, if only.

The Old Bailey, London's Central Criminal Court, first mentioned in its medieval form in 1585, strikes an intimidating chord in the heart of any non-forensic practitioner called upon to give expert witness. After all, hangings were a public spectacle in the street outside until 1868. It was early in my consultant career, and I had appeared in various courts before, at coroners' inquests, child care proceedings and magistrates' courts, but never at the most famous of them all.

Built on the site of London's old Newgate prison, one of its most famous trials was that of the Yorkshire Ripper. On the dome above the court stands a bronze statue of Lady Justice, holding a sword in her right hand and the scales of justice in her left. For some reason I expected a grand entrance, with a massive courtroom and lots of reporters outside its imposing edifice. There is the Great Hall decorated with many busts and statues of British monarchs, legal figures and others who were renowned for campaigning for improvement in prison conditions in the eighteenth and nineteenth centuries. Perhaps I was too close to it all, because my clearest memory was the narrowness of the entrance I had to go through. There was a queue of people waiting to get into the gallery to view the court proceedings, and there was another much faster-moving queue for those like myself who had business there. Dressed in my one smart suit, which only made an appearance at interviews and formal business occasions, I stood in the little lift as its doors closed, wondering what was in store for me that day.

231

The trial was to assess a defendant's fitness to plead. I had been called as an expert witness, to give evidence about a young man with learning disabilities who came from my practice area. He had been accused of abducting young children, and the courts wished to consider whether or not he was fit to plead and stand trial. If he were found fit to do so, he would go through the full criminal justice system. However, if he was deemed not fit to plead, the court would send him to a long-stay secure mental health facility for treatment. Although he was not known to the learning disability or psychiatric services, I had been approached to examine him and prepare a report as well as attend the court proceedings. When I had interviewed him in his prison cell a few weeks earlier I had been given access to all the statements relating to his offence. He had approached young boys on the pretence of being a policeman, and invited them back into the flat he shared with his mother and her partner. On the first occasion a few years earlier, the boy had stayed the whole day but was accompanied home when he began to feel afraid. The prisoner was given a probation period. However, on this occasion in question, he had kept the boy locked in a cupboard without food or drink, causing much distress to him and his relatives.

When I met him in the interview room at Brixton Prison, he was agitated and suspicious. He spoke about the persecutory voices he was hearing around him, super powers and visions of a tall woman talking to him. He claimed to have drunk a bottle of bleach and to have engaged in suicidal behaviours such as tying bed sheets together in an attempt to hang himself, and using an old razor blade on his wrists. However, none of these incidents were discovered, much less documented in his records. He denied the offence, and said he was in prison so that he could be kept out of harm's way. However, I noted his string of minor criminal offences, his long contact with probation services since his early teenage years and his superficial verbal ability.

It was difficult to assess whether his mental state was the result of imprisonment on remand, and the pressures of an impending court appearance, or whether he had been suffering from a psychotic illness before his arrest. He appeared unable to follow what I was saying and spent much of the time fearful of what the telephone or the panic button might do to him. The relationship between us in that sort of setting was obviously not a confidential one; perhaps that played a part in what he was prepared to disclose. Clearly he had intellectual impairment, had played truant from special schools and been physically and emotionally abused as a child. His alcoholic father had often locked him up; his mother appeared to have learning disabilities of her own. He was clearly vulnerable and had been easily led into a life of crime and exploited by others more able than himself.

He played down the offence when challenged, explaining he had only wanted a companion and adamantly denying any paedophilic tendencies. Gaunt and shifty, the bearded young man sitting in the dock looked a completely different man from the one I interviewed a few weeks earlier. He seemed more confident in his manner, alert to his environment and well presented. Taking the witness stand, with the gallery full of people, and the judge and barristers in their wigs, I had to remind myself to breathe and speak slowly. I knew I had to concentrate on the question asked, and answer only the question asked. I focused my mind on the judge sitting to my right.

The problem with a psychiatric assessment is that one tends to rely heavily on a patient's self-report of symptoms. Assessing someone with learning disabilities can pose considerable challenges, not only because of their limited language skills and hence their ability to understand what is being asked, but their limited ability to name an emotion or express themselves verbally. To add to this complexity, there may be perceptual and sequencing difficulties, so that they are unable to give information in a correct temporal sequence, missing out huge chunks of detail and giving unconnected narratives. There may be additional short-term memory problems, difficulties concentrating, sensory impairments and social skills deficits. To make the situation more difficult, people with learning disabilities respond to the perceived power and status imbalance that exists between themselves and the person they are talking to. In such situations, they are more likely to acquiesce and respond and say what they think is expected of them.

He was found fit to plead and eventually a separate trial went ahead and he was convicted. The judge was not inclined to give a non-custodial sentence, preferring instead to sentence him to an indefinite period of specialist care and rehabilitation at a secure hospital. At this stage, my services were called upon again, as I was the only consultant psychiatrist working in the field of learning disabilities, responsible for the London borough from which he came. However, inpatient facilities were, and still are, an extremely scarce resource, and I was unable to put together a secure package of care in the time frame stipulated by the Court.

There was uproar. The judge threatened to call for the Secretary of State for Health to take the stand to explain why such services were not available. The civil service cogwheels moved as I have never seen them move before. I had a phone call from the Chief Medical Officer – the highest doctor in the land, so to speak – enquiring about the situation. He was sympathetic to the difficulties, and volunteered to help secure an appropriate hospital placement. Before I knew it, a bed had been found for the convicted prisoner's transfer, to a specialist hospital outside of London. I knew it meant that someone else had either been denied the bed or transferred out prematurely. A few months later, the prisoner was moved yet again, into a high security hospital, as his dangerous and psychopathic tendencies became more apparent.

23

'When East is East and West is West'

'Grandmother, Neil has asked me to marry him,' I announced one evening during our medical student elective period in Hong Kong. The two months we spent in my homeland together had given Neil the opportunity to get to know my family and to be exposed to a different culture and a different way of life. The first time he visited he was not in the least impressed by our enthused excitement at eating in the night market on the waterfront. *Dai pai dongs* were everywhere, cooking and serving a concoction of rice, noodles, meats, fish and congee. We took our delicious bowls of steaming hot food to a makeshift table, chopsticks in hand, and proceeded to indulge in its wholesome flavours.

The air was cool with the breeze coming from the harbour, and the atmosphere was filled with the familiar noisy clatter of a popular evening haunt.

We had just arrived in the colony and it was Neil's first experience of eating out in Hong Kong. What with jetlag and the anxiety of meeting my family, his first memories of my homeland are of eating 'a scrappy meal on an overturned dustbin lid.' He soon acquired a taste for proper Cantonese cuisine, no longer relying on 'sweet and sour' from Chinese takeaways, the only dish he knew about at the time, although he disliked it immensely. He asked me what to say to compliment my grandmother's cooking, but Cantonese is a tonal language and he couldn't hear the difference. He ended up saying something to the effect that he liked to drink the dish water.

It was 1982. I had sung my first solo in years, at the Festival of Nine Lessons and Carols, high up in the rafters of the bell tower above the west door, to a congregation of almost 800 at the Cathedral; it had gone well, and I was barely aware of the delay between the sound of my voice in the tower and the organ at the other end of the nave. Neil and I then took the funicular tram to Victoria Peak for a brief evening stroll. Stars dotted the heavens, and the fairy lights of the Hong Kong skyline rolled out below us, seeping into the harbour and beyond and rising to the majestic dragon mountains of Kowloon, from which the peninsula got its name. Kowloon literally means 'nine dragons' in Cantonese, referring to the eight mountains which separated the colony from mainland China, the ninth dragon being the emperor himself.

There was a coolness and tranquillity in the December

air, and the extravagant Christmas neon lights which dominated the panoramic skyline of this Oriental pearl in the British crown created a magical kaleidoscope of anticipation that all would be well. There he proposed marriage.

'What is your view, grandmother? Is it good I should marry him?' I asked her.

My grandmother was getting ready for bed, and paused momentarily to consider my question. I had great respect for her wisdom and experience, and most of all I respected her position as the oldest member of the family clan.

'He is a good man,' grandmother said. 'I can see he is hardworking and careful with his money. He is also good-natured and caring. I think it is a good thing.' My grandmother had given us her blessing.

That evening we asked her to consult her almanac and choose an auspicious day to announce our engagement. Monocle in hand, my grandmother studied her red paperback book, which lay in an old biscuit tin at the foot of her bed. A few minutes later she had chosen the day. With our engagement date officially confirmed, and time difference allowing, Neil made the expensive overseas telephone call to his family in London to tell them our news.

A junior doctor's life is a nomadic existence. Each placement lasts for six months, and during this time one works intensely with a small group of staff, developing relationships that rarely survive. Friendships and professional alliances were quickly made and easily broken. It was during this time that my fiancé and I were planning our wedding. Whilst working busy medical and surgical jobs, we were making arrangements to fly out to Hong Kong for the occasion. I wanted my grandmother to be there.

Planning a wedding is a strange affair, as any married couple will testify. It starts off as a little gem of love between a couple, and gradually becomes a full-blown family affair, with tensions and conflicting wishes coming to the fore. We had little money, and even less time, to devote to such things. Whilst it is customary in Western cultures for the bride's family to host the wedding, it is the reverse in Chinese culture. My parents were clear that their duty to put me through further education had been fulfilled and they would not contribute financially. For the first time, my fiancé and I got a loan from the bank. I was appalled at the idea of starting our married life in debt, but it was a necessary move if we were to be married in Hong Kong. The air fares alone ate up almost half our financial allocation; the other half went on the Chinese banquet. We hosted ten tables, each seating twelve guests. I gave my grandmother six tables, so that she could invite her friends and our extended family to the celebration.

As white is the colour of mourning I chose instead to wear a Chinese *cheong sam*. Initially, I was going to have the dress tailored in Hong Kong, and my mother sent me copious samples of silk brocade embroidered with the emblems of luck and marriage: a phoenix, a peony and a chrysanthemum. But everything got too complicated, and I was worried there would be no time to have a fitting before the big day. In order to simplify matters, I ended up buying a red *cheong sam* from a shop in London's China Town. It cost me thirty-two pounds.

On the eve of our wedding, at the Cathedral Church

where I had sung every week, we were required to take an oath at the registry offices at the City Hall. We had only arrived in Hong Kong the day before, and were jetlagged, exhausted and disorientated. In the evening, after a simple dinner, when my fiancé had been safely returned to his hotel room, my grandmother combed my hair. I always wore my hair short, so there was not much to comb. But with each comb she muttered a blessing of good luck, and then she placed a flower in my hair – and gave me a sprig from our evergreen growing in a pot on the balcony, to symbolise fertility. My parents presented me with gifts; a pair of traditional gold bracelets and a white old-jade pendant. They presented us with an original Chinese painting scroll which now hangs in our dining room in London.

'Look!' I whispered aghast as we walked past a traditional Chinese herbalist and medicinal store. 'Who would eat cockroaches? Or are they water beetles?'

In the showcase in front of us were large jars filled with a range of roots, bark, shoots, shells, nuts, herbs, horns and antlers, animal organs and genitalia. Perhaps it was a reflection of the famines and floods in China's long history, but the Chinese seemed to find a use for almost anything – either as a medicine, food or aphrodisiac. It is said that the only thing one would not eat, is an animal that lived with its back to the sun, so we humans were safe, at least outside of the Japanese Occupation.

'You don't have to make a face like that!' my grandmother exclaimed as she saw my grimace. 'You've eaten them, only you just didn't know it at the time.'

'What! Me! I've eaten those things? Yuk! When?' I

uttered in alarm and disbelief, thinking back to the many soups and bitter brews my grandmother made from time to time, to harmonise our *chi*, or when I was ill. Sometimes the brews were so bitter I had to pinch my nose in order to swallow them. But there was often a sweet treat afterwards to help the medicine go down – a delicious individually-wrapped triplet of preserved plums, or a packet of the very best juicy raisins. I rarely went to the doctor when I was a child, apart from the pre-requisite inoculations. My grandmother treated all my ailments with traditional herbal remedies, Chinese medicines and 'a proper balanced diet'.

'When you didn't ask so many questions, that's when. They can be very good for you. Very good for a sore throat. Better than those pills and drugs you get from Western doctors.' And with that she stepped into the store with the agility and purpose of an experienced shopper.

The shop assistant greeted us with a smile as she worked her nimble fingers over a black abacus lying on the counter. As there were no other customers around, she was probably checking the shop's accounts. The clacking of the abacus tablets sounded a bit like a loud typewriter, with regular pauses to punctuate the rhythmic beat. Although my grandmother had never had any schooling, she had taught herself to read and write basic Chinese, and learnt to use an abacus with astonishing speed. All a necessary part of owning a business, I suspect, but how challenging and forward-thinking that must have been in her day.

The shop assistant put her abacus aside and began filling out a prescription written in large black Chinese script. She let us browse in an unhurried manner as she began opening a series of small drawers from one of the large cabinets behind her. A handful of red berries, a fistful of roots, petals, dried leaves and shredded bark. Everything was weighed on a tiny tin dish, attached to a long rod, marked with short lines and dots along its length. I watched as she balanced the pair of scales in her left hand whilst quickly moving the small weight along the rod with her right; exactly what my grandmother did every time she returned from market. She always checked the measure of everything she bought, on her own set of scales, and if the measure was not quite right she would return the item to the store at the next opportunity. I do not recall there ever being an argument when we went back the following day. Proprietors admitted to mistakes made by their employees and rectified them with profuse apologies, so as not to lose face. Perhaps it was just good business, or perhaps it was because my grandmother had lived amongst them for many years.

'One and twenty', the shop assistant called to the young man who had come in to pick up his prescription. 'This packet will be enough for two brews. Once in the morning, and once before retiring to bed.'

'Good. If I need more I will come back tomorrow,' the man said as he handed her two dollar coins. 'Do I boil this with two bowls of water?'

'Half a packet, three bowls of water, reduced down to one,' the assistant advised. My grandmother would have known that; she knew her herbs and medicines, and her advice was often sought by the younger generation, especially when they were away from home.

Reaching up above her head, the shop assistant pulled

down a small straw basket hanging above, and a bell rang gently in response. From across the shop, the owner, a middle-aged man in a traditional dark-coloured silk suit, peered over the rim of his spectacles. He was seated in a square kiosk jutting out from the centre of the back wall. Scribbling what must have been the invoice, the assistant clipped it onto a metal peg, and sent it overhead to her boss via a contraption of wire pulleys.

We made our way along Queen's Road, heading towards Central Market. It was an unusual route, as my grandmother often preferred the openness of the street market and the intimate atmosphere of Sheung Wan market. Central market was enclosed in an ugly building, where the pushing and shoving and general bustle of the maids and the occasional '*gweilo*', gave little opportunity to compare and haggle for the best buy. Immediately to our left were two dark alleyways, illuminated on either side by a row of bare light bulbs, their street stalls piled high with eggs; chicken eggs, duck eggs, quail eggs, salty eggs covered in thick black wet mud and the tantalising 'hundred-year-old' eggs enveloped in their husks of grain. I adored them.

At the mouth of the alleyway was a compact cigarette stall, literally the size of a crate. A woman who looked like she was well into her eighties managed it. Her kyphotic posture added to her diminutive stature as she sat on a low stool, dressed all in black. I passed her every day on my way back from school, and I would often pay the ten cents and choose a bag of preserved plums or crystalline ginger which hung from the wire strung across her cabinet of cigarette packets. My grandmother was of her generation, and they would exchange words whenever they saw one another. When time allowed, my grandmother would sit herself down beside the woman, and spend a few minutes with her exchanging reminiscences and listening to her various domestic crises or physical ailments.

The adjacent alleyway was renowned for its colourful feather dusters and fans, and it was featured on many tourist guides and routes. However, its colourful exterior hid a macabre and grotesque trade, for it was common knowledge amongst the locals who lived there that it was the place for the supply of fresh monkey brains. My grandmother never ate monkey brains, but she did occasionally cook pig brains to ensure a healthy memory, and at other times she would stew pig trotters with sweet ginger, whole eggs and fresh root ginger, a real delicacy and a treat both she and my mother enjoyed. We children were told we were too young to be in need of such things, as it was believed to restore *chi* and strength after the strains of childbirth.

'Grandfather must have been very pleased you gave him so many sons,' I said one day as my grandmother and I were preparing for the Maiden Festival.

'Of course he was. But he already had two living sons, by his first wife. One died. One was three and the other was about seven when I married your grandfather. But you know, he loved me even more when I had given him four or five more male children.'

'It was very important, having sons in those days, wasn't it, grandmother?' I asked.

She quickly confirmed my statement with a slight nod.

'Now, I think it doesn't really matter. These days, boy or girl, it's all the same, they're still your children. As long as they are good and respectful, that is all that matters. But in my day, women were discriminated against. Treated more like slaves. Kept at home, no schooling, and then under the rule of their mother-in-law. We had no rights, we always belonged to someone, and had nothing. But everything changes when you are lucky enough to produce a male heir. Somehow, after that, she is treated differently; she can take her place beside her husband, in every way, even in the Ancestral Hall.'

My grandmother paused, as though she were deep in thought, and sipped her bowl of *Bo Lai* tea. I could smell the analgesic Tokuhon medicinal plaster she had applied to her lower back that afternoon; a subtle blend of menthol, camphor and peppermint oils. I raised my eyes to the heavens, and wondered if the night sky would bring the two lovers together. Being the seventh day of the seventh lunar moon (Double Seven) we were preparing to celebrate Maiden Festival. The legend has been traced back to the Chou Dynasty (1122-222BC) and was my favourite story. It involves the stars, Vega (in the constellation Lyra) and Altair (in the constellation, Aquila.) It is about Ch'ien Niu, the cowherd (Altair) who fell in love with the Kitchen God's youngest daughter, Chih Nu (Vega), the spinning maid to the Queen of Heaven. She was the youngest of seven sisters. They were married on earth, and upon their return to heaven, they became so engrossed with one another that they abandoned their work. As a punishment, the Queen of Heaven drew a line across the heavens, forming a Celestial River separating the two lovers. The King, seeing their despair, granted them a meeting once a year. However, no ordinary bridge could be built. Fortunately, all the magpies in the sky were moved with compassion for the couple, and formed a Great Bird Bridge with their wings, otherwise known as the Milky Way. Should the sky be overcast, the bridge cannot be thrown, and the rain, in the shape of the lovers' tears, bears witness to the fact that they must endure another year of separation.

Not only was grandmother preparing a special meal for dinner, she had also purchased the customary biscuits and cakes which were needed for the evening's dedication to the Seven Sisters. Our trip to Central market that afternoon was in order to stop by a large department store for a new jar of Ponds' Cold Cream, which was also offered together with a selection of the freshest fruits and fragrant flowers.

Our meal was cooked slightly in advance, and offered on a tray to our family ancestors. They were invited to join the festivities with us; to enjoy the food and drink before the rest of the family sat down together to eat. My grandmother laid three pairs of chopsticks, three cups of tea, three cups of white rice wine, three bowls of rice and our spread of celebratory food. Earlier that morning, she had offered incense and kowtowed, banging her head against the hard stone floor three times, in front of our small shrine with her husband's ancestral tablet.

That evening, after dinner, we all sat up waiting until nearly midnight before setting up the square table. We didn't have enough room on our small balcony to stand the whole table under the open sky, so part of it remained in the living room. But it was a cool and peaceful night, and the heavens were littered with stars. Grandmother wiped the table clean with a kitchen rag and brought out a vase of fresh flowers; a sweet gingery scent rose above the fragrance of the other more colourful blooms. Everyone who lived in the flat joined in the preparations, apart from the men (my father and a cousin) who were not permitted to worship the Seven Sisters, but who could nevertheless join in the edible feast afterwards.

The girls (my sister, our cousin and I) set out a flask of tea, a green plant wrapped with a red ribbon and a brass incense burner. Across the table we laid out seven porcelain teacups as my grandmother placed the rest of the offerings on display. It was an exciting spread, the same excitement you feel on Christmas Day at the sight and smell of roast turkey with all the trimmings, or a Christmas pudding aflame in brandy.

Grandmother then lit twenty-one incense sticks and placed them in clusters of three in the burner whilst muttering prayers and blessings to the gods.

'Come now,' she called to us. 'Come and offer prayers to the Seven Sisters, and ask for the day when you will wed a good husband and be blessed with marital happiness.'

We took it in turns to kneel before the table, kowtowing three times and hitting our heads on the concrete balcony floor. With both hands placed carefully over each small cup we poured a little tea from each, onto the floor, as though the sisters had accepted our offering and drunk from the cup. My mother was a little unsure whether or not to join in as she was already married, but my grandmother's reply was the same every year: 'There's no harm in praying for continued marital happiness.'

The clock ticked away as we sat around the table, incense filling our eyes and nostrils and embers falling into the teacups that had been replenished after each offering. We children tried not to be too obvious as we glanced at the clock, wondering when my grandmother would give the go-ahead and allow us to start eating. I squeezed past the chairs and table and stepped out onto the balcony. The sky's darkness was speckled with a host of mysterious stars. I convinced myself I could see the Milky Way, and fantasised about a happy reunion for the legendary lovers.

Midnight struck. My grandmother got up from her squeaking rattan armchair, and offered a cup of tea, sprinkled with incense ash, to each maiden in the household, bestowing upon us good luck and blessings. When that had been done, she drank the rest of the cold dregs, saying it was no longer just ordinary tea, but tea touched by the spirits.

24

Chasing dreams

To the unaccustomed traveler, Hong Kong can seem a harsh place, with a cacophony of noises, smells and sights to assault the senses. Immediately the aircraft doors open, the distinct smell of seawater surrounding Kai Tak airport, tainted with an exotic fragrance from the famous harbour, would seep into every olfactory fibre. It is different today, as Kai Tak has given way to a new international airport built on a large artificial island, formed by levelling Chek Lap Kok and Lam Chau islands and reclaiming over nine square kilometres of the adjacent seabed. It opened in 1998 and is connected to the north side of Lantau Island. But the blanket of heat and humidity which hits a fraction of a second after the aircraft doors open still bears witness to the fact that one has arrived. Signboards in English and Chinese welcome the long-haul traveler to the luggage carousel. Countless faces of relatives and friends, anxious to catch the first glimpse of their loved ones as they come out through the arrivals gate, block every exit as one trundles suitcases and belongings on trolleys. Decibels rise. The distinctive intonations of the Cantonese dialect flood one's auditory canals, registering that you are in a foreign land. There is a sense of urgency. Though tired and jet-lagged, one feels the pace of life in Hong Kong, and the energy that keeps the colony so alive.

Within minutes of leaving the airport, you are among the crowds of pedestrians who line the streets, moving quickly and purposefully to their destinations. Traffic is everywhere, its volume staggering and its noise deafening. Their journeys are incredibly smooth despite the altercations between irate drivers as they cut into one another's space. Luxury automobiles and the occasional pink Rolls Royce may be seen amongst the red taxis and private Toyotas that fill the narrow streets.

One of the first things I noticed when I came to London was how slowly people moved in crowds. They would leave spaces everywhere. Hong Kong crowds move, and move quickly. Every available space is taken; there is no such thing as personal space. Well, not much anyway. To this day I can still lose my husband in a crowd as I weave my way through the maze, but he has learnt a skill or two to negotiate the situation. It took me a while to adapt to London; initially I was frustrated and impatient by the slow pace of life.

There is a Chinese proverb: 'what enters the eye shall never leave the heart'.

On my first visit to Great Britain I saw sheep for the first time, strange woolly animals grazing on pastures of verdant green on the gentle slopes of an English countryside. I have a romantic affinity for sheep, although I know very little about them and have no real desire to learn more either. My mother told me that when I was an infant my grandmother had given away one of my toys to a friend; a black sheep that had cost them the equivalent of almost a month's wages. Perhaps that is why I love calling out 'sheep!' whenever I spot them as we drive around the British Isles.

I also saw deer and squirrels and visited the iconic, regal, historic landmarks which to a foreign visitor make Britain what she is. The chimes of Big Ben on the River Thames embankment; the majesty of Westminster Abbey; the whispering gallery of St Paul's Cathedral; the glory of Hampton Court Palace; the poignancy of the White Cliffs of Dover. The majestic pomp and ceremony, the Changing of the Guard, the Edinburgh Military Tattoo, the Last Night of the Proms. I remember getting completely lost as I came out of Leicester Square tube station and stopped a tall, burly English policeman to asked for directions to Leicester Square, clutching a pristine A-Z 'bible' in my hand. It was my first British cinematic experience, in a massive, carpeted auditorium with soft, comfortable, allocated seats. But I could not understand why there was such a long programme before the film began. I had thought I was going to see the latest Pink Panther release at the Odeon, filmed partly in Hong Kong, but ended up with a 40-minute supporting film about skateboarding. It was so foreign to me that I thought I had absent-mindedly purchased the wrong ticket! Luckily, in those days there was only one screen, but it was massive. It was also possible to stay in the cinema all day, and watch the film again and again.

Travelling on a National Express coach bus, along open motorways and stopping at service stations, was a novelty I enjoyed immensely, and I went on numerous day excursions from London as well as long-distance journeys to other major UK cities. On the way back from one excursion, the coach stopped in an idyllic country village and the guide popped out to buy something from a farm, extolling the virtues of fresh produce. It is stuck in my mind because half the coach was standing directly under a rain cloud and the other in sunshine. I had never really appreciated clouds as discrete entities before, although of course they had to be!

Shopping the British way was completely new to me too. When a friend recommended I go to John Lewis for a raincoat, I thought she was talking about an acquaintance she knew, or a contact she had. It never occurred to me that it would be the name of a chain of stores. Likewise, I was very unfamiliar with the British tendency to use public houses (pubs) as landmarks when giving directions or suggesting a place to meet. I had no idea what 'The Standard' or 'The Queen's Head' could possibly be; they are even used as landmarks when giving driving directions, though they are often not well illustrated on a road map and completely useless if one does not know the area. Bargaining and bartering, so familiar and well-loved in Chinese transactions, were frowned upon, yet I did it all the time when I was shopping in London. I happily went into a department store, studied the merchandise on offer, chose the item and then asked what discount the salesperson could offer me. Often they obliged, after speaking with their manager.

My first visit to Great Britain in the summer of 1978 was a real eye-opener. I had a fantasy that all English people lived in mansions or dwellings like those depicted in Mary Poppins' Cherry Tree Lane, or in villages and country cottages with thatched roofs, gardens and picket fences; that the streets were cobbled but paved with gold; that iconic landmarks and greenery were everywhere, and that everyone spoke like the Queen or members of the Royal Family. I remember thinking how polite everyone was when I was travelling around the country, reserved but helpful, and so patiently queuing. And what avid readers they were too. Folk sitting or even standing on trains, their faces almost shoved into newspapers, magazines and paperback books so engrossed they did not make eye contact or conversation with fellow passengers. I was surprised they did not miss their stop!

It was something of a revelation to me that most did their own housework and cleaning. In Hong Kong, expatriates lived a privileged existence, in spacious well-maintained accommodation, with their children's school fees paid, and often with a generous package of extras such as air travel back home once a year and private health insurance. Many of my school friends had amahs and sometimes cooks and gardeners. Perhaps that was why when I was in the Brownies in primary school, the housekeeping badge was not the most popular, but the one I felt most comfortable with, even though it involved polishing shoes, polishing brass and making a bed.

The pervasive culture of living off credit was also very alien to me. Whilst I understood the need for mortgages, I couldn't get over how much pressure there was for ordinary people, even young adults, to take out bank loans and other credit in order to purchase something which was not necessary and which they couldn't afford. Within a few months of my introduction to this great country we were in the 'winter of discontent', not only because we had blizzards and deep snow, another first for me, but also a succession of damaging public sector strikes which the Labour government seemed unable to contain.

There are no records from my maternal grandmother's family, as they were destroyed by the Communists during the Great Leap Forward. My paternal side lays claim to Irish, Burmese, Portuguese, Dutch, Scottish and Indian ancestry. A distant relative traced it back to an Irish ancestor who was the mayor of Galway on the west coast of Ireland, and to the last man to be mauled to death by a lion in Mombasa. The animal is stuffed and is now an exhibit in the museum there.

Father was not yet out of his teens when I was born. He came to Hong Kong from Burma, following in the footsteps of his mentor and godfather, who had been posted as the British Council representative in the colony. The military coup in 1962 isolated his homeland from the outside world, and he was unable to go back to see his family. He never spoke about his childhood or family, but on occasions tried to recreate Burmese foods like the street dish *mohinga,* an aromatic rice vermicelli with a fish-based broth topped with boiled eggs and fritters, or *khow suey*, yellow rice noodles covered in a spice masala with a liberal sprinkle of freshly-squeezed lemon juice. In later years a great-aunt sent me her brother's account of the family's escape from Rangoon when the Japanese bombers arrived in 1941:

We were not only bombed but also machine-gunned, and whilst helping people off the streets around the Port, my brother saw a bullet pass through his short sleeve. A doctor's house in 51st Street received a direct hit and the houses nearby soon caught fire, so 52nd Street was evacuated to the nearest police station. My wife and children, age 5 and 2, had to walk more than 100 yards through the machine gun fire, and in the crowded confusion... were lost.

Each day I was trying to work my way the two miles home from my office, dodging the bombers, crossing the dead strewn all over the streets and not knowing whether I would find my family alive or dead.

It mentions my Irish great-grandfather and a number of his sons and families; my father was amongst the party which escaped from Rangoon into Calcutta, only to witness the Great Famine:

During our stay in Calcutta we were bombed by the Japanese many times and, here too, as there were no air raid shelters, thousands were killed. We also witnessed the Great Famine that struck India and this was something I shall never forget. Shortly afterwards there was the Great Killing, the fight between the Hindus and the Moslems. We were wisely advised not to interfere in any atrocities we might see and many times had to stand helpless as people were cut to pieces

before our eyes. This finally determined my wife to return to
Burma, our homeland, as soon as we could.

My father was a toddler then. I cannot begin to imagine
what it must have been like. He never spoke of it when I
was growing up, apart from the casual comment about
witnessing the cruelty of the Japanese during the war - he
saw them force someone to drink gallons of water, only to
then stamp on their stomach. He claimed not to remember
any of the Burmese language, rarely mentioned his family
and not a word about the mother who abandoned him.

My father went in search of his childhood over forty
years after he left Burma. Perhaps because of this, he was
also fond of searching for 'old Hong Kong'. He took delight
in sharing with me 'Love is a Many Splendored Thing,' a
1955 romance with William Holden as an American reporter
falling in love with the beautiful Eurasian doctor Han
Suyin, played by Jennifer Jones. Part of it was filmed in
Hong Kong, which was very unusual for its time. The
Foreign Correspondents' Club in Conduit Road was used as
the location for the hospital, but it was demolished in the
late 1960s. Hong Kong's many iconic and historic landmarks
have been lost over the years, as the colony gave way to
waves of land reclamation. My father searched for years,
yearning to see and own a copy of the 1955 film 'Soldier of
Fortune', with Clark Gable and Susan Hayward. It was
about the rescue of an American prisoner in China, but was
filled with many evocative street and waterfront scenes of
the island.

'You're such a big fan, one day you'll meet Julie Andrews', a friend said when I was about 14. I scoffed at her off-the-cuff, schoolgirl prediction. How could an insignificant, undeserving nobody like me, who had never set foot away from this small colony in the South China Sea ever possibly be in the same vicinity as an international superstar like Julie Andrews? She inhabited a different stratosphere; it was an unreachable, impossible fantasy I did not dare allow myself to dream.

Early in 1978, a senior executive from the HK Tourist Association confided in my father that he had made the necessary arrangements for a Hollywood team to film in Hong Kong. The whole thing was proving more challenging because of the Chinese New Year holidays. There was an additional complication as the director's wife had made a last-minute request to join her husband for a few days. She was due to arrive imminently. I was not yet 18. My little world, up till then so focused on revision for the A Level mock examinations, went into a spiral of dizzy disbelief. I don't think I revised much after that, and barely did the mock exams or myself justice, though I am not sure my teachers realised at the time.

The movie they were shooting was 'The Revenge of the Pink Panther.' The director was Blake Edwards; his wife was none other than Julie Andrews. This was quite literally my opportunity of a lifetime. I was determined to seize it with both hands, but part of me was also aware that in trying to realise my dream the whole experience might end in a crushing blow. What if Julie Andrews was nothing like the screen persona I had come to love and admire so much? The idiom 'be careful what you wish for' was certainly lurking in the background. But no matter, it was crunch time and I vowed if she did prove to be a disappointment, I would throw out my growing collection of fan memorabilia.

Immediately I wrote a brief 'welcome to Hong Kong' letter and sent it by post. She would be staying at the luxurious Peninsula Hotel in Tsim Sha Tsui on Kowloon side, close to the famous shopping areas and ocean liners. The Peninsula, known as The Pen, built in the 1920s as the ultimate hotel in the Far East, was known for its elegance, luxury, restaurants and fleet of Rolls Royce Silver Spurs. I had never set foot in a hotel before, and wouldn't have been the least bit surprised if the doormen in their crisp uniforms had turfed me out.

With my school examinations taking up much of the week, I only had the weekend in which to attempt to make contact. I thought it best to go in search of the film crew. Laden with heavy folders of fan memorabilia (newspaper cuttings mainly), I took myself off the Excelsior Hotel in Causeway Bay, where most of the cast and crew were staying. I sat nonchalantly in the lobby, trying to blend in with the hotel guests whilst eyeing the lift doors for a celebrity I might recognise. Eventually I summoned the courage to go up to reception to ask if the film crew were about. Luckily, just as I did so I spotted some of the cast – Robert Webber, Robert Loggia and Burt Kwouk – who must have felt sorry for me, because they gave me a copy of the filming schedule for the day. The main location was at an unfamiliar and remote stretch by the waterfront, miles away somewhere in Kowloon. I had no idea how to get there, and certainly couldn't afford the taxi fare. I telephoned my father at work, and he gave me directions by public transport.

It seemed to take forever to get there. I arrived to see some of the filming at a distance, and in conversation with some of the crew I learned that Julie had been and gone. I knew my parents would be expecting me to revise that evening and the next day, so reluctantly I went home. But when I returned, the flat was quiet and pretty empty. That meant it was not yet time to give up.

On a whim, I decided to telephone the hotel. I had no idea what I was going to say, but I was determined to try. Thumbing through the pages of our telephone directory, I dialled the number for the Peninsula hotel and was surprised to be put through to the suite. Blake Edwards answered. He told me Julie was out, but due back for tea. I thanked him and wished the film well. So close, and yet so far!

An hour later my parents had still not returned home. What did I have to lose? I phoned again, but the second time was not so easy. Who was I and why was I calling? 'Oh, it's okay... I spoke to Mr Edwards earlier, and he told me his wife would be back later for tea', I said. Such audacity! I wasn't sure how it went down. I was put on hold. Seconds later a woman answered. I was expecting their secretary, and asked to speak with Mrs Edwards.

'Speaking' came the reply. And then I heard her – I heard Julie Andrews, speaking to me on the phone! I blabbered something like, 'oh... Julie Andrews...' and went completely silent.

Julie asked if I was the young lady who had written to her at the hotel. She had responded, and her letter was on its way. She apologized for not being able to meet with me, that I must have just missed her on location and that she was flying home the next day. She was gracious, warm and friendly and we ended up chatting for almost twenty minutes. I was hooked for life.

25

New York – October 1995

Seventeen years later, I was in New York. Sweat drenched my face and hair as I ran the four blocks along 42nd Street, between our hotel and Grand Central Station, my heart thumping to keep pace with the unfamiliar exertion. I was so glad I had started going regularly to the gym a few months before. Taxis were nowhere to be found, as the streets of the city were snarled up with luxury executive cars taking diplomats and other VIPs to the United Nations 50th anniversary celebration. I hardly noticed the clouds of white steam billowing from the pavements, or the people in the streets rushing home at the end of their working day.

I had just received a telephone call from my husband which had made my mind focus on one thing; to get to the station as soon as I could, to be with our son. We had left him after a simple lunch in the care of a relative, who lived outside Manhattan, whilst we took in one of the many Broadway shows on offer. But this show was special. We had flown from London so that I could witness Julie Andrews' return to the Broadway stage. She was due to open in a new musical called 'Victor Victoria' and we were fortunate enough to have obtained prime seats for a preview performance within days of the premiere.

But fate conspired against us. Although we had boarded the train in plenty of time to get back to Manhattan, we were delayed by almost two hours because the Amtrak engine broke down. Prominent posters of 'Victor Victoria' seemed to greet my every glance, as I looked through the large glass panes and cursed the US railway system. The carefully-chosen and purchased clothes we had packed for this most special event hung flaccidly in our hotel room, the excitement and uniqueness which was to have imbued them with life so near and yet so far. We had chosen a hotel right opposite the theatre, so as to be in the centre of everything.

Unable to hail a taxi when we eventually got out of Grand Central Station, we ran all the way to the theatre, still in our denim jeans and sweatshirts, with no time to change. It had already started. It was bitterly disappointing to be standing at the back of the auditorium knowing there were two seats for us, centre and three rows from the front. The show was a sell-out, the hottest tickets on Broadway.

My only consolation came a few minutes later when Blake Edwards, the show's director, entered the theatre and stood beside me for a good while before accepting a makeshift seat from one of the production team. We did manage to get to our seats after the intermission, but many of the dazzling song and dance numbers which Julie performed in the first half were witnessed from behind a pillar.

Two hours later we returned to our hotel room, my head spinning with the exuberance of a large, traditional musical stage show, my soul restored. My husband went to meet our son's train that evening. We had spoken to our relatives and confirmed the arrangements and were told that our son had had a fall whilst with them, and had hurt his elbow. He had slept for a while that afternoon, but was on his way back to us. So the telephone call that came was totally unexpected.

'You'd better get over here, quick,' my husband said to me with a graveness in his voice I had heard only a few times before.

'What's wrong?' I asked, a dawning of dread creeping up within me.

'He's very pale. He's broken his elbow and he's in shock. They're sending an ambulance over for him now.'

I remember every detail of that horrendous evening, from the moment I saw our boy's waxen and terrified little face to the nightmarish experiences of Bellevue Hospital's casualty department. Both my husband and I had worked in casualty departments before, but we had never witnessed patients with gunshot wounds chained to trolleys as they were being treated. Checking our son in for treatment was tantamount to filling in an application for a major financial loan. Insurance details were foremost in the receptionist's mind, but luckily I had had enough sense to gather our travel insurance policy together before making the dash to the station. However, the treatment our son received in the department was first class, and cannot be faulted.

'So, young man, which grade are you in?' the doctor asked in her American twang.

Grade? How does the first year after reception equate to the American education system?

'Grade One,' piped up the six-year-old on the casualty trolley.

The doctor seemed to accept this without question, and proceeded to examine his swollen elbow.

'So, are you planning to go trick or treat?' she continued.

'No' came the answer again. I didn't know whether our son knew what 'trick or treat' was, as we never celebrated Halloween in London. This example, so simple and so American, made a deep impression upon me. How often do we make assumptions about another person's culture, especially when they appear to be speaking the same language as ourselves?

'Oh, this is so comfortable,' our boy said, with a relaxed smile on his face as the morphine injection began to relieve his pain. The examination couch was narrow and hard; it was a humorous and touching moment amidst all the pain and anxiety.

Transferring to the paediatric ward later that night was not so comfortable. I stayed with him for the next four days, catnapping in an armchair beside his bed. His elbow was obviously disfigured and very swollen. The ward staff kept him 'nil by mouth' with the expectation that he would be operated upon in the morning; his fractures needed to be reduced and pinned. But the days came and went, and all we got were short, uninformative comments from an army of doctors, flapping about in their white coats as they descended upon the ward and stopped by each patient's bed for a brief time. They checked our son's X-rays, mumbled to themselves and told us they could not operate until the swelling had subsided. It did not make the slightest difference to them that we were medical practitioners in the United Kingdom, and our inside knowledge confirmed our suspicions that all was not as it seemed.

We asked to bleep the orthopaedic surgeon on call, and eventually after much waiting about, got some junior doctor who spouted out some lame excuse; when our son was sobbing in pain the nursing staff seemed oblivious to our request for analgesia, saying they would be doing their medication round soon –and they started right down the other end of the ward. Neither of us realised how frightening, and handicapping, it can be to be a patient in a medical system one did not understand. No one made it easy; there was little information shared and yet we supposedly spoke the same language – medically and non-medically speaking.

Spending one's whole day and night in a hospital ward can be very disorientating. My husband went back to the hotel to sleep, but I only left our son's side for an hour or two, walking back to the hotel to get showered and a change of clothes. Early one evening, the paediatric ward put on a videotape of Disney's 'Lion King'. It was the first and only time I had seen the show and I thought it a strange choice for a hospital setting. I sat through it with our son, being acutely aware that the concept of 'the circle of life', was constantly being rammed down my throat. Dissonance imploded within me.

A rather large Hispanic girl was sitting in the common room with us all. She was mobile, independent and looked as though she was in her teens. Her exuberant and disinhibited presence felt very inappropriate and uncomfortable, as she sang loudly to all the songs, seemingly oblivious to the younger, more vulnerable patients around her.

Thank God for friends. A friend from my school days in Hong Kong was living in New Jersey at the time and we were due to meet. I telephoned her to apologise for having to cancel the evening we had planned together. She was horrified to learn we were at Bellevue, and said she knew a fairly senior orthopaedic surgeon who, she was sure, would come to see our son. Through him we came to understand that there were no senior doctors around in the hospital. What we were waiting for was for the weekly visiting consultant, who would give the go-ahead for the operation. Through my friend's connections, we were able to arrange an immediate transfer for our son to the nearby University Hospital, where he received prompt treatment by experienced staff. The next day we took him back to the hotel, five days after his fall, the operation done, pins sticking out of his elbow and his arm in such a heavy cast that he was lopsided whenever he stood up.

I can empathise with my patients now, having smelt the fear of hospitals and the vulnerability of being at the receiving end. Any operation is risky, and any general anaesthetic is not to be taken lightly. Our child's life was at risk – and I was acutely aware of it when I held his little hand, and told him the magical story of the rainbow fish as he fell asleep under his oxygen mask. And then I left him, in the hands of complete strangers. All I could do then was wait.

Waiting is very hard. Time, fear and uncertainty can play awful tricks. That experience taught me a great deal, and I try now in my clinical practice to prepare my patients and their carers for any investigation or hospital procedure. I give as much thought to how the information and experience is perceived by them, and shared with them, as to the clinical interview itself. My work with handicap and disability brings me in daily contact with loss and threatened loss, bereavement and the human capacity to cope, and to find joy in the smaller things in life many of us take for granted.

A few hours after we arrived back at the hotel room as a family once more, I went out for an early evening walk to clear my head. Despite the price we paid, our accommodation was a poky back room barely big enough for the two double beds. The single window overlooked a brick wall. I needed to get out for a breath of fresh air. I needed to feel alive; my senses had been numbed and disorientated by the hospital experience.

Still in my denim jeans and obligatory sweatshirt, I walked out into Times Square. The metropolis buzzed around me. I felt so much at home. To me, New York had the vitality and pace of Hong Kong, but with the spaciousness of London. Instinctively, I crossed over to the Marriot Marquis Hotel, looming high above the city's throbbing heart of Broadway. Wandering towards the Marquis theatre, I saw the red carpets and the police, the minders and the stretch-limousines. I saw the television cameras and the broadcasting vans parked at the corner near the stage door. There were throngs of people milling around the entrance to the theatre, and the shining lights around the posters of 'Victor Victoria' sparkled in the early evening dusk. The lobby was filled with people – people who were people in New York and elsewhere, no doubt.

Casually, I continued to wander round the gallery and into the numerous rooms filled with reporters, technicians and television screens. For the few minutes I sneaked in, I watched Julie Andrews – bedazzling and beguiling – on her triumphant return to Broadway, 35 years after her reign in 'The Boyfriend', 'My Fair Lady' and 'Camelot'. Now, despite everything, at least I could say I was there on opening night.

26

East meets West

We had two framed photographs on display in our flat in Sheung Wan District. One was a large black and white portrait of my grandfather. It is the only existing picture we have of him and for as long as I can remember, it took pride of place in our home. The other was a postcard-sized black and white photo of the man I was named after, meeting the Queen of the British Empire. I don't know much about my great-godfather, but he was known as JJ. I am told that for a short while we lived with him in his spacious flat near Stanley. He must have left Hong Kong soon after, and died back in Britain when I was six years old. I remember my father being very upset, and the agony he went through deciding what to do with the organ that was bequeathed to him in his godfather's will. In the end he sold it, but he had the trunk of sheet music and books shipped over.

JJ was the British Council representative in Rangoon, Burma, and the choirmaster there. His posting to Hong Kong in the late 1950s, and my father following in his footsteps, resulted in my parents meeting. My mother was working in the British Council as a secretary, with a speedy shorthand she constantly practised at home and efficient office administration skills. When I visited Britain in the summer of 1978 I had the opportunity of being the house guest for a few days of JJ's sister, a lady we called Aunty Dock. Already 80, she was a very active and social lady, who wore bright colours and took pride in her appearance. I was fascinated by her makeup and hair, and her circle of friends. She drove me around the local area sightseeing and took me to a number of social events during my stay. She didn't tell me much about her brother, but did mention her son, who was or had been Dean of the medical school in Manchester, I can't quite remember now.

However, it was obvious she was particularly proud of the achievements of her young grandson, Richard Branson, from her daughter Eve. Richard apparently set up his first business venture at the age of 16, and is best known now as an entrepreneur and the founder of the Virgin Group. Aunty Dock had a small collection of newspaper cuttings and memorabilia which she shared with me. It was in the early days of Virgin records, the chain of stores he opened in the early 1970s, with the release of 'Tubular Bells' on the Virgin Record label. When subsequently I stayed with distant relatives in Croydon, I made a point of visiting the local Virgin record store. Aunty Dock also came to our wedding reception in London, and quite by chance, it was at the same establishment where she and her husband had celebrated their marriage.

JJ was also the organist and choirmaster at St John's Cathedral, one of the oldest buildings in Hong Kong. In fact, it is probably one of the few that have survived Hong Kong's entire colonial history intact. It was built to cater primarily for the needs of a non-Chinese, mainly British community and a large military garrison. When I returned decades later, after the handover of the colony back to China, I was somewhat impressed and reassured to find it offered weekly services in Mandarin. The cathedral marked the half way point for me when I walked home from school each day. Its colourful stained glass east window is etched in my mind; a memorial to those who endured and gave their lives during the Japanese Occupation of Hong Kong, the original having been destroyed during the war. It is the first sight one sees on entering the west door, the main entrance from where the choir began the weekly processional hymn.

Each Sunday morning, my sister and I would walk all the way from home, allowing enough time to cool down and put on our choir robes before the Sung Eucharist at nine o'clock. The walk involved a steep climb up Battery Path, lined with lush trees and ferns. Often we stopped by a hawker, squatting with his basket of bamboo leaves. He created the most amazing grasshoppers from the thin blades of green. We couldn't afford to buy one, but I do remember owning one as a treat, and the disappointment I felt when it eventually dried and lost its form and appeal.

As the calm oasis of greenery and tower of the Cathedral came into sight, so would a group of female beggars dressed in black 'sam fu', some with empty tins and others with outstretched palms. Beggars were a common sight, especially on the pavements in Central District, near shops and the Star Ferry. At times it felt like a contest for who could display the most disabling condition worthy of monetary donation; there were men with open wounds and amputations lying on sheets of newspaper, and others hobbling or crawling along the streets hitting their begging tins on the ground. The able-bodied ones pursued passers-by, pestering them to give. I remember the exposé in the news about how much some of them earned and how after a day's begging they would return to their air-conditioned flats and television sets. We were taught never to give money to them. But one birthday, I was given a wallet, which in my eyes could have passed for crocodile-skin had it not been for its shiny, red plastic. However, because it is a bad omen to give an empty wallet or purse as a gift, my parents had put in a range of coinage as well as a low denomination banknote. I felt so plush, and so privileged. I walked to church that Sunday morning with my wallet in my Burmese hand-woven shan bag, bursting to share my joy and good fortune with the world. I spotted an elderly woman begging, and promptly fished out my wallet to give her a coin. Before I knew it, a group of them had converged on me and soon all my coins had gone, even the one I had set aside for the church collection. They muttered and flapped their hands dismissively when I said I had no more to give.

My secondary school was housed in the former British Military Hospital, built in 1907 upon a hill in the mid-levels.

It was an attractive red brick Edwardian building with arched verandas and balconies overlooking the harbour. It opened as a school in 1967, to provide children of expatriates living in Hong Kong with the same educational curriculum as the British system. Most graduates went on to university education back in the United Kingdom. As a second language we learnt French; Mandarin or Cantonese was not an option at the time. In the early years, we studied the history and geography of Britain. We had long academic terms and an even longer summer break, allowing our teachers a good two months to travel back home and escape the height of the heat, humidity and typhoon season. Many of my friends socialised after school, or played cricket, hockey and rugby. In the evenings and at weekends they frequented country clubs and establishments where we never got a look in. I barely knew they existed until when one year, whilst at primary school, I got an invitation to a pool party at the Ladies' Recreational Club, to celebrate a classmate's birthday.

When I left the strictness of my last primary school year, where the onus was on discipline and academic achievement with weekly tests and desks re-arranged to reflect one's results, I met a teacher who would in the years to follow, become a lifelong mentor and personal friend. She was an American teacher of English language and English literature. Instead of concentrating on grammar and academic abilities, she was more interested in what each of us had to say. In that first year of secondary school, how we said it was less important. It was a complete shock to the system, and it left me very confused. She rarely used set pieces from text books and was creative and unconventional in manner and approach. Homework would consist of analysing the lyrics to popular songs played on the radio. This posed a problem for me, because apart from typhoon bulletins we never listened to the radio at home. I resorted to asking my choir friends, who were all much older than me, for words to their favourite songs, such as Paul Simon's 'I am a rock' and James Taylor's 'You've got a friend'. She allowed us to sit where we liked in the classroom, even on our desks and on top of lockers. She asked our opinion and encouraged debate, proposing the most absurd statements and allowing my classmates to express themselves in language I found totally inappropriate and unacceptable for eleven and twelve-year-olds. I hardly said a thing. I hardly asked a question. I was trying to understand this whole new world, and where I fitted in, whilst not putting this teacher in the position where she would lose face if I asked something she could not answer adequately.

For the first time, I also had male teachers. My mathematics teacher in that first year was quick to throw the blackboard duster at us if we were not paying attention; he also took to flicking pieces of chalk at students, and never missed. I was terrified about what would happen when I couldn't complete my homework, having chosen probably the most complex 3D model to construct out of paper. My parents wrote him a note to explain, and I was literally trembling when I gave it to him. It turned out he was very impressed by my ambition and perseverance, and I never had any problems with him after that.

I liked a challenge. I was never one to take the easy path. I liked taking things apart to see how they worked, and then putting them back together again. My construction kit, in its red box complete with a little black hammer, gave me hours of play as a young child. When we had a choice at school, between domestic science and metalwork, I chose the latter and enjoyed soldering and hammering with the boys to create my copper ashtray which I later polished and presented to my father. I did enjoy the cookery classes though, and taking back to the family baked treats and puddings we never made at home.

In secondary school we were all encouraged to learn a new musical instrument, so I decided on the trombone. I was able to have one on loan from the music department, but it was so heavy to carry to and from school each week that I gave up after one term.

All the girls had to play netball and hockey. I wasn't very good at either but preferred hockey, mainly because I liked the feel of my hockey stick, especially its weight. I thought it would come in handy as a useful weapon if ever I was to be attacked or had to make a quick getaway. That wasn't very realistic as I didn't have it with me all the time, but it was a reassuring thought.

In spite of the heat and humidity I enjoyed the walk home from school, particularly as the route between school and the cathedral was away from the frantic bustle of the city, and afforded some peace and shade under the banyan trees. Their wood has no practical use, but the tree spirit lives in Chinese culture and often, amidst their magnificent roots, would be a small shrine. I have vivid memories of a Chinese film about an elderly woman who at the end of the story is absorbed into the tree trunk, thus confirming her magical powers to be those of the tree spirit.

My journey took me along Bowen Road, and at times I

would make a two-mile detour, backtracking along a narrow mountain trail, to Amah's Rock, (now known as Lover's Rock), a granite standing stone 9 meters tall and overlooking a cliff. It is believed to be the home of the God of Love, and is frequented by young couples. Around Maiden Festival, women made offerings of roast chicken, suckling pig, oranges and joss sticks, praying for eligible husbands, faithful partners or fertility. I often felt a little disappointed if I made the extra effort to climb up close to the boulder, because to me it looked much more impressive from the ground. On a Friday, my arrival at the Cathedral would allow me an hour to start my weekend homework in the coolness of the cathedral library or reading room, before choir practice began. It was preceded by a simple spread of dainty sandwiches and pots of English tea, taken with milk. On other days, I continued down Battery Path and into Central District, filled with noise and traffic and people. However, it didn't have the frenetic, kaleidoscopic feel it does today. Traffic police, uniformed, gloved and standing in their isolated pagoda-like pedestals in the middle of the road, directed drivers and pedestrians alike.

27

Medical School finals - 1983

A pack of snarling, hungry dogs had cornered me again. I don't know where they came from. five of them, lean, mean and very nasty. One minute I was walking from the council estate on Uamvar Street where we lived in East London, and the next minute I heard the pounding of paws around me; teeth bared, saliva drooling. I hated this place. The whole area stank. The horrible claustrophobic lift smelt of stale urine and alcohol, vulgar, racist graffiti covered the walls, and dark corners allowed unsavoury characters to loiter, dealing and shooting drugs and no doubt mugging anyone who looked a easy target.

Three years before, my flatmate and I had been offered a 'hard-to-let' two-bedroomed council flat, because it was on the seventh floor, and with the lift constantly breaking down, it was not a property they could offer to families with young children. Students like us had put our names on the local authority housing waiting list, as we would be resident in the inner London borough for at least five years. I was in Hong Kong when my flatmate wrote to tell me the exciting news that we had been offered a flat only a year after putting our names down together. It was sooner than we had anticipated. 'It's not in a particularly nice area,' she had said, 'but the flat is big, and my parents will help us do it up.'

I arrived back in London a little early, so I could give notice to my landlady and help decorate. Despite the jetlag I was anxious to see the property, so soon after depositing my luggage at my bedsit, I took the underground train and walked the short distance from the station. What met my eyes was a sight I will never forget. My heart sank, and I felt sick to the stomach. Had my parents struggled so hard to get us all a better life and send me for further education in Britain, only for me to end up in the slums of the East End of London?

Our flat was big for two people, and we made a real effort to paint it with light, bright colours. Second-hand furniture filled our living room, and gradually we were able to purchase the basics needed for the bedrooms too. Our own kitchen meant I would no longer live on boil-in-a-bag meals cooked in a saucepan, and indeed my flatmate enjoyed recreating her family recipes using suet and oxtail. Her father secured a heavy metal plate to our front door, in an attempt to give extra protection. It did feel more secure, but in reality, when we were victims of a break-in, it probably allowed the burglars easier entry as it came off its hinges due to its weight. From my bedroom window I could see the Grand Union Canal. In the cover of darkness, I often saw people climb over the brick wall to the water's edge and passing plastic bags over the top before disappearing from view.

We lived there for three years, doing the weekly Sunday jaunt to the local Crisp Street Market Square about a mile away. It was a market made of concrete, with shops and cheap rubbish for sale. The launderette we frequented fitted well with the poverty and deprivation of the area. Working-class East Enders sat side by side, picking their teeth, rolling tobacco and thumbing through tacky Sunday tabloids, filled with photos of big-bosomed girls, scantily clad. We sat amongst them waiting for the tumble dryer to complete its cycle and trying not to be too conspicuous as we studied from the medical textbooks resting innocently upon our laps. Then we would fold all the clothes and bedding, stuff them into large blue plastic carrier bags and trundle back to the flat, crossing the canal by a long bridge which seemed to link all the local estate blocks. Every so often, I would catch the sun setting across the concrete horizon. Its beauty made one forget the momentary reality in which we lived.

That early summer morning in 1983 was an important one. I was all psyched up for one of the many examinations that made up our Medical Finals. I was cool and collected on the outside, but those awful dogs must have sniffed the rush of adrenaline that churned within.

'Go away!' I said firmly, visualising my own bio-feedback mechanisms at work. I tried to slow my heart rate, and breathed as calmly as I could. But the animals had circled me, blocking every turn.

'Leave me alone! Just go away!' I commanded loudly, for I did not want to shout and lose control. Sweat crowned my forehead. I told myself it was just nerves because of the exams, and I sang 'I have confidence' in my mind, imagining the feisty nature with which Julie Andrews had sung the song in the 'The Sound of Music'. I have always used that song, to get me through many trying moments. And it worked. The dogs lost interest, and scampered away to bully some other poor soul who had happened to venture in their territory.

Our examinations included multiple choice questions, short answer papers, long papers, short clinical cases, long clinical cases and a *viva voce* for each of the subjects; drugs and therapeutics, medicine, surgery and obstetrics and gynaecology. There were no continual assessments as there are now. That morning my exam patient was a woman who was well into her pregnancy. She had been one of the patients who, having been admitted onto the antenatal ward because of an ante-partum haemorrhage, agreed to be a patient for the examination. I took her history and examined her – and then waited for the two examiners to arrive. One was a professor of obstetrics from a well-known London teaching hospital and the other was a local consultant whose intolerance of medical students' ignorance and stupidity was legendary. It was usual for the student to have to demonstrate some physical hands-on examination technique, but I prayed they would not ask me to perform a pelvic examination on the woman, or to demonstrate the insertion of a vaginal speculum. Should they require me to do so, I hoped the woman would refuse consent. After all, these skills had been learnt, practised and assessed by our tutors during our placements, and had been signed off as satisfactorily completed.

Thankfully, these days, medical students are observed performing such intimate procedures on a life-size mannequin. I understand though that the situation in the United States of America is quite different. There, professional actors are paid to be patients for this purpose. Not only do they permit such procedures to be performed on them, they are instrumental in grading the student on his/her skills, technique and bedside manner.

28

London - 1987

'Doctor, can you come and see Michelle?' asked the ward manager when I answered my bleep during an outpatient clinic at the institution for people with learning disabilities. It was known as 'mental handicap' in those days.

'Is it urgent?' I asked, thinking of the list of people I still had to see that morning. 'What's the problem?'

'She's very irritable. She's been pulling her hair out and not letting us get near.'

'I'll be there as soon as I can.'

I finished my outpatient clinic, collected blood samples from relatives to test for Fragile X syndrome, checked through test results that had come from the labs so they could be actioned or filed away as necessary, and then made my way to the ward.

The institution was a monument to the nineteenth century care of the 'mentally defective'. Its Grade II listed building was sparsely furnished, creaking and looked in need of urgent renovations. It had been a 'cradle to grave' hospital in its heyday, catering for the physical, mental, spiritual and educational needs of all its patients. Many had been institutionalised for being what was termed 'morally defective'; teenagers who had borne children out of wedlock, or girls who had been a little too difficult to control. Others had been incarcerated almost from birth, professionals believing and coercing parents into thinking that it was the 'right thing to do under the circumstances' for those who were deemed 'ineducable'. For many patients, this hospital would be the only home they would ever know. But unlike other large institutions of its kind, it was not set in acres of fields out of sight and out of mind. This hospital was located in the centre of the local community, with the dangerous, fearful and intolerant 'normal' world just beyond its wrought iron gates.

Ringing the doorbell to one of the ground floor 'houses', I waited for the house-manager to let me in. A rotund female nurse from Mauritius opened the door and invited me to their little office upstairs.

'Come, Michelle,' she called in a rather loud and heavily-accented voice. 'Doctor's here to see you.'

I picked up the thick set of notes from the desk. It was crammed with reports and programme sheets from her 'further education centre' activities, bowel and weight charts. Yet there was very little in her notes to tell me about her personal history; about why she had been admitted in the first place, about her physical, emotional and psychological needs, about her abilities and level of functioning.

A woman of about 22 years old was standing uncomfortably beside the open door. She rocked from side to side, groaning and drooling, looking from the house-manager to me, unable to verbalise her distress. I introduced myself and held out my hand towards her.

'What's wrong, Michelle?' I said quietly, noticing patches of baldness on her head and the thinning blond hair. Gingivitis was clearly evident as she opened her mouth again and groaned. She grabbed my arm and placed my hand on her protruding abdomen, rubbing it up and down over her thin summer cotton dress.

'Is your tummy hurting?' I asked again. 'Come, let me have a look.'

The dormitory was empty. All the other residents were engaged in their various day activities in the hospital grounds. Michelle threw herself onto the first bed we came to, the hem of her dress riding up her thighs. She parted her legs.

'She won't let us put a pad on,' explained the house-manager. 'She's doubly incontinent, but she won't even let us bathe her without a struggle. She only gets in the bath when she goes home.'

'How often is that?' I asked, noticing the redness of her crotch.

'Oh, Michelle goes home every weekend. Her mother looks after her, but she doesn't stay the night. Grandfather is there to help out.'

I saw the distended abdomen lying compliantly on the bed in front of me. I remembered the rule of thumb we had been taught in medical school about the causes of a distended abdomen, and ran through the 'Fs' in my mind; fat, flatulence, faeces, foetus... My hand palpated gently. A shocking realisation dawned as I calculated she must be almost twenty-eight weeks pregnant. No one had mentioned pregnancy. It was clear this had been missed. I felt the baby kicking, and as I did so Michelle grabbed a bunch of her hair and looked confused and worried.

The weeks and months that followed were challenging for us all. Michelle was too advanced for anyone to seriously consider a termination of pregnancy as an option, even if we were able to find an obstetrician willing to undertake such a late procedure. We had to try to communicate with her in some way, to help her understand what she and her body were going through, and what would happen when the baby was born. Would she be able to tolerate a normal vaginal delivery, or should we plan for an elective surgical intervention? It was clear Michelle was too disabled to care for herself, let alone her baby, and there were issues of immediate fostering and adoption, and how we would have to prepare Michelle to say goodbye. Then there were the nightmarish issues of consent. Could Michelle consent to anything that complicated? Did Michelle have capacity to consent to sexual relationships? Who was the father of this baby? Had Michelle been the victim of a rape, or was this the product of long-term sexual abuse?

I discussed her care and management with my consultant and our team of specialist nurses, social workers and clinical psychologists. Who would be engaging in intimate relationships with a severely mentally-handicapped woman who was doubly incontinent? She was always escorted on the hospital grounds, and lived in a female only dormitory. She had no particular friends, and did not socialise with the male residents. It was not unusual for the more able female patients to have sexual encounters with male patients on the hospital grounds, sometimes in exchange for a cigarette.

Soon after the diagnosis, her pregnancy was dated by ultrasound scanning, and the police were called to investigate. Interviews with her mother led us to confirm that she was mildly learning disabled herself, and all personal care was carried out by the grandfather who lived in the same house. We had to act, even without proof, and stopped all her weekend visits home. At first we allowed family contact at the hospital with a member of staff, but they became more and more uncomfortable when the police investigations continued. Eventually, Michelle lost all contact with her family, at a time when she probably needed the safety of familiarity in her life.

When my six-month training placement ended I moved to another training post in the psychiatric training rotation, just after Michelle gave birth to a normal, healthy baby girl by elective caesarean section. The infant was taken into the care of social services immediately, and her grandfather was eventually charged. I never had a chance to say goodbye to Michelle when I left, but I was reassured in the knowledge that she was having regular one-to-one sessions with a clinical psychologist who was experienced and caring, and interested in her emotional wellbeing.

29

Casualty

My second year after qualifying as a doctor. It was early evening, and I was two hours into my shift at a busy casualty department of a district general hospital. We were the only neurosurgical unit for miles, and so took every stretcher case and blue light, from heart attacks to serious head injuries. The walking wounded came in through the hospital's front doors, and more often than not complained about the length of time they had to wait before being seen. They had no idea what turmoil and drama lay behind the wall that separated them from the cubicles of the main casualty department. Much of the time we were overwhelmed by the sheer volume of ambulance cases brought in through our emergency doors; patients covered in foil to prevent hypothermia; the elderly strapped in wheelchairs and wrapped in blankets, with obvious signs of stroke; others in stretchers with collars around their necks and intravenous lines already in their veins, clothing soaked with blood and exposed fragments of bone.

The casualty department, especially in the evening and at night, was staffed by a team of very experienced nurses and often rather inexperienced doctors. The post felt an easy option and offered a breather from the relentless junior doctor 'rite of passage'. Unlike other posts with 72–80 hour stretches and no protected rest periods, working in casualty required us to work in shifts: a week of days, a week of nights (9pm-9am) and a variable period of split shifts in between, which meant being on duty from nine to one and again from five to eleven the same day. When a 'blue light' was due the nurse in charge would allocate a number of staff to be on standby, often with a minute or two's notice.

That night, a young woman was rushed into the department having suffered a heart attack. A team of us dashed into the resuscitation room and began cardiac massage until more senior staff were on hand to take charge. Access to a vein was paramount, as well as getting an airway into the windpipe. The defibrillator was always at hand. Given the patient's age, we fought for much longer than usual to try to save her, but to no avail.

As the equipment and resuscitation paraphernalia were being put away, the anaesthetist encouraged us to have a go inserting the tube into the airway. It was a necessary part of clinical training, at a time when mannequins were not widely available, and often the only chance one had to learn and practice the skill was when a patient was being prepared for surgery. But it was often difficult to dissociate from trying to save a living person, only to end up practising a skill on a dead body.

We left the nurses to inform the relatives – they were often better at it. They seemed to have the time to spend with them; certainly they were not afraid to comfort them or to show emotion. Unfortunately, it also meant junior doctors never got a chance to learn and practice such skills. I also remember consultants I have worked for sitting with patients behind closed doors, or drawn curtains, breaking bad news about a particular diagnosis or terminal illness, but we were never involved. That night, the nurses had comforted the young woman's sister, who turned out to be her twin. The department was in chaos, as she promptly developed all the acute symptoms her deceased twin sister had just an hour before.

Casualty is a strange place. It is the most acute end of clinical practice, and provides a wealth of experience as long as one is prepared for the gamut of emotions and the juxtaposition of the most trivial symptom with life-threatening conditions requiring immediate action. I enjoyed my six months immensely, and I have the deepest admiration for those who have made a career in this most challenging field of medicine. In those early years of my clinical practice I enjoyed watching the American television soap drama series 'St Elsewhere', about a group of newly-qualified doctors in a fictional underrated Boston hospital, St. Eligius, and their first year in hospital practice, disorientated by chronic sleep deprivation, constant bleeps and real-life dramas. It was known for its gritty, realistic drama and seemed to capture what it was really like for us at the time, yet it did so with such humour and gentleness. It was the precursor for many of the medical dramas we have on our television screens now, and portrayed the medical profession as admirable people with good intentions in serving their patients, but with their own personal and professional problems. There was a lot of black humour, inside jokes as well as real humanity. I remember thinking how the nation's hospitals and casualty departments were run by people like me, so inexperienced and yet out there, in the front line. It was a sobering and rather scary reality.

Perhaps I am looking at my early clinical experiences through rose-coloured spectacles, but I can still feel the buzz of a busy casualty department. I can hear the drunken demands of disinhibited patients on a Friday night, the sirens of a blue light, the grumbles of the walking wounded tiring of the same television programmes being screened in the waiting room and the hushed whispers or anxious, aggressive behaviours of concerned and desperate relatives. There was such need out there – a constant demand for medical attention. Sometimes, those who shouted loudest were far healthier than the poor overworked doctors who eventually came to attend to them. We very rarely took days out sick. Hospitals rarely employed locum doctors to cover an absence unless it was for an extended period of planned leave, and even that was exceptional. It was not so much the guilt of being away from patients. Taking a day off meant leaving other medical colleagues, already heavily burdened, to deal with more.

One evening I was sagging under the weight of it all. My husband had urged me to go into work. 'You'll be all right,' he said. 'You'll survive'.

I shouldn't have to survive. I was coughing and spluttering; my head was throbbing, my body was feverish and achy, and it was difficult to concentrate on the task at hand. It was 10pm. I had just been told off by the surgical team for asking them to review a young man with a severe head injury, for a second opinion, because I should have known better and discharged him with a head injury warning card. I could hear the house officer as he left, criticizing and mumbling to the three medical students shadowing his 'on call' duties, saying how I was usually a reliable casualty officer, making only appropriate referrals. And the demands kept coming; nurses came up time and again to remind me to see cubicle number so and so, or someone required pain killers, or there was an X-ray to look at. My head spun round, and patient and staff voices became a kaleidoscope of noise around me. I felt so physically ill and at breaking point – and finally, I burst into tears.

Hoping no one had noticed, I took myself off into the sanctuary of an unoccupied minor surgery suite next door and sat for a few minutes regaining my composure. After all, I only had a few hours to go. My husband, who was working the opposite shift in Casualty, and I would only pass each other as ships in the night as we came on and off duty, not even having enough time to remind the other to buy a pint of milk. But it didn't go unnoticed. There was a young staff nurse working that night who saw my distress and came in after me, to offer some comfort and solace. She didn't stay long, but just knowing there was somebody else out there, in the department, on the same shift, who was in some small way keeping an eye on my well-being helped get me through the rest of the shift.

When I went back I was immediately involved in the aftermath of a severe road traffic accident. After a hefty dose of paracetamol and as many hours of daytime sleep as I could get, I was back on duty for my next stint twelve hours later.

My time in casualty holds many memories – many deaths, but many successes too. We often do not remember the latter, and the media are complicit in this biased selective memory. Headlines are full of disasters, malpractice and medical or hospital scandals. No one reads much about how well they have been treated in spite of the circumstances, or the hard work and dedication of doctors and nurses. Actually, the public do have a soft spot for nurses, mainly I think because patients see them more often, and understand what they do and the important role they play in the delivery of everyday care. They have less understanding of the stresses and working conditions doctors face. We get very little thanks, but we certainly know it if there are complaints.

I have particular memories of my time as a casualty officer in a busy accident and emergency department. In particular, I remember the numerous aortic aneurysms we saw come through the department; patients with such large pulsating masses in their abdomens that were in danger of rupturing at any moment. The multiple stroke victims, young overdoses, children distressed by whooping cough or distraught parents of children with febrile convulsions (fits due to a fever). As a neurosurgical unit, we saw a range of head injuries, from those who were mildly concussed to those who had been involved in serious road traffic accidents. But there were three clinical encounters that made a lasting impression on me, and steered my growing interest to specialize in mental health.

The first was an unkempt-looking man in his thirties, dressed in a striped pyjama top and sitting in a casualty trolley, waiting to be examined. I found out from the ambulance men that he was known to suffer from chronic schizophrenia, a severe mental illness in which the boundaries between fantasy and reality are fragmented. That evening he had put his music on full volume, which prompted the neighbours to call the police. He had then taken a chainsaw and cut off his penis. There was hardly any blood, and one of the policemen almost stepped on his dismembered part lying flaccid on the floor in the dark. When I examined him, he spoke not a word. He didn't even look distressed, and was clearly in a catatonic stupor. Luckily, he had been found in time and the urologists were able to suture his penis back on in an emergency operation that night. I never knew what happened to him, although I assume he was transferred into psychiatric care when his physical health allowed.

The second involved a young nurse who was resident in the hospital campus. She had been found by her friends crawling along the corridors of the nurses' home, completely naked, talking about strange happenings in her bedroom. She spoke of objects moving on the shelf of their own accord, and other visual hallucinations. I was able to persuade her to go into the local psychiatric hospital for a brief admission, but again have no idea what actually happened to her. However, my management of her presentation in the casualty department as a fairly inexperienced doctor must have got me through my interview a few months later, when

I applied for my first psychiatric training post, as they were impressed that I had found out she had been diagnosed with an acute drug-induced psychosis.

Substance misuse played a significant part in the third case I remember well. I saw this patient in casualty when I was a surgical houseman. It was my first job after qualifying, and it was scary – especially being 'on take'. It was an absurd situation really. Casualty officers at least one year my senior would be making referrals to me as the surgeon on call. I would trot down to the casualty department after a day assisting my consultant in the operating theatre to assess a new patient and decide whether or not to admit them into hospital, or indeed whether emergency surgery was warranted. One day, in the early hours of the morning, I was bleeped to see a young man who had been brought in by ambulance and accompanied by the police. The casualty officer suggested I called my more senior colleague on duty with me to see him too, so I knew something more serious than appendicitis or a perforated ulcer was waiting for me. The patient was a young man who had been sniffing glue with some friends. Together they had broken into a local warehouse, setting off the intruder alarm. With the police hot on their trail, the individuals involved jumped through an open window to the street below in an attempt to escape. They were all caught, but this patient was not so lucky. He had jumped out of the window, only to impale himself on the spikes of an iron railing below. The wounds in his abdomen and thigh looked quite innocuous – small and hardly bleeding at all – but when we took him into the operating theatre, we were there for hours suturing each laceration.

Our boss was away for a few weeks, and we had a locum consultant surgeon take charge. He was a tall, brusque man with an engaging grin and an athletic stature. He seemed approachable enough, and certainly did not mind being called into the hospital from his warm bed in the wee hours of a cold winter's night. But something changed when he got into his surgical greens and scrubbed up with a mask over his face. He insisted on operatic music being blasted into the theatre as he worked, he threw blood-soaked cotton swabs at the nursing staff and was generally abusive to everyone in sight. I couldn't believe the complete change in his demeanour; it reminded me of drivers behind a steering wheel. In the relative safety of their own vehicles, the most placid of people can become aggressive, careless and quite dangerous.

The young patient stayed long enough for his wounds to heal, and discharged himself from the hospital prematurely. I am not sure if the police ever caught up with him.

Fourteen years after first setting foot at The London Hospital as a naïve overseas medical student, I walked out of Whitechapel underground station and took in the East End air. The street stalls were being set up for another day. Not much had changed around me, but it felt so different. I remembered the first patient I had encountered in my training; I was prepped with a checklist of questions in my head and went to take a medical history from her. She told me she had something wrong with her ticker. I didn't know what she was talking about. This wasn't the English language I had learnt at school. I used to bump into her often after that, at the station, as she attended for her various appointments. She always asked how my studies were going. Now the façade of the old hospital building, once such a foreboding and inspiring sight, gleamed in the early morning sunshine and beckoned my return. I had been appointed as a consultant psychiatrist, to the teaching hospital in which I had trained, a hospital that had been founded almost 250 years earlier. It was the first medical school in England connected to a hospital, and I was going to work amongst colleagues who were formerly my teachers. I was very conscious of the psychiatric department's international reputation and its eminent professors. They were leaders in the treatment of psychosexual disorders, bereavement, loss, abnormal grief reactions and psychiatric aspects of epilepsy. The department had a strong and passionate workforce of dedicated academics, researchers and clinicians. It marked a dynamic and promising start to my consultant career.

30

A Chinese parable

At the time of famine in China, a young woman is confronted with a moral dilemma: does she offer her breast milk to her old mother, who is starving, or does she save her remaining child, given her other child is already dead on the ground?

My husband returned from a trans-cultural training seminar one afternoon and posed to me the parable they had discussed that day. I smiled and said without the slightest hesitation what the only answer could be that the milk is offered to the old woman. He was aghast, as every one of his English colleagues, including him, had chosen the child.

'In Chinese culture it is offered to the old woman,' I explained, 'because filial piety is unquestioned. One's responsibility to one's parents is paramount, and transcends one's responsibilities to one's children.'

He looked at me as though I were from another planet.

'But you know,' I added as a qualifying statement to soothe his unease. 'If my grandmother were that old woman, she would refuse it and give it to the child.'

Apart from a court judge, only one's parents have the authority to punish and reprimand. When I was a child my mother was the one who either adopted, or chose, the role of disciplinarian. She administered this role, and her punishment, with an unflinching rod of iron. The rod was a bamboo cane, so thick it held its shape firmly, yet so thin it cracked through the air like a whip. The wheals it left on the backs of my legs and buttocks prevented me from sitting down comfortably for days afterwards. It seemed not a week went by when one of us children, including my cousins, would not be the target of her rage. And it was a rage that seemed to flare up from nothing at all, or in response to the most minimal provocation. The ritual included the 'bringing in of the stick', which hung on a hook behind the partition door adjacent to our face flannels. A daily reminder perhaps. A deathly quiet would descend upon the household and dread seeped from every floorboard. An interlude between the angry shouting and the physical punishment.

The cane was offered to her with both hands, as if to say 'please discipline me, for I have done wrong.' The beating would last for as long as it took to bring tears to the eyes, and sobbing pleas for mercy, and just that little bit more. Neither my father nor my grandmother interfered, except on one occasion, when I remember my grandmother coming out from the kitchen, apron still tied to her waist, wiping her wet hands and calling 'Hasn't she had enough, now.

Stop this beating. Do you not realise that you are beating your own flesh and blood?'

Quickly as the beatings came, they stopped equally abruptly when I was about 11 or 12. When we moved from Bonham Strand to our spacious government flat in Pokfulam, the cane was left behind the door, and I knew then that that chapter of my life was over. In their adult lives my cousins have maintained that the corporal punishment they received was just and fair and appropriate. Whether or not this was so, it certainly was acceptable in those days. Caning was allowed in schools, and I can still hear the thunderous footsteps of our short, rotund headmistress as she was called upon to administer the cane on a fellow student when I was at primary school. I was never at the receiving end, but I do remember being sent downstairs to her office to let her know the culprit was ready.

At home, the beatings were replaced by outbursts of black temper that would seethe for hours until a full apology was offered. Without much provocation I found myself at the receiving end of accusatory assertions and criticism as my mother worked herself up into a rage, bringing into the tirade confidences that had been shared. It was not possible to de-escalate such a situation and I stood there in silence with eyes downcast, trying not to let her words hurt me. As the years went by these outbursts got shorter and less intense. Now she has mellowed and is very different in nature and temperament, but to this day I can remember my dreams of running away – running with my sister and grandmother, in the dead of night, as we lost ourselves in the shadows of the alleyways and market streets. And I had recurring dreams of leaving my body fast asleep, as my soul flew away to new adventures and far-away lands. The Chinese believe that when one sleeps, the soul leaves the body, through the top of the head, to wander the earth – and what is experienced is very real. Whilst separated, the body is vulnerable to possession by evil spirits.

When my grandmother died in the summer of 1988, it came as a sudden and devastating blow. She had taken to visiting Guangzhou annually, to stay with family, thus giving my parents a chance to have a holiday abroad. In the Year of the Dragon, her birthday, officially her eighty-eighth (although she was probably two or more years older), fell on the eighth day of the eighth month of the eighty-eighth year. All Chinese regard serial eights as tremendously lucky, and for Grandmother's birthday to fall on this most auspicious day, it meant this was going to be her luckiest year. I was so excited for her. A big celebration had been planned for when she and my parents returned to Hong Kong later that summer. But it was not to be.

One weekend, I felt a dull and heavy pain within me, yet I could not name it, having never felt it before. I was unsettled and troubled all day, and unable to sleep. I knew something was not right, but I did not know what. My mother told me she had the most awful pain in her chest, soon after she landed at the airport on her return home. Within hours, she received a telephone call from her eldest brother in Guangzhou, to tell her that my grandmother had died. Only three weeks before she had been with grandmother in Guangzhou. Grandmother had bought a piece of fabric for herself – simple, plain, black and very coarse. She showed it to my mother and asked her to sew her death dress. Mum lost her temper and said she did not have the time. She told my grandmother that she would have to ask one of her granddaughters in China to do this instead. However, before she left my grandmother in Guangzhou she went out with her, and together they chose a less austere fabric, with a finer, softer and gentler touch.

On the day of her death, Grandmother had enjoyed the company of an old family friend. They spent the day together, catching up on news and sharing reminisces. I am told there was much laughter that afternoon. She had a happy time, and was looking forward to returning to Hong Kong within a few days. Minutes after her elderly friend left, Grandmother called out in pain and evidently knew she was dying; she said as much. The traditional healer who had been summoned to attend to her gave her an injection for her pain, but said he feared her flow of *chi* was broken. And in less time than it takes for a child to be born, my grandmother was gone.

My life was thrown into the darkest and deepest abyss. Everything was turned upside down; the bottom had fallen out of my life, and a part of me died with her.

Epilogue: a pilgrimage

'It is when the world within us is destroyed, when it is dead and loveless, when our loved ones are in fragments, and we ourselves in helpless despair – it is then that we must recreate our world anew, reassemble the pieces, infuse life into dead fragments... recreate life.'

(Hannah Segal, 1981)

I wrote the first draft of this manuscript within six weeks of my grandmother's death, and then flew back to Hong Kong for her Requiem Mass, held in a newly-built temple dedicated to the Goddess of Mercy. My grandmother had visited a few months earlier and had been very taken by the serenity of the environment and the surrounding area. I took comfort in the ceremony and elaborate rituals, and thought it fitting that a group of monks and nuns should chant all day for her salvation. I folded gold paper nuggets for her treasure chests, and admired the paper offerings which would accompany her in the after-life. A year later, my grandmother's ashes were interred in a tomb next to her husband, overlooking the ancestral village. My cousins travelled there to pay their respects. Six thousand miles away, at the exact hour they were standing at her tomb, our son was born. I cannot believe it was just coincidence.

Four years later, my husband and I and our young son flew Cathay Pacific Airways, direct from London to Hong Kong. It was our first family visit to my homeland, and my first return since my grandmother's funeral. We caught the fast train to Guangzhou. As a new day dawned, we boarded an old farm truck, allowed access into the ancient 'Five Rams' city on market day because its licence plate bore the necessary letter of the alphabet. With its suspension system almost completely gone and the engine continually stalling, we bumped along for three hours on bead-covered seats, yet the discomfort of our journey barely filtered into consciousness. Large divots spanned the road ahead, narrowed by bicycle lanes, construction sites and people, oblivious to traffic. Small stretches of motorway and a ten-minute crossing on a tug-driven pontoon across a murky river near Zhaoqing afforded brief but welcome relief. Shanty towns, isolated villages, paddy fields and distant mountains shrouded in mist gave way to factory sites, quarries filled with billowing orange dust and new towns. A world shrouded in palpable, visible pollution suddenly cleared to reveal avenues of lush green trees. Local Chinese people squatted along the roadside, some brushing their teeth and others breakfasting on bowls of steaming hot noodles or congee.

As we turned into our destination, mud-covered sows sauntered heavily across our path. Chickens and cockerels ran amok. Water buffalo watched our coming from their cool resting-place in the river tributary.

Ninth Uncle met us, a sprightly man in his mid-sixties who walked with an out-turned gait and swinging arms. The family resemblance was striking. He had travelled overnight by boat the day before, from Guangzhou, to prepare for our arrival, uncertain if the letter detailing our visit had been received. A quick calculation informed us that one hundred and sixty members of our family still lived here.

'Here' was my ancestral village: a small duck pond, uneven stone steps winding up through small stone houses, open wooden doors, images of Door Gods and the symbols of the Five Happinesses hanging from granite lintel. Questioning villagers enquired of unfamiliar faces. Once my grandmother's name was spoken, their questions turned to friendly greetings and their impassive wrinkled faces, bronzed by the sun, broke into toothless grins. They invited us into their homes, proudly offering their restroom facilities: a toilet ring covering a bucket or an indoor gutter.

The doors to my grandmother's marital home were flung wide open. In spite of the children noisily running around and the voices of the village elders in reminiscent chatter, I sensed a quiet, hallowed ambience – an inner peace. I had entered a sacred place. I felt my grandmother's strong presence. The poignancy of the occasion awoke a sadness within me and loss etched my heart. I reached out for the thin sticks of incense - the link between our earthly and spiritual world – and struck a match to light them. I made my offering in front of our ancestral shrine, and to my grandmother's spirit.

At the far end of her bedroom, dimly lit and sparsely furnished, my attention was drawn to a box, rich in colour and ornately carved. It had been used to carry her ashes the one hundred and sixty kilometres from Guangzhou. I spent time imagining what had been, sitting on her bed, climbing up the narrow flight of steps onto a small balcony, touching the simple items of furniture, the tiny mirror on the wall and the chest in which my grandmother's wedding garments had been stored. Exactly as it was under Imperial rule. Savouring every detail, I was acutely aware of the privilege and pride I felt. I felt a sense of belonging; of being part of such an unspoilt piece of history; a living history. Exhibits previously seen only in museums became reality. And it was my reality. I had come home to claim my heritage.

No visual shade of someone lost
But he, the spirit himself may come,
Where all the nerve of sense is numb;
Spirit to spirit, ghost to ghost.
Descend, and touch, and enter; here
The wish too strong for words to name;
That in this blindness of the frame,
My ghost may feel that thine is near.
- The Chinese poet Li Chi (70-50 BC)

It was time to make the pilgrimage to my grandmother's grave, the reason we had come to Guangzhou. My uncles, whom I had never met before this visit, had been somewhat surprised but deeply moved by my filial piety. I couldn't understand why. It felt so natural to me. After all, it was my grandmother who had raised me.

The vastness of the rural landscape stretched behind us and the gentle slopes of the Choi Sek mountain range guided our footsteps. Paths were so overgrown; we sometimes could not see one another, yet there was a sense of safety in kinship. Neither the heat from the midday sun nor the water snake close by could dampen our enthusiasm. Cousins told stories of grandmother's visits to the village when the borders were closed, and many tales of her wisdom and counsel, with only the trickle of irrigation water accompanying their laughter. It was an inspiring, joyous journey. For the first time I saw that my grandmother had been a grandmother to them all, and I felt sure she was with us.

We arrived before I realised I was standing by her tombstone. Her details were etched in Chinese script below a circle of red, signifying a life cycle complete. And it was a complete life: one which had seen the whole of China's twentieth century history. A life borne into poverty and servitude, but a courageous spirit had risen from the ashes of human pain and tragedy.

I breathed in her memory, filling my lungs with a strength I have never forgotten. My eyes feasted on the tranquillity of this idyllic final resting place and my soul rejoiced in its propriety. There I paid my own tribute in incense and prayers. Together, fifty of her descendants swept her grave and offered a roast suckling pig, fruits and fresh flowers. Firecrackers ricocheted through the air, chasing away evil and proclaiming our presence and homage for all to witness.

For the first time I was at one with heaven, earth and my ancestral spirit.

Printed in Great Britain
by Amazon